To

_____

From

_____

Also by Rick Warren

The Purpose Driven Church

Rick Warren's Bible Study Methods

What on Earth Am I Here For?

Living with Purpose Series

God's Answers to Life's Difficult Questions

God's Power to Change Your Life

THE PURPOSE DRIVEN LIFE
expanded edition

WHAT ON EARTH AM I HERE FOR?

LARGE PRINT EDITION

RICK WARREN

ZONDERVAN®

ZONDERVAN.com/
AUTHORTRACKER
follow your favorite authors

ZONDERVAN

The Purpose Driven Life
Copyright © 2002, 2011, 2012 by Rick Warren

This title is also available as a Zondervan ebook.
Visit www.zondervan.com/ebooks.

This title is also available in a Zondervan audio edition.
Visit www.zondervan.fm.

Requests for information should be addressed to:

Zondervan, *Grand Rapids, Michigan 49530*

This expanded edition: ISBN 978-0-310-33550-4 (softcover)

Library of Congress has cataloged the original edition as follows:

Warren, Richard, 1954 –
    The purpose driven life : what on earth am I here for? / Rick Warren.— Large print ed.
        p. cm.
    Includes bibliographical references.
    ISBN 978-0-310-25525-3
    1. Christian life. 2. Large type books. I. Title.
BV4501.3.W37 2003
    248.4 – dc21   2003008400

The Scripture versions cited in this book are identified in appendix 3, which hereby becomes a part of this copyright page.

Any Internet addresses (websites, blogs, etc.) and telephone numbers in this book are offered as a resource. They are not intended in any way to be or imply an endorsement by Zondervan, nor does Zondervan vouch for the content of these sites and numbers for the life of this book.

Cover design: Brian Montes
Cover illustration: iStockphoto®
Interior illustration: iStockphoto®
Interior design: Beth Shagene

Printed in the United States of America

---

12 13 14 15 16 17 18 19 /DCI/ 24 23 22 21 20 19 18 17 16 15 14 13 12 11 10 9 8 7 6 5 4 3 2 1

THIS BOOK IS DEDICATED TO YOU.

Before you were born, God planned *this moment* in your life. It is no accident that you are holding this book. God *longs* for you to discover the life he created you to live — here on earth, and forever in eternity.

> *It's in Christ that we find out who we are and what we are living for. Long before we first heard of Christ, ... he had his eye on us, had designs on us for glorious living, part of the overall purpose he is working out in everything and everyone.*
>
> EPHESIANS 1:11 (MSG)

I am grateful to the hundreds of writers and teachers, both classical and contemporary, who have shaped my life and helped me learn these truths. I thank God and you for the privilege of sharing them with you.

Now with QR Codes that link to 42 exclusive 3-minute videos featuring Rick Warren, this QR Code and video-enhanced edition includes all the wisdom of the original book, plus new insights Warren has gleaned since he first wrote *The Purpose Driven Life.* What on earth are you

here for? Read, see, and hear the answers from Rick Warren himself.

Using your smartphone camera, simply scan the QR Code by taking a picture of the code in the book, and the video for that chapter will automatically appear in your smartphone browser.

You can download a free QR Code reader app onto your phone from your phone's app store. For additional information on QR Codes, how they are used, and links to various QR Code readers, visit *www.qrcode.zondervan.com.*

Contents

PURPOSE #2: You Were Formed for God's Family

PURPOSE #3: You Were Created to Become Like Christ

PURPOSE #4: **You Were Shaped for Serving God**

PURPOSE #5: **You Were Made for a Mission**

PURPOSE #4: You Were Shaped for Serving God

PURPOSE #5: You Were Made for a Mission

A Journey with Purpose
Getting the Most from This Book

THIS IS MORE THAN A BOOK; IT IS A GUIDE TO A *40-DAY spiritual journey* that will enable you to discover the answer to life's most important question: What on earth am I here for? By the end of this journey you will know God's purpose for your life and will understand the big picture — how all the pieces of your life fit together. Having this perspective will reduce your stress, simplify your decisions, increase your satisfaction, and, most important, prepare you for eternity.

Your Next 40 Days

Today the average life span is 25,550 days. That's how long you will live if you are typical. Don't you think it would be a wise use of time to set aside 40 of those days to figure out what God wants you to do with the rest of them?

The Bible is clear that God considers 40 days a

spiritually significant time period. Whenever God wanted to prepare someone for his purposes, he took 40 days:

- Noah's life was transformed by 40 days of rain.

- Moses was transformed by 40 days on Mount Sinai.

- The spies were transformed by 40 days in the Promised Land.

- David was transformed by Goliath's 40-day challenge.

- Elijah was transformed when God gave him 40 days of strength from a single meal.

- The entire city of Nineveh was transformed when God gave the people 40 days to change.

- Jesus was empowered by 40 days in the wilderness.

- The disciples were transformed by 40 days with Jesus after his resurrection.

The next 40 days will transform *your* life.

This book is divided into 40 brief chapters (plus two bonus chapters). I strongly urge you to *read only one chapter a day,* so you will have time to *think about* the implications for your life. The Bible says, *"Let God transform you into a new person by changing the way you think. Then you will know what God wants you to do."*[1]

One reason most books don't transform us is that we are so eager to read the next chapter, we don't pause and take the time to seriously consider what we have just read.

We rush to the next truth without reflecting on what we have learned.

Don't just *read* this book. *Interact with it.* Underline it. Write your own thoughts in the margins. Make it *your* book. Personalize it! The books that have helped me most are the ones that I reacted to, not just read.

Five Features to Help You

At the end of each chapter is a section called "Thinking about My Purpose." There you will find:

- **A Point to Ponder.** This is a nugget of truth that summarizes a principle of purpose-driven living that you can reflect on throughout your day. Paul told Timothy, *"Reflect on what I am saying, for the Lord will give you insight into all this."*[2]

- **A Verse to Remember.** This is a Bible verse that teaches a truth from that chapter. If you really want to improve your life, memorizing Scripture may be the most important habit you can begin. You can either copy these verses onto small cards to carry with you, or purchase a *Purpose Driven Life Scripture Keeper Plus.*

- **A Question to Consider.** These questions will help you think about the implications of what you have read and how it applies to you personally. Let me encourage you to write your answers in the margin of this book or in a notebook, or obtain a copy of *The Purpose Driven Life Journal*, a companion book designed for this purpose. Writing down your thoughts is the best way to clarify them.

• **A Message to Hear.** These 42 audio messages will give you more of my teaching related to each chapter. Each message varies from 40 to 50 minutes in length.

In appendix 1 you will find:

• **Discussion Questions.** I strongly urge you to get one or more friends to join you in reading this book during the next 40 days. A journey is always better when it is *shared*. With a partner or a small reading group you can discuss what you read and bounce ideas off each other. This will help you grow stronger and deeper spiritually. Real spiritual growth is *never* an isolated, individualistic pursuit. Maturity is produced through relationships and community.

The best way to explain God's purpose for your life is to allow the Scripture to speak for itself, so in this book the Bible is quoted extensively, using over a thousand different verses from fifteen English translations and paraphrases. I have varied the versions used for several important reasons, which I explain in appendix 3.

I Have Been Praying for You

As I wrote this book, I often prayed that you would experience the incredible sense of hope, energy, and joy that comes from discovering what God put you on this planet to do. There's nothing quite like it. I am excited because I know all the great things that are going to happen to you. They happened to me, and I have never been the same since I discovered the purpose of my life.

Because I know the benefits, I want to challenge you to stick with this spiritual journey for the next 40 days, not missing a single daily reading. Your life is worth taking the time to think about it. Make it a daily appointment on your schedule. If you will commit to this, let's sign a covenant together. There is something significant about signing your name to a commitment. If you get a partner to read through this with you, have him or her sign it too. Let's get started together!

A New Edition for a New Generation
An Explanation from Rick

*"We're not keeping this to ourselves;
we're passing it along to the next generation!"*

PSALM 78:4 (MSG)

RECENTLY A 22-YEAR-OLD NAMED MARK CONNECTED with me through social media and asked, "How do I know what my purpose in life is?" As we chatted, I learned that his parents had read this book, but he had not read it, since he was only 12 years old when it was published.

Every new generation must rediscover God's purposes for themselves. But God also adds that the older generation is responsible to pass on what they have learned *"so that each generation can set its hope anew on God"* (Psalm 78:7 NLT).

Since *The Purpose Driven Life* was first published, our world has changed dramatically. God's eternal purposes are still unchanged, but we have many new tools and channels to help people understand those purposes.

I have added four new features to this expanded edition:

- A video introduction to each of the 42 chapters *(see links).*

- An audio Bible study at the end of each chapter *(see links).* These give you over 30 additional hours of my teaching.

- Two new bonus chapters on the most common barriers to living on purpose.

- Access to an online community where you can discuss your journey to purpose, get feedback, and receive support.

I dedicate this new edition to all of you who, like Mark, are the new generation, but are asking the question every age has asked: *What on earth am I here for?* I am honored to serve you.

> *"The LORD is good.*...
> *His faithfulness continues*
> *to each generation."*
>
> PSALM 100:5 (NLT)

 TWITTER @RICKWARREN

 FACEBOOK PASTOR RICK WARREN

 LINKEDIN

My Covenant

With God's help, I commit the next 40 days of my life to discovering God's purpose for my life.

_____

YOUR NAME

_____

PARTNER'S NAME

Rick Warren

_____

RICK WARREN

"Two are better off than one, because together they can work more effectively. If one of them falls down, the other can help him up.... Two people can resist an attack that would defeat one person alone. A rope made of three cords is hard to break."

ECCLESIASTES 4:9 (TEV)

WHAT ON EARTH AM I HERE FOR?

A life devoted to things is a dead life, a stump;
a God-shaped life is a flourishing tree.
PROVERBS 11:28 (MSG)

Blessed are those who trust in the Lord....They
are like trees planted along a riverbank, with
roots that reach deep into the water. Such trees
are not bothered by the heat or worried by long
months of drought. Their leaves stay green, and
they go right on producing delicious fruit.
JEREMIAH 17:7 – 8 (NLT)

WHAT ON EARTH AM I HERE FOR?

*A life devoted to things is a dead life, a stump;
a God-shaped life is a flourishing tree.*

PROVERBS 11:28 (MSG)

*Blessed are those who trust in the Lord. . . .They
are like trees planted along a riverbank, with
roots that reach deep into the water. Such trees
are not bothered by the heat or worried by long
months of drought. Their leaves stay green, and
they go right on producing delicious fruit.*

JEREMIAH 17:7 – 8 (NLT)

It All Starts with God

For everything, absolutely everything,
above and below, visible and invisible, . . .
everything got started in him and
finds its purpose in him.

COLOSSIANS 1:16 (MSG)

purposedriven.com/
day1

Unless you assume a God, the question
of life's purpose is meaningless.

BERTRAND RUSSELL, ATHEIST

IT'S NOT ABOUT YOU.

The purpose of your life is far greater than your own personal fulfillment, your peace of mind, or even your happiness. It's far greater than your family, your career, or even your wildest dreams and ambitions. If you want to know why you were placed on this planet, you must begin with God. You were born *by* his purpose and *for* his purpose.

The search for the purpose of life has puzzled people for thousands of years. That's because we typically begin at the wrong starting point — ourselves. We ask self-centered questions like What do *I* want to be? What should *I* do with *my* life? What are *my* goals, *my* ambitions, *my* dreams for *my* future? But focusing on ourselves will never reveal our life's purpose. The Bible says, *"It is God who directs the lives of his creatures; everyone's life is in his power."*[1]

Contrary to what many popular books, movies, and seminars tell you, you won't discover your life's meaning by looking within yourself. You have probably tried that already. You didn't create yourself, so there is no way you can tell yourself what you were created for! If I handed you an invention you had never seen before, you wouldn't know its purpose, and the invention itself wouldn't be able to tell you either. Only the creator or the owner's manual could reveal its purpose.

I once got lost in the mountains. When I stopped to ask for directions to the campsite, I was told, *"You can't get there from here. You must start from the other side of the mountain!"* In the same way, you cannot arrive at your life's purpose by starting with a focus on yourself. You must begin with God, your Creator. You exist only because God wills that you exist. You were made *by* God and *for* God—and until you understand that, life will never make sense. It is only in God that we discover our origin, our identity, our meaning, our purpose, our

> Focusing on ourselves will never reveal our life's purpose.

significance, and our destiny. Every other path leads to a dead end.

Many people try to use God for their own self-actualization, but that is a reversal of nature and is doomed to failure. You were made for God, not vice versa, and life is about letting God use you for *his* purposes, not your using him for your own purpose. The Bible says, *"Obsession with self in these matters is a dead end; attention to God leads us out into the open, into a spacious, free life."*[2]

I have read many books that suggest ways to discover the purpose of my life. All of them could be classified as "self-help" books because they approach the subject from a self-centered viewpoint. Self-help books, even Christian ones, usually offer the same predictable steps to finding your life's purpose: Consider your dreams. Clarify your values. Set some goals. Figure out what you are good at. Aim high. Go for it! Be disciplined. Believe you can achieve your goals. Involve others. Never give up.

Of course, these recommendations often lead to great success. You can usually succeed in reaching a goal if you put your mind to it. But being successful and fulfilling your life's purpose are *not at all* the same issue! You could reach all your personal goals, becoming a raving success by the world's standard, and

> *You were made by God and for God—and until you understand that, life will never make sense.*

still miss the purposes for which God created you. You need more than self-help advice. The Bible says, *"Self-help is no help at all. Self-sacrifice is the way, my way, to finding yourself, your true self."*[3]

This is not a self-help book. It is not about finding the right career, achieving your dreams, or planning your life. It is not about how to cram more activities into an overloaded schedule. Actually, it will teach you how to do *less* in life — by focusing on what matters most. It is about becoming what *God* created you to be.

How, then, do you discover the purpose you were created for? You have only two options. Your first option is *speculation.* This is what most people choose. They conjecture, they guess, they theorize. When people say, "I've always thought life is ...," they mean, "This is the best guess I can come up with."

For thousands of years, brilliant philosophers have discussed and speculated about the meaning of life. Philosophy is an important subject and has its uses, but when it comes to determining the purpose of life, even the wisest philosophers are just guessing.

Dr. Hugh Moorhead, a philosophy professor at Northeastern Illinois University, once wrote to 250 of the best-known philosophers, scientists, writers, and intellectuals in the world, asking them, "What is the meaning of life?" He then published their responses in a book. Some offered their best guesses, some admitted that they just made up a purpose for life, and others were honest enough to say they were clueless. In fact, a number of famous intellectuals asked Professor Moorhead to write back and tell them if he discovered the purpose of life![4]

Fortunately, there is an alternative to speculation about the meaning and purpose of life. It's *revelation.* We can turn to what God has revealed about life in his Word. The easiest way to discover the purpose of an invention is to ask the creator of it. The same is true for discovering your life's purpose: Ask God.

God has not left us in the dark to wonder and guess. He has clearly revealed his five purposes for our lives through the Bible. It is our Owner's Manual, explaining why we are alive, how life works, what to avoid, and what to expect in the future. It explains what no self-help or philosophy book could know. The Bible says, *"God's wisdom ... goes deep into the interior of his purposes.... It's not the latest message, but more like the oldest — what God determined as the way to bring out his best in us."*[5]

God is not just the starting point of your life; he is the *source* of it. To discover your purpose in life you must turn to God's Word, not the world's wisdom. You must build your life on eternal truths, not pop psychology, success-motivation, or inspirational stories. The Bible says, *"It's in Christ that we find out who we are and what we are living for. Long before we first heard of Christ and got our hopes up, he had his eye on us, had designs on us for glorious living, part of the overall purpose he is working out in everything and everyone.*"[6] This verse gives us three insights into your purpose.

1. You discover your identity and purpose through a relationship with Jesus Christ. If you don't have such a relationship, I will later explain how to begin one.

2. God was thinking of you long before you ever thought about him. His purpose for your life predates your conception. He planned it before you existed, *without your input!* You may choose your career, your spouse, your hobbies, and many other parts of your life, but you don't get to choose your purpose.

3. The purpose of your life fits into a much larger, cosmic purpose that God has designed for eternity. That's what this book is about.

Andrei Bitov, a Russian novelist, grew up under an atheistic Communist regime. But God got his attention one dreary day. He recalls, "In my twenty-seventh year, while riding the metro in Leningrad (now St. Petersburg) I was overcome with a despair so great that life seemed to stop at once, preempting the future entirely, let alone any meaning. Suddenly, all by itself, a phrase appeared: *Without God life makes no sense.* Repeating it in astonishment, I rode the phrase up like a moving staircase, got out of the metro and walked into God's light."[7]

You may have felt in the dark about *your* purpose in life. Congratulations, you're about to walk into the light.

DAY 1

Thinking about My Purpose

POINT TO PONDER: It's not about me.

VERSE TO REMEMBER: *"Everything got started in him and finds its purpose in him."* COLOSSIANS 1:16B (MSG)

QUESTION TO CONSIDER: In spite of all the advertising around me, how can I remind myself that life is really about living for God, not myself?

MESSAGE TO HEAR: *www.purposedriven.com/day1*

You Are Not an Accident

I am your Creator.
You were in my care
even before you were born.

ISAIAH 44:2A (CEV)

purposedriven.com/
day2

God does not play dice.

ALBERT EINSTEIN

YOU ARE NOT AN ACCIDENT.

Your birth was no mistake or mishap, and your life is no fluke of nature. Your parents may not have planned you, but God did. He was not at all surprised by your birth. In fact, he expected it.

Long before you were conceived by your parents, you were conceived in the mind of God. He thought of you first. It is not fate, nor chance, nor luck, nor coincidence that you are breathing at this very moment. You are alive because God wanted to create you! The Bible says, *"The LORD will fulfill his purpose for me."*[1]

God prescribed every single detail of your body. He deliberately chose your race, the color of your skin, your hair, and every other feature. He custom-made your body just the way he wanted it. He also determined the natural talents you would possess and the uniqueness of your personality. The Bible says, *"You know me inside and out, you know every bone in my body; You know exactly how I was made, bit by bit, how I was sculpted from nothing into something."*[2]

Because God made you for a reason, he also decided *when* you would be born and *how long* you would live. He planned the days of your life in advance, choosing the exact time of your birth and death. The Bible says, *"You saw me before I was born and scheduled each day of my life before I began to breathe. Every day was recorded in your Book!"*[3]

God also planned *where* you'd be born and where you'd live for his purpose. Your race and nationality are no accident. God left no detail to chance. He planned it all for *his* purpose. The Bible says, *"From one man he made every nation,… and he determined the times set for them and the exact places where they should live."*[4] Nothing in your life is arbitrary. It's all for a purpose.

Most amazing, God decided *how* you would be born. Regardless of the circumstances of your birth or who your parents are, God had a plan in creating you. It doesn't matter whether your parents were good, bad, or indifferent. God knew that those two individuals possessed *exactly* the right genetic makeup to create the custom "you" he had in mind. They had the DNA God wanted to make you.

While there are illegitimate parents, there are no illegitimate children. Many children are unplanned by their parents, but they are not unplanned by God. God's purpose took into account human error, and even sin.

Long before you were conceived by your parents, you were conceived in the mind of God.

God never does anything accidentally, and he never makes mistakes. He has a reason for everything he creates. Every plant and every animal was planned by God, and every person was designed with a purpose in mind. God's motive for creating you was his love. The Bible says, *"Long before he laid down earth's foundations, he had us in mind, had settled on us as the focus of his love."*[5]

God was thinking of you even *before* he made the world. In fact, that's why he created it! God designed this planet's environment just so we could live in it. We are the focus of his love and the most valuable of all his creation. The Bible says, *"God decided to give us life through the word of truth so we might be the most important of all the things he made."*[6] This is how much God loves and values you!

God is not haphazard; he planned it all with great precision. The more physicists, biologists, and other scientists learn about the universe, the better we understand how it is uniquely suited for our existence, custom-made with the *exact* specifications that make human life possible.

Dr. Michael Denton, senior research fellow in human molecular genetics at the University of Otago in New Zealand, has concluded, "All the evidence available in the biological sciences supports the core proposition ... that the cosmos is a specially designed whole with life and mankind as its fundamental goal and purpose, a whole in which all facets of reality have their meaning and explanation in this central fact."[7] The Bible said the same thing thousands of years earlier: *"God formed the earth.... He did not create it to be empty but formed it to be inhabited."*[8]

Why did God do all this? Why did he bother to go to all the trouble of creating a universe for us? Because he is a God of love. This kind of love is difficult to fathom, but it's fundamentally reliable. You were created as a special object of God's love! God made you so he could love you. This is a truth to build your life on.

The Bible tells us, *"God is love."*[9] It doesn't say God *has* love. He *is* love! Love is the essence of God's character. There is perfect love in the fellowship of the Trinity, so God didn't *need* to create you. He wasn't lonely. But he wanted to make you in order to express his love. God says, *"I have carried you since you were born; I have taken care of you from your birth. Even when you are old, I will be the same. Even when your hair has turned gray, I will take care of you. I made you and will take care of you.*"[10]

If there was no God, we would all be "accidents," the result of astronomical random chance in the universe. You could stop reading this book, because life would have no purpose or meaning or significance. There would be no right or wrong, and no hope beyond your brief years here on earth.

But there *is* a God who made you for a reason, and your life has profound meaning! We discover that meaning and purpose *only* when we make God the reference point of our lives. The Message paraphrase of Romans 12:3 says, *"The only accurate way to understand ourselves is by what God is and by what he does for us."*

This poem by Russell Kelfer sums it up:

> You are who you are for a reason.
> You're part of an intricate plan.
> You're a precious and perfect unique design,
> Called God's special woman or man.
>
> You look like you look for a reason.
> Our God made no mistake.
> He knit you together within the womb,
> You're *just* what he wanted to make.
>
> The parents you had were the ones he chose,
> And no matter how you may feel,

They were custom-designed with God's plan
  in mind,
And they bear the Master's seal.

No, that trauma you faced was not easy.
And God wept that it hurt you so;
But it was allowed to shape your heart
So that into his likeness you'd grow.

You are who you are for a reason,
You've been formed by the Master's rod.
You are who you are, beloved,
Because there is a God![11]

DAY 2

Thinking about My Purpose

POINT TO PONDER: I am not an accident.

VERSE TO REMEMBER: *"I am your Creator. You were in my care even before you were born."* ISAIAH 44:2 (CEV)

QUESTION TO CONSIDER: I know that God uniquely created me. What areas of my personality, background, and physical appearance am I struggling to accept?

MESSAGE TO HEAR: *www.purposedriven.com/day2*

DAY 3

What Drives Your Life?

*I observed that the basic motive
for success is the driving force
of envy and jealousy!*

ECCLESIASTES 4:4 (LB)

purposedriven.com/
day3

*The man without a purpose
is like a ship without a rudder—
a waif, a nothing, a no man.*

THOMAS CARLYLE

EVERYONE'S LIFE IS DRIVEN BY SOMETHING.

Most dictionaries define the verb *drive* as "to guide, to control, or to direct." Whether you are driving a car, a nail, or a golf ball, you are guiding, controlling, and directing it at that moment. What is the driving force in your life?

Right now you may be driven by a problem, a pressure, or a deadline. You may be driven by a painful memory, a haunting fear, or an unconscious belief. There are hundreds of circumstances, values, and emotions that can drive your life. Here are five of the most common ones:

Many people are driven by guilt. They spend their entire lives running from regrets and hiding their shame. Guilt-driven people are manipulated by memories. They allow their past to control their future. They often unconsciously punish themselves by sabotaging their own success. When Cain sinned, his guilt disconnected him from God's presence, and God said, *"You will be a restless wanderer on the earth."*[1] That describes most people today — wandering through life without a purpose.

We are products of our past, but we don't have to be prisoners of it. God's purpose is not limited by your past. He turned a murderer named Moses into a leader and a coward named Gideon into a courageous hero, and he can do amazing things with the rest of your life, too. God specializes in giving people a fresh start. The Bible says, *"What happiness for those whose guilt has been forgiven!...What relief for those who have confessed their sins and God has cleared their record."*[2]

Many people are driven by resentment and anger. They hold on to hurts and never get over them. Instead of releasing their pain through forgiveness, they rehearse it over and over in their minds. Some resentment-driven people *"clam up"* and internalize their anger, while others *"blow up"* and explode it onto others. Both responses are unhealthy and unhelpful.

Resentment always hurts you more than it does the person you resent. While your offender has probably forgotten the offense and gone on with life, you continue to stew in your pain, perpetuating the past.

Listen: Those who have hurt you in the past cannot continue to hurt you now *unless* you hold on to the pain through resentment. Your past is past! Nothing will change it. You are only hurting yourself with your bitterness. For your own sake, learn from it, and then let it go. The Bible says, *"To worry yourself to death with resentment would be a foolish, senseless thing to do."*[3]

Many people are driven by fear. Their fears may be a result of a traumatic experience, unrealistic expectations, growing up in a high-control home, or even genetic predisposition. Regardless of the cause, fear-driven people often miss great opportunities because they're afraid to venture out. Instead they play it safe, avoiding risks and trying to maintain the status quo.

Fear is a self-imposed prison that will keep you from becoming what God intends for you to be. You *must* move against it with the weapons of faith and love. The Bible says, *"Well-formed love banishes fear. Since fear is crippling, a fearful life — fear of death, fear of judgment — is one not yet fully formed in love."*[4]

Many people are driven by materialism. Their desire to acquire becomes the whole goal of their lives. This drive to always want more is based on the misconceptions that having more will make me more happy, more important, and more secure, but all three ideas are untrue. Possessions only provide *temporary* happiness. Because things do not change, we eventually become bored with them and then want newer, bigger, better versions.

It's also a myth that if I get more, I will be more important. Self-worth and net worth are not the same. Your value is not determined by your valuables, and God says the most valuable *things* in life are not things!

The most common myth about money is that having more will make me more secure. It won't. Wealth can be lost instantly through a variety of uncontrollable factors. Real security can only be found in that which can never be taken from you — your relationship with God.

> *Nothing matters more than knowing God's purposes for your life, and nothing can compensate for not knowing them.*

Many people are driven by the need for approval. They allow the expectations of parents or spouses or children or teachers or friends to control their lives. Many adults are still trying to earn the approval of unpleasable parents. Others are driven by peer pressure, always worried by what others might think. Unfortunately, those who follow the crowd usually get lost in it.

I don't know all the keys to success, but one key to failure is to try to please everyone. Being controlled by the opinions of others is a guaranteed way to miss God's purposes for your life. Jesus said, *"No one can serve two masters."*[5]

There are other forces that can drive your life but all lead to the same dead end: unused potential, unnecessary stress, and an unfulfilled life.

This 40-day journey will show you how to live a *purpose-driven* life — a life guided, controlled, and directed by God's purposes. Nothing matters more than knowing God's purposes for your life, and nothing can compensate for not knowing them — not success, wealth, fame, or pleasure. Without a purpose, life is motion without meaning, activity without direction, and events without reason. Without a purpose, life is trivial, petty, and pointless.

The Benefits of Purpose-Driven Living

There are five great benefits of living a purpose-driven life:

Knowing your purpose gives meaning to your life. We were made to have meaning. This is why people try dubious methods, like astrology or psychics, to discover it. When life has meaning, you can bear almost anything; without it, nothing is bearable.

A young man in his twenties wrote, "I feel like a failure because I'm struggling to become something, and I don't even know what it is. All I know how to do is to get by. Someday, if I discover my purpose, I'll feel I'm beginning to live."

Without God, life has no purpose, and without

purpose, life has no meaning. Without meaning, life
has no significance or hope. In the Bible, many different
people expressed this hopelessness. Isaiah complained,
*"I have labored to no purpose; I have spent my strength in
vain and for nothing."*[6] Job said, *"My life drags by — day
after hopeless day"*[7] and *"I give up; I am tired of living.
Leave me alone. My life makes no sense."*[8] The greatest
tragedy is not death, but life without purpose.

Hope is as essential to your life as air and water. You
need hope to cope. Dr. Bernie Siegel found
he could predict which of his cancer patients
would go into remission by asking, "Do you
want to live to be one hundred?" Those with
a deep sense of life purpose answered yes
and were the ones most likely to survive. Hope comes
from having a purpose.

DAY 3:
*What Drives
Your Life?*

If you have felt hopeless, hold on! Wonderful changes
are going to happen in your life as you begin to live it on
purpose. God says, *"I know what I am planning for you....
'I have good plans for you, not plans to hurt you. I will give
you hope and a good future.'"*[9] You may feel you are facing
an impossible situation, but the Bible says, *"God ... is able
to do far more than we would ever dare to ask or even
dream of — infinitely beyond our highest prayers, desires,
thoughts, or hopes."*[10]

Knowing your purpose simplifies your life. It
defines what you do and what you don't do. Your purpose
becomes the standard you use to evaluate which activities

are essential and which aren't. You simply ask, "Does this activity help me fulfill one of God's purposes for my life?"

Without a clear purpose you have no foundation on which you base decisions, allocate your time, and use your resources. You will tend to make choices based on circumstances, pressures, and your mood at that moment. People who don't know their purpose try to do too much —and *that* causes stress, fatigue, and conflict.

It is impossible to do everything people want you to do. You have just enough time to do God's will. If you can't get it all done, it means you're trying to do more than God intended for you to do (or, possibly, that you're watching too much television). Purpose-driven living leads to a simpler lifestyle and a saner schedule. The Bible says, *"A pretentious, showy life is an empty life; a plain and simple life is a full life."*[11] It also leads to peace of mind: *"You, LORD, give perfect peace to those who keep their purpose firm and put their trust in you."*[12]

Knowing your purpose focuses your life. It concentrates your effort and energy on what's important. You become effective by being selective.

It's human nature to get distracted by minor issues. We play *Trivial Pursuit* with our lives. Henry David Thoreau observed that people live lives of *"quiet desperation,"* but today a better description is *aimless distraction.* Many people are like gyroscopes, spinning around at a frantic pace but never going anywhere.

Without a clear purpose, you will keep changing

directions, jobs, relationships, churches, or other externals — hoping each change will settle the confusion or fill the emptiness in your heart. You think, *Maybe this time it will be different,* but it doesn't solve your real problem — a lack of focus and purpose.

The Bible says, *"Don't live carelessly, unthinkingly. Make sure you understand what the Master wants."*[13]

The power of focusing can be seen in light. Diffused light has little power or impact, but you can concentrate its energy by focusing it. With a magnifying glass, the rays of the sun can be focused to set grass or paper on fire. When light is focused even more as a laser beam, it can cut through steel.

There is nothing quite as potent as a focused life, one lived on purpose. The men and women who have made the greatest difference in history were the most focused. For instance, the apostle Paul almost single-handedly spread Christianity throughout the Roman Empire. His secret was a focused life. He said, *"I am focusing all my energies on this one thing: Forgetting the past and looking forward to what lies ahead."*[14]

If you want your life to have impact, *focus* it! Stop dabbling. Stop trying to do it all. Do less. Prune away even good activities and do only that which matters most. Never confuse activity with productivity. You can be busy without a purpose, but what's the point? Paul said, *"Let's keep focused on that goal, those of us who want everything God has for us."*[15]

Knowing your purpose motivates your life. Purpose always produces passion. Nothing energizes like a clear purpose. On the other hand, passion dissipates when you lack a purpose. Just getting out of bed becomes a major chore. It is usually meaningless work, not overwork, that wears us down, saps our strength, and robs our joy.

George Bernard Shaw wrote, "This is the true joy of life: the being used up for a purpose recognized by yourself as a mighty one; being a force of nature instead of a feverish, selfish little clot of ailments and grievances, complaining that the world will not devote itself to making you happy."

Knowing your purpose prepares you for eternity. Many people spend their lives trying to create a lasting legacy on earth. They want to be remembered when they're gone. Yet, what ultimately matters most will not be what others say about your life but what *God* says. What people fail to realize is that all achievements are eventually surpassed, records are broken, reputations fade, and tributes are forgotten. In college, James Dobson's goal was to become the school's tennis champion. He felt proud when his trophy was prominently placed in the school's trophy cabinet. Years later, someone mailed him that trophy. They had found it in a trashcan when the school was remodeled. Jim said, *"Given enough time, all your trophies will be trashed by someone else!"*

Living to create an earthly legacy is a shortsighted goal. A wiser use of time is to build an *eternal* legacy. You weren't put on earth to be remembered. You were put here to prepare for eternity.

One day you will stand before God, and he will do an audit of your life, a final exam, before you enter eternity. The Bible says, *"Remember, each of us will stand personally before the judgment seat of God.... Yes, each of us will have to give a personal account to God."*[16] Fortunately, God wants us to pass this test, so he has given us the questions in advance. From the Bible we can surmise that God will ask us two crucial questions:

First, *"What did you do with my Son, Jesus Christ?"* God won't ask about your religious background or doctrinal views. The only thing that will matter is, did you accept what Jesus did for you and did you learn to love and trust him? Jesus said, *"I am the way and the truth and the life. No one comes to the Father except through me."*[17]

Second, *"What did you do with what I gave you?"* What did you do with your life — all the gifts, talents, opportunities, energy, relationships, and resources God gave you? Did you spend them on yourself, or did you use them for the purposes God made you for?"

Preparing you for these two questions is the goal of this book. The first question will determine *where* you spend eternity. The second question will determine *what you do* in eternity. By the end of this book you will be ready to answer both questions.

DAY 3

Thinking about My Purpose

POINT TO PONDER: Living on purpose is the path to peace.

VERSE TO REMEMBER: *"You, LORD, give perfect peace to those who keep their purpose firm and put their trust in you."* ISAIAH 26:3 (TEV)

QUESTION TO CONSIDER: What would my family and friends say is the driving force of my life? What do I want it to be?

MESSAGE TO HEAR: *www.purposedriven.com/day3*

Made to Last Forever

God has ... planted eternity
in the human heart.
ECCLESIASTES 3:11 (NLT)

Surely God would not have created such
a being as man to exist only for a day!
No, no, man was made for immortality.
ABRAHAM LINCOLN

purposedriven.com/
day4

THIS LIFE IS NOT ALL THERE IS.

Life on earth is just the dress rehearsal before the real production. You will spend far more time on the other side of death — *in eternity* — than you will here. Earth is the staging area, the preschool, the tryout for your life in eternity. It is the practice workout before the actual game; the warm-up lap before the race begins. This life is preparation for the next.

At most, you will live a hundred years on earth, but you will spend forever in eternity. Your time on earth is, as Sir Thomas Browne said, "but a small parenthesis in eternity." You were made to last forever.

The Bible says, *"God has ... planted eternity in the human heart."*[1] You have an inborn instinct that longs for immortality. This is because God designed you, in his image, to live for eternity. Even though we know everyone eventually dies, death always seems unnatural and unfair. The reason we feel we should live forever is that God wired our brains with that desire!

One day your heart will stop beating. That will be the end of your body and your time on earth, but it will not be the end of you. Your earthly body is just a temporary residence for your spirit. The Bible calls your earthly body a "tent," but refers to your future body as a "house." The Bible says, *"When this tent we live in — our body here on earth — is torn down, God will have a house in heaven for us to live in, a home he himself has made, which will last forever."*[2]

While life on earth offers many choices, eternity offers only two: heaven or hell. Your relationship to God on earth will determine your relationship to him in eternity. If you learn to love and trust God's Son, Jesus, you will be invited to spend the rest of eternity with him. On the other hand, if you reject his love, forgiveness, and salvation, you will spend eternity apart from God forever.

C. S. Lewis said, "There are two kinds of people: those who say to God *'Thy will be done'* and those to whom God says, *'All right then, have it your way.'*" Tragically, many people will have to endure eternity without God because they chose to live without him here on earth.

When you fully comprehend that there is more to life than just here and now, and you realize that life is just preparation for eternity, you will begin to live differently. You will start *living in light of eternity,* and that will color how you handle every relationship, task, and circumstance. Suddenly many activities, goals, and even problems that seemed so important will appear trivial, petty, and unworthy of your attention. The closer you live to God, the smaller everything else appears.

> *This life is preparation for the next.*

When you live in light of eternity, your values change. You use your time and money more wisely. You place a higher premium on relationships and character instead of fame or wealth or achievements or even fun. Your priorities are reordered. Keeping up with trends, fashions, and popular values just doesn't matter as much anymore. Paul said, *"I once thought all these things were so very important, but now I consider them worthless because of what Christ has done."*[3]

If your time on earth were all there is to your life, I would suggest you start living it up immediately. You could forget being good and ethical, and you wouldn't have to worry about any consequences of your actions. You could indulge yourself in total self-centeredness because your actions would have no long-term repercussions. But — *and this makes all the difference* — death is not the end of you! Death is not your termination, but your transition into eternity, so there are *eternal* consequences to everything you do on earth. Every act of our lives strikes some chord that will vibrate in eternity.

The most damaging aspect of contemporary living is short-term thinking. To make the most of your life, you must keep the vision of eternity continually in your mind and the value of it in your heart. There's far more to life than just here and now! Today is the visible tip of the iceberg. Eternity is all the rest you don't see underneath the surface.

When you live in light of eternity, your values change.

What is it going to be like in eternity with God? Frankly, the capacity of our brains cannot handle the wonder and greatness of heaven. It would be like trying to describe the Internet to an ant. It's futile. Words have not been invented that could possibly convey the experience of eternity. The Bible says, *"No mere man has ever seen, heard or even imagined what wonderful things God has ready for those who love the Lord."*[4]

However, God has given us glimpses of eternity in his Word. We know that right now God is preparing an eternal home for us. In heaven we will be reunited with loved ones who are believers, released from all pain and suffering, rewarded for our faithfulness on earth, and reassigned to do work that we will enjoy doing. We *won't* lie around on clouds with halos playing harps! We will enjoy unbroken fellowship with God, and he will enjoy us for an unlimited, endless forever. One day Jesus will say, *"Come, you who are blessed by my Father; take your inheritance, the kingdom prepared for you since the creation of the world."*[5]

C. S. Lewis captured the concept of eternity on the last page of the Chronicles of Narnia, his seven-book children's fiction series: "For us this is the end of all the stories.... But for them it was only the beginning of the real story. All their life in this world ... had only been the cover and the title page: now at last they were beginning Chapter One of the Great Story, which no one on earth has read, which goes on forever and in which every chapter is better than the one before."[6]

God has a purpose for your life on earth, but it doesn't end here. His plan involves far more than the few decades you will spend on this planet. It's more than "the opportunity of a lifetime"; God offers you an opportunity *beyond* your lifetime. The Bible says, *"[God's] plans endure forever; his purposes last eternally."*[7]

DAY 4:

Made to Last Forever

The only time most people think about eternity is at funerals, and then it's often shallow, sentimental thinking, based on ignorance. You may feel it's morbid to think about death, but actually it's unhealthy to live in denial of death and not consider what is inevitable.[8] Only a fool would go through life unprepared for what we all know will eventually happen. You need to think *more* about eternity, not less.

Just as the nine months you spent in your mother's womb were not an end in themselves but preparation for life, so this life is preparation for the next. If you have a relationship with God through Jesus, you don't need to fear death. It is the door to eternity. It will be the last hour of your time on earth, but it won't be the last of you. Rather than being the end of your life, it will be your birthday into eternal life. The Bible says, *"This world is not our home; we are looking forward to our everlasting home in heaven."*[9]

Measured against eternity, our time on earth is just a blink of an eye, but the consequences of it will last forever. The deeds of this life are the destiny of the next. We should be *"realizing that every moment we spend in these earthly bodies is time spent away from our eternal home in heaven with Jesus."*[10] Years ago a popular slogan encouraged people to live each day as "the first day of the rest of your life." Actually, it would be wiser to live each day as if it were the last day of your life. Matthew Henry said, "It ought to be the business of every day to prepare for our final day."

DAY 4

Thinking about My Purpose

POINT TO PONDER: There is more to life than just here and now.

VERSE TO REMEMBER: *"This world is fading away, along with everything it craves. But if you do the will of God, you will live forever."* 1 JOHN 2:17 (NLT)

QUESTION TO CONSIDER: Since I was made to last forever, what is the one thing I should stop doing and the one thing I should start doing today?

MESSAGE TO HEAR: *www.purposedriven.com/day4*

DAY 5

Seeing Life from God's View

What is your life?

JAMES 4:14B (NIV)

purposedriven.com/
day5

*We don't see things as they are,
we see them as we are.*

ANAÏS NIN

THE WAY YOU *SEE* YOUR LIFE *SHAPES* YOUR LIFE.

How you define life determines your destiny. Your perspective will influence how you invest your time, spend your money, use your talents, and value your relationships.

One of the best ways to understand other people is to ask them, *"How do you see your life?"* You will discover that there are as many different answers to that question as there are people. I've been told life is a circus, a minefield, a roller coaster, a puzzle, a symphony, a journey, and a dance. People have said, "Life is a carousel:

Sometimes you're up, sometimes you're down, and sometimes you just go round and round" or "life is a ten-speed bicycle with gears we never use" or "life is a game of cards: You have to play the hand you are dealt."

If I asked how you picture life, what image would come to your mind? That image is your *life metaphor.* It's the view of life that you hold, consciously or unconsciously, in your mind. It's your description of how life works and what you expect from it. People often express their life metaphors through clothes, jewelry, cars, hairstyles, bumper stickers, even tattoos.

Your unspoken life metaphor influences your life more than you realize. It determines your expectations, your values, your relationships, your goals, and your priorities. For instance, if you think life is a party, your primary value in life will be *having fun.* If you see life as a race, you will value *speed* and will probably be in a hurry much of the time. If you view life as a marathon, you will value *endurance.* If you see life as a battle or a game, *winning* will be very important to you.

What is your view of life? You may be basing your life on a faulty life metaphor. To fulfill the purposes God made you for, you will have to challenge conventional wisdom and replace it with the *biblical* metaphors of life. The Bible says, *"Do not conform yourselves to the standards of this world, but let God transform you inwardly by a complete change of your mind. Then you will be able to know the will of God."*[1]

The Bible offers three metaphors that teach us God's view of life: Life is a *test,* life is a *trust,* and life is a *temporary assignment.* These ideas are the foundation of purpose-driven living. We will look at the first two in this chapter and the third one in the next.

Life on earth is a Test. This life metaphor is seen in stories throughout the Bible. God continually tests people's character, faith, obedience, love, integrity, and loyalty. Words like *trials, temptations, refining,* and *testing* occur more than 200 times in the Bible. God tested Abraham by asking him to offer his son Isaac. God tested Jacob when he had to work extra years to earn Rachel as his wife.

DAY 5:
Seeing Life from God's View

Adam and Eve failed their test in the garden of Eden, and David failed his tests from God on several occasions. But the Bible also gives us many examples of people who passed a great test, such as Joseph, Ruth, Esther, and Daniel.

Character is both developed and revealed by tests, and *all* of life is a test. You are *always* being tested. God constantly watches your response to people, problems, success, conflict, illness, disappointment, and even the weather! He even watches the simplest actions such as when you open a door for others, when you pick up a piece of trash, or when you're polite toward a clerk or waitress.

We don't know all the tests God will give you, but we

can predict some of them, based on the Bible. You will be tested by major changes, delayed promises, impossible problems, unanswered prayers, undeserved criticism, and even senseless tragedies. In my own life I have noticed that God tests my *faith* through problems, tests my *hope* by how I handle possessions, and tests my *love* through people.

A very important test is how you act when you can't *feel* God's presence in your life. Sometimes God intentionally draws back, and we don't sense his closeness. A king named Hezekiah experienced this test. The Bible says, *"God withdrew from Hezekiah in order to test him and to see what was really in his heart."*[2] Hezekiah had enjoyed a close fellowship with God, but at a crucial point in his life God left him alone to test his character, to reveal a weakness, and to prepare him for more responsibility.

When you understand that life is a test, you realize that *nothing* is insignificant in your life. Even the smallest incident has significance for your character development. *Every* day is an important day, and every second is a growth opportunity to deepen your character, to demonstrate love, or to depend on God. Some tests

> *Character is both developed and revealed by tests, and all of life is a test.*

seem overwhelming, while others you don't even notice. But all of them have eternal implications.

The good news is that God wants you to pass the tests of life, so he never allows the tests you face to be greater than the grace he gives you to handle them. The Bible says, *"God keeps his promise, and he will not allow you to be tested beyond your power to remain firm; at the time you are put to the test, he will give you the strength to endure it, and so provide you with a way out."*[3]

Every time you pass a test, God notices and makes plans to reward you in eternity. James says, *"Blessed are those who endure when they are tested. When they pass the test, they will receive the crown of life that God has promised to those who love him."*[4]

Life on earth is a Trust. This is the second biblical metaphor of life. Our time on earth and our energy, intelligence, opportunities, relationships, and resources are all gifts from God that he has entrusted to our care and management. We are stewards of whatever God gives us. This concept of stewardship begins with the recognition that God is the owner of everything and everyone on earth. The Bible says, *"The world and all that is in it belong to the LORD; the earth and all who live on it are his."*[5]

We never really *own* anything during our brief stay on earth. God just *loans* the earth to us while we're here. It was God's property before you arrived, and God will loan it to someone else after you die. You just get to enjoy it for a while.

When God created Adam and Eve, he entrusted the

care of his creation to them and appointed them trustees of his property. The Bible says, *"[God] blessed them, and said, 'Have many children, so that your descendants will live all over the earth and bring it under their control. I am putting you in charge.'"*[6]

The first job God gave humans was to manage and take care of God's "stuff" on earth. This role has never been rescinded. It is a part of our purpose today. Everything we enjoy is to be treated as a *trust* that God has placed in our hands. The Bible says, *"What do you have that God hasn't given you? And if all you have is from God, why boast as though you have accomplished something on your own?"*[7]

Years ago, a couple let my wife and me use their beautiful beachfront home in Hawaii for a vacation. It was an experience we could

The more God gives you, the more responsible he expects you to be.

never have afforded, and we enjoyed it immensely. We were told, "Use it just like it's yours," so we did! We swam in the pool, ate the food in the refrigerator, used the bath towels and dishes, and even jumped on the beds in fun! But we knew all along that it wasn't *really* ours, so we took special care of everything. We enjoyed the benefits of using the home without owning it.

Our culture says, "If you don't own it, you won't take care of it." But Christians live by a higher standard: "Because *God* owns it, I must take the best care of it that I can." The Bible says, *"Those who are trusted with something valuable must show they are worthy of that trust."*[8] Jesus often referred to life as a trust and told many stories to illustrate this responsibility toward God. In the story of the talents,[9] a businessman entrusts his wealth to the care of his servants while he's away. When he returns, he evaluates each servant's responsibility and rewards them accordingly. The owner says, *"Well done, good and faithful servant! You have been faithful with a few things; I will put you in charge of many things. Come and share your master's happiness."*[10]

At the end of your life on earth you will be evaluated and rewarded according to how well you handled what God entrusted to you. That means *everything* you do, even simple daily chores, has eternal implications. If you treat everything as a *trust,* God promises three rewards in eternity. First, you will be given God's *affirmation:* He will say, "Good job! Well done!" Next, you will receive a *promotion* and be given greater responsibility in eternity: "I will put you in charge of many things." Then you will be honored with a *celebration:* "Come and share your Master's happiness."

Most people fail to realize that money is both a *test* and a *trust* from God. God uses finances to teach us to trust him, and for many people, money is the greatest test of all. God watches how we use money to test how trustworthy we are. The Bible says, *"If you are untrustworthy about worldly wealth, who will trust you with the true riches of heaven?"*[11]

This is a very important truth. God says there is a direct relationship between how I use my money and the quality of my spiritual life. How I manage my money (*"worldly wealth"*) determines how much God can trust me with spiritual blessings (*"true riches"*). Let me ask you: Is the way you manage your money preventing God from doing more in your life? Can you be trusted with spiritual riches?

Jesus said, *"From everyone who has been given much, much will be demanded; and from the one who has been entrusted with much, much more will be asked."*[12] Life is a test and a trust, and the more God gives you, the more responsible he expects you to be.

DAY 5

Thinking about My Purpose

POINT TO PONDER: Life is a test and a trust.

VERSE TO REMEMBER: *"Unless you are faithful in small matters, you won't be faithful in large ones."*
LUKE 16:10A (NLT)

QUESTION TO CONSIDER: What has happened to me recently that I now realize was a test from God? What are the greatest matters God has entrusted to me?

MESSAGE TO HEAR: *www.purposedriven.com/day5*

Life Is a Temporary Assignment

LORD, remind me how brief my time on earth will be. Remind me that my days are numbered, and that my life is fleeing away.

PSALM 39:4 (NLT)

I am here on earth for just a little while.

PSALM 119:19 (TEV)

purposedriven.com/
day6

LIFE ON EARTH IS A TEMPORARY ASSIGNMENT.

The Bible is full of metaphors that teach about the brief, temporary, transient nature of life on earth. Life is described as *a mist, a fast runner, a breath,* and *a wisp of smoke.* The Bible says, *"For we were born but yesterday.... Our days on earth are as transient as a shadow."*[1]

To make the best use of your life, you must never forget two truths: First, compared with eternity, life is extremely brief. Second, earth is only a temporary residence. You won't be here long, so don't get too attached. Ask God to help you see life on earth as he sees

63

it. David prayed, *"Lord, help me to realize how brief my time on earth will be. Help me to know that I am here for but a moment more."*[2]

Repeatedly the Bible compares life on earth to temporarily living in a foreign country. This is not your permanent home or final destination. You're just passing through, just visiting earth. The Bible uses terms like *alien, pilgrim, foreigner, stranger, visitor,* and *traveler* to describe our brief stay on earth. David said, *"I am but a foreigner here on earth,"*[3] and Peter explained, *"If you call God your Father, live your time as temporary residents on earth."*[4]

In California, where I live, many people have moved from other parts of the world to work here, but they keep their citizenship with their home country. They are required to carry a visitor registration card (called a "green card"), which allows them to work here even though they aren't citizens. Christians should carry *spiritual* green cards to remind us that our citizenship is in heaven. God says his

> Your identity is in eternity, and your homeland is heaven.

children are to think differently about life from the way unbelievers do. *"All they think about is this life here on earth. But we are citizens of heaven, where the Lord Jesus Christ lives."*[5] Real believers understand that there is far more to life than just the few years we live on this planet.

Your identity is in eternity, and your homeland

is heaven. When you grasp this truth, you will stop worrying about "having it all" on earth. God is very blunt about the danger of living for the *here and now* and adopting the values, priorities, and lifestyles of the world around us. When we flirt with the temptations of this world, God calls it spiritual adultery. The Bible says, *"You're cheating on God. If all you want is your own way, flirting with the world every chance you get, you end up enemies of God and his way."*[6]

DAY 6:
Life Is a Temporary Assignment

Imagine if you were asked by your country to be an ambassador to an enemy nation. You would probably have to learn a new language and adapt to some customs and cultural differences in order to be polite and to accomplish your mission. As an ambassador you would not be able to isolate yourself from the enemy. To fulfill your mission, you would have to have contact and relate to them.

But suppose you became so comfortable with this foreign country that you fell in love with it, preferring it to your homeland. Your loyalty and commitment would change. Your role as an ambassador would be compromised. Instead of representing your home country, you would start acting like the enemy. You'd be a traitor.

The Bible says, *"We are Christ's ambassadors."*[7] Sadly, many Christians have betrayed their King and his kingdom. They have foolishly concluded that because they live on earth, it's their home. It is not. The Bible is clear: *"Friends, this world is not your home, so don't make yourselves cozy in it. Don't indulge your ego at the expense of your soul."*[8] God warns us to not get too attached to what's around us because it is temporary. We're told, *"Those in frequent contact with the things of the world should make good use of them without becoming attached to them, for this world and all it contains will pass away."*[9]

Compared with other centuries, life has never been easier for much of the Western world. We are constantly entertained, amused, and catered to. With all the fascinating attractions, mesmerizing media, and enjoyable experiences available today, it's easy to forget that the pursuit of happiness is not what life is about. Only as we remember that life is a test, a trust, and a temporary assignment will the appeal of these things lose their grip on our lives. We are preparing for something even better. *"The things we see now are here today, gone tomorrow. But the things we can't see now will last forever."*[10]

The fact that earth is not our ultimate home explains why, as followers of Jesus, we experience difficulty, sorrow, and rejection in this world.[11] It also explains why some of God's promises seem unfulfilled, some prayers seem unanswered, and some circumstances seem unfair. This is not the end of the story.

In order to keep us from becoming too attached to earth, God allows us to feel a significant amount of discontent and dissatisfaction in life — longings that will *never* be fulfilled on this side of eternity. We're not completely happy here because we're not supposed to be! Earth is not our final home; we were created for something much better.

A fish would never be happy living on land, because it was made for water. An eagle could never feel satisfied if it wasn't allowed to fly. You will never feel completely satisfied on earth, because you were made for more. You will have happy moments here, but nothing compared with what God has planned for you.

> Earth is not our final home; we were created for something much better.

Realizing that life on earth is just a temporary assignment should radically alter your values. Eternal values, not temporal ones, should become the deciding factors for your decisions. As C. S. Lewis observed, "All that is not eternal is eternally useless." The Bible says, *"We fix our eyes not on what is seen, but on what is unseen. For what is seen is temporary, but what is unseen is eternal."*[12]

It is a fatal mistake to assume that God's goal for your life is material prosperity or popular success, as the world defines it. The abundant life has nothing to do with *material* abundance, and faithfulness to God does not guarantee success in a career or even in ministry. Never focus on temporary crowns.[13]

Paul was faithful, yet he ended up in prison. John the Baptist was faithful, but he was beheaded. Millions of faithful people have been martyred, have lost everything, or have come to the end of life with nothing to show for it. *But the end of life is not the end!*

In God's eyes, the greatest heroes of faith are not those who achieve prosperity, success, and power in this life, but those who treat this life as a temporary assignment and serve faithfully, expecting their promised reward in eternity. The Bible says this about God's Hall of Fame: *"All these great people died in faith. They did not get the things that God promised his people, but they saw them coming far in the future and were glad. They said they were like visitors and strangers on earth.... they were waiting for a better country — a heavenly country. So God is not ashamed to be called their God, because he has prepared a city for them."*[14] Your time on earth is not the complete story of your life. You must wait until heaven for the rest of the chapters. It takes faith to live on earth as a foreigner.

An old story is often repeated of a retiring missionary coming home to America on the same boat as the president of the United States. Cheering crowds, a military band, a red carpet, banners, and the media welcomed the president home, but the missionary slipped off the ship unnoticed. Feeling self-pity and resentment, he began complaining to God. Then God gently reminded him, "But my child, *you're not home yet.*"

You will not be in heaven two seconds before you cry out, *"Why did I place so much importance on things that were so temporary?* What was I thinking? Why did I waste so much time, energy, and concern on what wasn't going to last?"

When life gets tough, when you're overwhelmed with doubt, or when you wonder if living for Christ is worth the effort, remember that you are not home yet. At death you won't leave home — you'll *go* home.

DAY 6

Thinking about My Purpose

POINT TO PONDER: This world is not my home.

VERSE TO REMEMBER: *"So we fix our eyes not on what is seen, but on what is unseen. For what is seen is temporary, but what is unseen is eternal."* 2 CORINTHIANS 4:18 (NIV)

QUESTION TO CONSIDER: How should the fact that life on earth is just a temporary assignment change the way I am living right now?

MESSAGE TO HEAR: *www.purposedriven.com/day6*

DAY 7

The Reason for Everything

Everything comes from God alone.
Everything lives by his power,
and everything is for his glory.

ROMANS 11:36 (LB)

purposedriven.com/
day7

The LORD has made everything
for his own purposes.

PROVERBS 16:4 (NLT)

IT'S ALL FOR HIM.

The ultimate goal of the universe is to show the glory of God. It is the reason for everything that exists, including you. God made it *all* for his glory. Without God's glory, there would be nothing.

What is the glory of God? It is who God is. It is the essence of his nature, the weight of his importance, the radiance of his splendor, the demonstration of his power, and the atmosphere of his presence. God's glory is the expression of his goodness and all his other intrinsic, eternal qualities.

Where is the glory of God? Just look around. *Everything* created by God reflects his glory in some way. We see it everywhere, from the smallest microscopic form of life to the vast Milky Way, from sunsets and stars to storms and seasons. Creation reveals our Creator's glory. In nature we learn that God is powerful, that he enjoys variety, loves beauty, is organized, and is wise and creative. The Bible says, *"The heavens declare the glory of God."*[1]

> Living for God's glory is the greatest achievement we can accomplish with our lives.

Throughout history, God has revealed his glory to people in different settings. He revealed it first in the garden of Eden, then to Moses, then in the tabernacle and the temple, then through Jesus, and now through the church.[2] It was portrayed as a consuming fire, a cloud, thunder, smoke, and a brilliant light.[3] In heaven, God's glory provides all the light needed. The Bible says, *"The city does not need the sun or the moon to shine on it, for the glory of God gives it light."*[4]

God's glory is best seen in Jesus Christ. He, the Light of the World, illuminates God's nature. Because of Jesus, we are no longer in the dark about what God is really like. The Bible says, *"The Son is the radiance of God's glory."*[5] Jesus came to earth so we could fully understand God's glory. *"The Word became human and lived among us. We saw his glory ... a glory full of grace and truth."*[6]

God's *inherent* glory is what he possesses because he is God. It is his nature. We cannot add anything to this glory, just as it would be impossible for us to make the sun shine brighter. But we are commanded to *recognize* his glory, *honor* his glory, *declare* his glory, *praise* his glory, *reflect* his glory, and *live* for his glory.[7] Why? Because God deserves it! We owe him every honor we can possibly give. Since God made all things, he deserves all the glory. The Bible says, *"You are worthy, O Lord our God, to receive glory and honor and power. For you created everything."*[8]

> When anything in creation fulfills its purpose, it brings glory to God.

In the entire universe, only two of God's creations fail to bring glory to him: fallen angels (demons) and us (people). All sin, at its root, is failing to give God glory. It is loving anything else more than God. Refusing to bring glory to God is prideful rebellion, and it is the sin that caused Satan's fall — and ours, too. In different ways we have all lived for our own glory, not God's. The Bible says, *"All have sinned and fall short of the glory of God."*[9]

None of us have given God the full glory he deserves from our lives. This is the worst sin and the biggest mistake we can make. On the other hand, living for God's glory is the greatest achievement we can accomplish with our lives. God says, *"They are my own people, and I created them to bring me glory,"*[10] so it ought to be the supreme goal of our lives.

How Can I Bring Glory to God?

Jesus told the Father, *"I brought glory to you here on earth by doing everything you told me to do."*[11] Jesus honored God by fulfilling his purpose on earth. We honor God the same way. When anything in creation fulfills its purpose, it brings glory to God. Birds bring glory to God by flying, chirping, nesting, and doing other bird-like activities that God intended. Even the lowly ant brings glory to God when it fulfills the purpose it was created for. God made ants to be ants, and he made you to be you. St. Irenaeus said, "The glory of God is a human being fully alive!"

There are many ways to bring glory to God, but they can be summarized in God's five purposes for your life. We will spend the rest of this book looking at them in detail, but here is an overview:

We bring God glory by worshiping him. Worship is our first responsibility to God. We worship God by enjoying him. C. S. Lewis said, "In commanding us to glorify him, God is inviting us to enjoy him." God wants our worship to be motivated by love, thanksgiving, and delight, not duty.

John Piper notes, "God is most glorified in us when we are most satisfied in him."

Worship is far more than praising, singing, and praying to God. Worship is a lifestyle of *enjoying* God, *loving* him, and *giving* ourselves to be used for his purposes. When you use your life for God's glory, everything you do can become an act of worship. The Bible says, *"Use your whole body as a tool to do what is right for the glory of God."*[12]

We bring God glory by loving other believers. When you were born again, you became a part of God's family. Following Christ is not just a matter of believing; it also includes *belonging* and learning to love the family of God. John wrote, *"Our love for each other proves that we have gone from death to life."*[13] Paul said, *"Accept each other just as Christ has accepted you; then God will be glorified."*[14]

It is your responsibility to learn how to love as God does, because God is love, and it honors him. Jesus said, *"As I have loved you, so you must love one another. By this all men will know that you are my disciples, if you love one another."*[15]

We bring God glory by becoming like Christ. Once we are born into God's family, he wants us to grow to spiritual maturity. What does that look like? Spiritual maturity is becoming like Jesus in the way we think, feel, and act. The more you develop Christlike character, the more you will bring glory to God. The Bible says, *"As the Spirit of the Lord works within us, we become more and more like him and reflect his glory even more."*[16]

God gave you a new life and a new nature when you accepted Christ. Now, for the rest of your life on earth, God wants to continue the process of changing your character. The Bible says, *"May you always be filled with the fruit of your salvation — those good things that are produced in your life by Jesus Christ — for this will bring much glory and praise to God."*[17]

We bring God glory by serving others with our gifts. Each of us was uniquely designed by God with talents, gifts, skills, and abilities. The way you're "wired" is not an accident. God didn't give you your abilities for selfish purposes. They were given to benefit others, just as others were given abilities for your benefit. The Bible says, *"God has given gifts to each of you from his great variety of spiritual gifts. Manage them well so that God's generosity can flow through you.... Are you called to help others? Do it with all the strength and energy that God supplies. Then God will be given glory."*[18]

DAY 7: The Reason for Everything

We bring God glory by telling others about him. God doesn't want his love and purposes kept a secret. Once we know the truth, he expects us to share it with others. This is a great privilege — introducing others to Jesus, helping them discover their purpose, and preparing them for their eternal destiny. The Bible says, *"As God's grace brings more and more people to Christ,... God will receive more and more glory."*[19]

What Will You Live for?

Living the rest of your life for the glory of God will require a change in your priorities, your schedule, your relationships, and everything else. It will sometimes mean choosing a difficult path instead of an easy one. Even Jesus struggled with this. Knowing he was about to be crucified, he cried out: *"My soul has become troubled; and what shall I say, 'Father, save Me from this hour'? But for this purpose I came to this hour. Father, glorify Thy name."*[20]

Jesus stood at a fork in the road. Would he fulfill his purpose and bring glory to God, or would he shrink back and live a comfortable, self-centered life? You face the same choice. Will you live for your own goals, comfort, and pleasure, or will you live the rest of your life for God's glory, knowing that he has promised eternal rewards? The Bible says, *"Anyone who holds on to life just as it is destroys that life. But if you let it go, … you'll have it forever, real and eternal."*[21]

It's time to settle this issue. *Who* are you going to live for — yourself or God? You may hesitate, wondering whether you will have strength to live for God. Don't worry. God will give you what you need if you will just make the choice to live for him. The Bible says, *"Everything that goes into a life of pleasing God has been miraculously given to us by getting to know, personally and intimately, the One who invited us to God."*[22]

Jesus will give you everything you need to live for him.

Right now, God is inviting you to live for his glory

by fulfilling the purposes he made you for. It's really the only way to live. Everything else is just *existing*. Real life begins by committing yourself completely to Jesus Christ. If you are not sure you have done this, all you need to do is *receive* and *believe*. The Bible promises, *"To all who received him, to those who believed in his name, he gave the right to become children of God."*[23] Will you accept God's offer?

First, believe. Believe God loves you and made you for his purposes. Believe you're not an accident. Believe you were made to last forever. Believe God has chosen you to have a relationship with Jesus, who died on the cross for you. Believe that no matter what you've done, God wants to forgive you.

Second, receive. Receive Jesus into your life as your Lord and Savior. Receive his forgiveness for your sins. Receive his Spirit, who will give you the power to fulfill your life purpose. The Bible says, *"Whoever accepts and trusts the Son gets in on everything, life complete and forever!"*[24] Wherever you are reading this, I invite you to bow your head and quietly whisper the prayer that will change your eternity: *"Jesus, I believe in you and I receive you."* Go ahead.

If you sincerely meant that prayer, congratulations! Welcome to the family of God! You are now ready to discover and start living God's purpose for your life. I urge you to tell someone about it. You're going to need support. If you email me (see appendix 2), I will send you a little booklet I wrote called *Your First Steps for Spiritual Growth.*

DAY 7

Thinking about My Purpose

POINT TO PONDER: It's all for him.

VERSE TO REMEMBER: *"For everything comes from God alone. Everything lives by his power, and everything is for his glory."* ROMANS 11:36 (LB)

QUESTION TO CONSIDER: Where in my daily routine can I become more aware of God's glory?

MESSAGE TO HEAR: *www.purposedriven.com/day7*

YOU WERE PLANNED FOR GOD'S PLEASURE

For God has planted them like strong and graceful oaks for his own glory.

ISAIAH 61:3 (LB)

Planned for God's Pleasure

*You created everything,
and it is for your pleasure that
they exist and were created.*

REVELATION 4:11 (NLT)

The Lord takes pleasure in his people.

PSALM 149:4A (TEV)

purposedriven.com/
day8

You were planned for God's pleasure.

The moment you were born into the world, God was there as an unseen witness, *smiling* at your birth. He wanted you alive, and your arrival gave him great pleasure. God did not *need* to create you, but he *chose* to create you for his own enjoyment. You exist for his benefit, his glory, his purpose, and his delight.

Bringing enjoyment to God, living for his pleasure, is the first purpose of your life. When you fully understand this truth, you will never again have a problem with feeling insignificant. It proves your worth. If you are *that* important to God, and he considers you valuable enough to keep with him for eternity, what greater significance could you have? You are a child of God, and you bring pleasure to God like nothing else he has ever created. The Bible says, *"Because of his love God had already decided that through Jesus Christ he would make us his children — this was his pleasure and purpose."*[1]

One of the greatest gifts God has given you is the ability to enjoy pleasure. He wired you with five senses and emotions so you can experience it. He wants you to enjoy life, not just endure it. The reason you are able to enjoy pleasure is that God made you *in his image.*

We often forget that God has emotions, too. He feels things very deeply. The Bible tells us that God grieves, gets jealous and angry, and feels compassion, pity, sorrow, and sympathy as well as happiness, gladness, and satisfaction. God loves, delights, gets pleasure, rejoices, enjoys, and even laughs![2]

> *Anything you do that brings pleasure to God is an act of worship.*

Bringing pleasure to God is called "worship." The Bible says, *"The LORD is pleased only with those who worship him and trust his love."*[3]

Anything you do that brings pleasure to God is an act of worship. Like a diamond, worship is *multifaceted.* It would take volumes to cover *all* there is to understand about worship, but we will look at the primary aspects of worship in this section.

Anthropologists have noted that worship is a universal urge, hard-wired by God into the very fiber of our being —an inbuilt need to connect with God. Worship is as natural as eating or breathing. If we fail to worship God, we always find a substitute, even if it ends up being ourselves. The reason God made us with this desire is that he desires worshipers! Jesus said, *"The Father seeks worshipers."*[4]

Depending on your religious background, you may need to expand your understanding of "worship." You may think of church services with singing, praying, and listening to a sermon. Or you may think of ceremonies, candles, and communion. Or you may think of healing, miracles, and ecstatic experiences. Worship can include these elements, but worship is *far more* than these expressions. Worship is a lifestyle.

Worship is far more than music. For many people, worship is just a synonym for music. They say, "At our church we have the worship first, and then the teaching." This is a big misunderstanding. *Every* part of a church service is an act of worship: praying, Scripture reading, singing, confession, silence, being still, listening to a sermon, taking notes, giving an offering, baptism, communion, signing a commitment card, and even greeting other worshipers.

Actually, worship predates music. Adam worshiped in the garden of Eden, but music isn't mentioned until Genesis 4:21 with the birth of Jubal. If worship were just music, then all who are nonmusical could never worship. Worship is far more than music.

Even worse, "worship" is often misused to refer to a particular *style* of music: "First we sang a hymn, then a *praise and worship* song." Or, "I like the fast praise songs but enjoy the slow worship songs the most." In this usage, if a song is fast or loud or uses brass instruments, it's considered "praise." But if it is slow and quiet and intimate, maybe accompanied by guitar, that's worship. This is a common misuse of the term "worship."

Worship has nothing to do with the style or volume or speed of a song. God loves all kinds of music because he invented it all — fast and slow, loud and soft, old and new. You probably don't like it all, but God does! If it is offered to God in spirit and truth, it is an act of worship.

Worship is far more than music.

Christians often disagree over the style of music used in worship, passionately defending their preferred style as the most biblical or God-honoring. But there is no biblical style! There are no musical notes in the Bible; we don't even have the instruments they used in Bible times.

Frankly, the music style you like best says more about *you* — your background and personality — than it does about God. One ethnic group's music can sound like noise to another. But God likes variety and enjoys it all.

There is no such thing as "Christian" music; there are only Christian lyrics. It is the words that make a song sacred, not the tune. There are no spiritual tunes. If I played a song for you without the words, you'd have no way of knowing if it were a "Christian" song.

Worship is not for your benefit. As a pastor, I receive notes that say, "I loved the worship today. I got a lot out of it." This is another misconception about worship. It isn't for our benefit! We worship for God's benefit. When we worship, our goal is to bring pleasure to God, not ourselves.

If you have ever said, "I didn't get anything out of worship today," you worshiped for the wrong reason. Worship isn't for you. It's for God. Of course, most "worship" services also include elements of fellowship, edification, and evangelism, and there *are* benefits to worship, but we don't worship to please ourselves. Our motive is to bring glory and pleasure to our Creator.

In Isaiah 29 God complains about worship that is halfhearted and hypocritical. The people were offering God stale prayers, insincere praise, empty words, and man-made rituals without even thinking about the meaning. God's heart is not touched by tradition in worship, but by passion and commitment. The Bible says, *"These people come near to me with their mouth and honor me with their lips, but their hearts are far from me. Their worship of me is made up only of rules taught by men."*[5]

Worship is not a *part* of your life; it *is* your life. Worship is not just for church services. We are told to *"worship him continually"*[6] and to *"praise him from sunrise to sunset."*[7] In the Bible people praised God at work, at home, in battle, in jail, and even in bed! Praise should be the first activity when you open your eyes in the morning and the last activity when you close them at night.[8] David said, *"I will thank the Lord at all times. My mouth will always praise him."*[9]

Every activity can be transformed into an act of worship when you do it for the praise, glory, and pleasure of God. The Bible says, *"So whether you eat or drink or whatever you do, do it all for the glory of God."*[10] Martin Luther said, "A dairymaid can milk cows to the glory of God."

DAY 8:

Planned for God's Pleasure

How is it possible to do everything to the glory of God? By doing everything *as if you were doing it for Jesus* and by carrying on a continual conversation with him while you do it. The Bible says, *"Whatever you do, work at it with all your heart, as working for the Lord, not for men."*[11]

This is the secret to a lifestyle of worship — doing everything as if you were doing it for Jesus. The Message paraphrase says, *"Take your everyday, ordinary life — your sleeping, eating, going-to-work, and walking-around life — and place it before God as an offering."*[12] Work becomes worship when you dedicate it to God and perform it with an awareness of his presence.

When I first fell in love with my wife, I thought of her constantly: while eating breakfast, driving to school, attending class, waiting in line at the market, pumping gas — I could not stop thinking about this woman! I often talked to myself about her and thought about all the things I loved about her. This helped me feel close to Kay even though we lived several hundred miles apart and attended different colleges. By constantly thinking of her, I was *abiding in her love*. This is what real worship is all about — *falling in love with Jesus*.

DAY 8

Thinking about My Purpose

POINT TO PONDER: I was planned for God's pleasure.

VERSE TO REMEMBER: *"The LORD takes pleasure in his people."* PSALM 149:4A (TEV)

QUESTION TO CONSIDER: What common task could I start doing as if I were doing it directly for Jesus?

MESSAGE TO HEAR: *www.purposedriven.com/day8*

DAY 9

What Makes God Smile?

> *May the LORD smile on you....*
> NUMBERS 6:25 (NLT)

> *Smile on me, your servant;*
> *teach me the right way to live.*
> PSALM 119:135 (MSG)

purposedriven.com/
day9

THE SMILE OF GOD IS THE GOAL OF YOUR LIFE.

Since pleasing God is the first purpose of your life, your most important task is to discover how to do that. The Bible says, *"Figure out what will please Christ, and then do it."*[1] Fortunately, the Bible gives us a clear example of a life that gives pleasure to God. The man's name was Noah.

In Noah's day, the entire world had become morally bankrupt. Everyone lived for their own pleasure, not God's. God couldn't find *anyone* on earth interested in pleasing him, so he was grieved and regretted making

88

man. God became so disgusted with the human race that he considered wiping it out. But there was one man who made God smile. The Bible says, *"Noah was a pleasure to the Lord."*[2]

God said, "This guy brings me pleasure. He makes me smile. I will start over with his family." Because Noah brought pleasure to God, you and I are alive today. From his life we learn the five acts of worship that make God smile.

God smiles when we love him supremely. Noah loved God more than anything else in the world, even when *no one else* did! The Bible tells us that for his entire life, *"Noah consistently followed God's will and enjoyed a close relationship with Him."*[3]

This is what God wants most from you: a relationship! It's the most astounding truth in the universe —

> What God wants most from you is relationship.

that our Creator wants to fellowship with us. God made you to love you, and he longs for you to love him back. He says, *"I don't want your sacrifices — I want your love; I don't want your offerings — I want you to know me."*[4]

Can you sense God's passion for you in this verse? God deeply loves you and *desires* your love in return. He *longs* for you to know him and spend time with him. This is why learning to love God and be loved by him should be the greatest objective of your life. Nothing else comes close in importance. Jesus called it the greatest commandment. He said, *"Love the Lord your God with all your heart and with all your soul and with all your mind. This is the first and greatest commandment."*[5]

God smiles when we trust him completely. The second reason Noah pleased God was that he trusted God, even when it didn't make sense. The Bible says, *"By faith, Noah built a ship in the middle of dry land. He was warned about something he couldn't see, and acted on what he was told.... As a result, Noah became intimate with God."*[6]

Imagine this scene: One day God comes to Noah and says, "I'm disappointed in human beings. In the entire world, no one but you thinks about me. But Noah, when I look at you, I start smiling. I'm pleased with your life, so I'm going to flood the world and start over with your family. I want you to build a giant ship that will save you and the animals."

There were three problems that could have caused Noah to doubt. First, Noah had never seen rain, because prior to the Flood, God irrigated the earth from the ground up.[7] Second, Noah lived hundreds of miles from the nearest ocean. Even if he could learn to build a ship, how would he get it to water? Third, there was the problem of rounding up all the animals and then caring for them. But Noah didn't complain or make excuses. He trusted God completely, and that made God smile.

Trusting God completely means having faith that he knows what is best for your life. You expect him to keep his promises, help you with problems, and do the impossible when necessary. The Bible says, *"He takes pleasure in those that honor Him; in those who trust in His constant love."*[8]

It took Noah 120 years to build the ark. I imagine he faced many discouraging days. With no sign of rain year after year, he was ruthlessly criticized as a "crazy man who thinks God speaks to him." I imagine Noah's children were often embarrassed by the giant ship being built in their front yard. Yet Noah kept on trusting God.

> *Trusting God completely means having faith that he knows what is best for your life.*

In what areas of your life do you need to trust God completely? Trusting is an act of worship. Just as parents are pleased when children trust their love and wisdom, your faith makes God happy. The Bible says, *"Without faith it is impossible to please God."*[9]

God smiles when we obey him wholeheartedly. Saving the animal population from a worldwide flood required great attention to logistics and details. Everything had to be done *just as God prescribed it.* God didn't say, "Build any old boat you'd like, Noah." He gave very detailed instructions as to the size, shape, and materials of the ark as well as the different numbers of animals to be brought on board. The Bible tells us Noah's response: *"So Noah did everything exactly as God had commanded him."*[10]

Notice that Noah obeyed *completely* (no instruction was overlooked), and he obeyed *exactly* (in the way and time God wanted it done). That is wholeheartedness. It is no wonder God smiled on Noah.

If God asked you to build a giant boat, don't you think you might have a few questions, objections, or reservations? Noah didn't. He obeyed God wholeheartedly. That means doing whatever God asks without reservation or hesitation. You don't procrastinate and say, "I'll pray about it." You do it without delay. Every parent knows that delayed obedience is really disobedience.

God doesn't owe you an explanation or reason for everything he asks you to do. Understanding can wait, but obedience can't. Instant obedience will teach you more about God than a lifetime of Bible discussions. In fact, you will never understand some commands until you obey them first. Obedience unlocks understanding.

Often we try to offer God *partial* obedience. We want to pick and choose the commands we obey. We make a list of the commands we like and obey those while ignoring the ones we think are unreasonable, difficult, expensive, or unpopular. I'll attend church but I won't tithe. I'll read my Bible but won't forgive the person who hurt me. Yet partial obedience is disobedience.

Wholehearted obedience is done joyfully, with enthusiasm. The Bible says, *"Obey him gladly."*[11] This is the attitude of David: *"Just tell me what to do and I will do it, Lord. As long as I live I'll wholeheartedly obey."*[12]

James, speaking to Christians, said, *"We please God by what we do and not only by what we believe."*[13] God's Word is clear that you can't earn your salvation. It comes only by grace, not your effort. But as a child of God you can bring pleasure to your heavenly Father through obedience. Any act of obedience is also an act of worship. Why is obedience so pleasing to God? Because it proves you really love him. Jesus said, *"If you love me, you will obey my commandments."*[14]

God smiles when we praise and thank him continually. Few things feel better than receiving heartfelt praise and appreciation from someone else. God loves it, too. He smiles when we express our adoration and gratitude to him.

Noah's life brought pleasure to God because he lived with a heart of praise and thanksgiving. Noah's first act after surviving the Flood was to express his thanks to God by offering a sacrifice. The Bible says, *"Then Noah built an altar to the LORD ... and sacrificed burnt offerings on it."*[15]

Because of Jesus' sacrifice, we don't offer animal sacrifices as Noah did. Instead we are told to offer God *"the sacrifice of praise"*[16] and *"the sacrifice of thanksgiving."*[17] We praise God for *who he is*, and we thank God for *what he has done*. David said, *"I will praise*

God's name in song and glorify him with thanksgiving. This will please the LORD."[18]

An amazing thing happens when we offer praise and thanksgiving to God. When we give God enjoyment, our own hearts are filled with joy!

My mother loved to cook for me. Even after I married Kay, when we would visit my parents, Mom prepared incredible home-cooked feasts. One of her great pleasures in life was watching us kids eat and enjoy what she prepared. The more we enjoyed eating it, the more enjoyment it gave her.

But we also enjoyed pleasing Mom by expressing our enjoyment of her meal. It worked both ways. As I would eat the great meal, I would rave about it and praise my mother. I intended not only to enjoy the food but to please my mother. Everyone was happy.

Worship works both ways, too. We enjoy what God has done for us, and when we express that enjoyment to God, it brings him joy — but it also increases *our* joy. The book of Psalms says, *"The righteous are glad and rejoice in his presence; they are happy and shout for joy."*[19]

God smiles when we use our abilities. After the Flood, God gave Noah these simple instructions: *"Be fruitful and increase in number and fill the earth.... Everything that lives and moves will be food for you. Just as I gave you the green plants, I now give you everything."*[20]

God said, "It's time to get on with your life! Do the things I designed humans to do. Make love to your spouse. Have babies. Raise families. Plant crops and eat meals. Be humans! This is what I made you to be!"

You may feel that the only time God is pleased with you is when you're doing "spiritual" activities — like reading the Bible, attending church, praying, or sharing your faith. And you may think God is unconcerned about the other parts of your life. Actually, God enjoys watching *every* detail of your life, whether you are working, playing, resting, or eating. He doesn't miss a single move you make. The Bible tells us, *"The steps of the godly are directed by the* LORD. *He delights in every detail of their lives."*[21]

Every human activity, except sin, can be done for God's pleasure if you do it with an attitude of praise. You can wash dishes, repair a machine, sell a product, write a computer program, grow a crop, and raise a family for the glory of God.

> God enjoys watching every detail of your life.

Like a proud parent, God especially enjoys watching you use the talents and abilities he has given you. God intentionally gifted us differently for his enjoyment. He has made some to be athletic and some to be analytical. You may be gifted at mechanics or mathematics or music or a thousand other skills. All these abilities can bring a smile to God's face. The Bible says, *"He has shaped each person in turn; now he watches everything we do."*[22]

You don't bring glory or pleasure to God by hiding your abilities or by trying to be someone else. You only bring him enjoyment by being you. Anytime you reject any part of yourself, you are rejecting God's wisdom and sovereignty in creating you. God says, *"You have no right to argue with your Creator. You are merely a clay pot shaped by a potter. The clay doesn't ask, 'Why did you make me this way?'"*[23]

In the film *Chariots of Fire,* Olympic runner Eric Liddell says, "I believe God made me for a purpose, but he also made me fast, and when I run, I feel God's pleasure." Later he says, "To give up running would be to hold him in contempt." There are no *unspiritual* abilities, just misused ones. Start using yours for God's pleasure.

DAY 9:
What Makes
God Smile?

God also gains pleasure in watching you *enjoy* his creation. He gave you eyes to enjoy beauty, ears to enjoy sounds, your nose and taste buds to enjoy smells and tastes, and the nerves under your skin to enjoy touch. Every act of enjoyment becomes an act of worship when you thank God for it. In fact, the Bible says, *"God ... generously gives us everything for our enjoyment."*[24]

God even enjoys watching you sleep! When my children were small, I remember the deep satisfaction of watching them sleep. Sometimes the day had been filled with problems and disobedience, but asleep they looked contented, secure, and peaceful, and I was reminded of how much I love them.

My children didn't have to do anything for me to enjoy

them. I was happy to just watch them *breathing*, because I loved them so much. As their little chests would rise and fall, I'd smile, and sometimes tears of joy filled my eyes. When you are sleeping, God gazes at you with love, because you were his idea. He loves you as if you were the only person on earth.

Parents do not require their children to be perfect, or even mature, in order to enjoy them. They enjoy them at every stage of development. In the same way, God doesn't wait for you to reach maturity before he starts liking you. He loves and enjoys you at every stage of your spiritual development.

You may have had unpleasable teachers or parents as you were growing up. Please don't assume God feels that way about you. He knows you are incapable of being perfect or sinless. The Bible says, *"He certainly knows what we are made of. He bears in mind that we are dust."*[25]

What God looks at is the attitude of your heart: Is pleasing him your deepest desire? This was Paul's life goal: *"More than anything else, however, we want to please him, whether in our home here or there."*[26] When you live in light of eternity, your focus changes from "How much pleasure am I getting out of life?" to "How much pleasure is God getting out of my life?"

God is looking for people like Noah in the twenty-first century — people willing to live for the pleasure of God. The Bible says, *"The Lord looks down from heaven on all mankind to see if there are any who are wise, who want to please God."*[27]

Will you make pleasing God the goal of your life? There is nothing that God won't do for the person totally absorbed with this goal.

DAY 9

Thinking about My Purpose

POINT TO PONDER: God smiles when I trust him.

VERSE TO REMEMBER: *"The Lord is pleased with those who worship him and trust his love."* PSALM 147:11 (CEV)

QUESTION TO CONSIDER: Since God knows what is best, in what areas of my life do I need to trust him most?

MESSAGE TO HEAR: *www.purposedriven.com/day9*

The Heart of Worship

Give yourselves to God....
Surrender your whole being
to him to be used
for righteous purposes.

ROMANS 6:13 (TEV)

purposedriven.com/
day10

THE HEART OF WORSHIP IS SURRENDER.

Surrender is an unpopular word, disliked almost as much as the word *submission.* It implies losing, and no one wants to be a *loser. Surrender* evokes the unpleasant images of admitting defeat in battle, forfeiting a game, or yielding to a stronger opponent. The word is almost always used in a negative context. Captured criminals *surrender* to authorities.

In today's competitive culture we are taught to never give up and never give in — so we don't hear much about surrendering. If winning is everything, surrendering is *unthinkable.* We would rather talk about winning, succeeding, overcoming, and conquering than yielding, submitting, obeying, and surrendering. But surrendering to God is the heart of worship. It is the natural response to God's amazing love and mercy. We give ourselves to him, not out of fear or duty, but in love, *"because he first loved us."*[1]

After spending eleven chapters of the book of Romans explaining God's incredible grace to us, Paul urges us to fully surrender our lives to God in worship: *"So then, my friends, because of God's great mercy to us ... offer yourselves as a living sacrifice to God, dedicated to his service and pleasing to him. This is the true worship that you should offer."*[2]

> Offering yourself to God is what worship is all about.

True worship — bringing God pleasure — happens when you give yourself completely to God. Notice the first and last words of that verse are the same: *offer.*

Offering yourself to God is what worship is all about.

This act of personal surrender is called many things: consecration, making Jesus your Lord, taking up your cross, dying to self, yielding to the Spirit. What matters is that you do it, not what you call it. God wants your life — all of it. Ninety-five percent is not enough.

There are three barriers that block our total surrender to God: fear, pride, and confusion. We don't realize how much God loves us, we want to control our own lives, and we misunderstand the meaning of surrender.

Can I trust God? Trust is an essential ingredient to surrender. You won't surrender to God unless you trust him, but you can't trust him until you know him better. Fear keeps us from surrendering, but *love casts out all fear.* The more you realize how much God loves you, the easier surrender becomes.

How do you know God loves you? He gives you many evidences: God says he loves you;[3] you're never out of his sight;[4] he cares about every detail of your life;[5] he gave you the capacity to enjoy all kinds of pleasure;[6] he has good plans for your life;[7] he forgives you;[8] and he is lovingly patient with you.[9] God loves you infinitely more than you can imagine.

The greatest expression of this is the sacrifice of God's Son for you. *"God proves his love for us in that while we still were sinners Christ died for us."*[10] If you want to know how much you matter to God, look at Christ with his arms outstretched on the cross, saying, "I love you this much! I'd rather die than live without you."

God is not a cruel slave driver or a bully who uses brute force to coerce us into submission. He doesn't try to break our will, but woos us to himself so that we might offer ourselves freely to him. God is a lover and a liberator, and surrendering to him brings freedom, not bondage. When we completely surrender ourselves to

Jesus, we discover that he is not a tyrant, but a savior; not a boss, but a brother; not a dictator, but a friend.

Admitting our limitations. A second barrier to total surrender is our pride. We don't want to admit that we're just creatures and not in charge of everything. It is the oldest temptation: *"You'll be like God!"*[11] That desire — to have complete control — is the cause of so much stress in our lives. Life is a struggle, but what most people don't realize is that our struggle, like Jacob's, is really a struggle with God! We want to be God, and there's no way we are going to win that struggle.

A. W. Tozer said, "The reason why many are still troubled, still seeking, still making little forward progress is because they haven't yet come to the end of themselves. We're still trying to give orders, and interfering with God's work within us."

We aren't God and *never* will be. We are humans. It is when we try to be God that we end up most like Satan, who desired the same thing.

We accept our humanity intellectually, but not emotionally. When faced with our own limitations, we react with irritation, anger, and resentment. We want to be taller (or shorter), smarter, stronger, more talented, more beautiful, and wealthier. We want to have it all and do it all, and we become upset when it doesn't happen. Then when we notice that God gave others characteristics we don't have, we respond with envy, jealousy, and self-pity.

What it means to surrender. Surrendering to God is not passive resignation, fatalism, or an excuse for laziness. It is not accepting the status quo. It may mean the exact opposite: sacrificing your life or suffering in order to change what needs to be changed. God often calls surrendered people to do battle on his behalf. Surrendering is not for cowards or doormats. Likewise, it does not mean giving up rational thinking. God would not waste the mind he gave you! God does not want robots to serve him.

Surrendering is not repressing your personality. God wants to use your unique personality. Rather than its being diminished, surrendering enhances it. C. S. Lewis observed, "The more we let God take us over, the more truly ourselves we become — because he made us. He invented all the different people that you and I were intended to be.... It is when I turn to Christ, when I give up myself to His personality, that I first begin to have a real personality of my own."

Surrendering is best demonstrated in obedience. You say *"yes, Lord"* to whatever he asks of you. To say *"no, Lord"* is to speak a contradiction. You can't call Jesus your Lord when you refuse to obey him. After a night of failed fishing, Simon modeled surrender when Jesus told him to try again: *"Master, we've worked hard all night and haven't caught anything. But because you say so, I will let down the nets."*[12] Surrendered people obey God's word, even if it doesn't make sense.

Another aspect of a fully surrendered life is trust. Abraham followed God's leading without knowing *where* it would take him. Hannah waited for God's perfect timing without knowing *when*. Mary expected a miracle without knowing *how*. Joseph trusted God's purpose without knowing *why* circumstances happened the way they did. Each of these people were fully surrendered to God.

You know you're surrendered to God when you rely on God to work things out instead of trying to manipulate others, force your agenda, and control the situation. You let go and let God work. You don't have to always be "in charge." The Bible says, *"Surrender yourself to the Lord, and wait patiently for him."*[13] Instead of trying harder, you trust more. You also know you're surrendered when you don't react to criticism and rush to defend yourself. Surrendered hearts show up best in relationships. You don't edge others out, you don't demand your rights, and you aren't self-serving when you're surrendered.

Surrender is best demonstrated in obedience and trust.

The most difficult area to surrender for many people is their money. Many have thought, "I want to live for God but I also want to earn enough money to live comfortably and retire someday." Retirement is not the goal of a surrendered life, because it competes with God for the primary attention of our lives. Jesus said, *"You cannot* serve *both God and money*"[14] and *"Wherever your treasure is, your heart will be also."*[15]

The supreme example of self-surrender is Jesus. The night before his crucifixion Jesus surrendered himself to God's plan. He prayed, *"Father, everything is possible for you. Please take this cup of suffering away from me. Yet I want your will, not mine."*[16]

Jesus didn't pray, "God, if you're *able* to take away this pain, please do so." He had already affirmed that God can do anything! Instead he prayed, "God, if it is in *your* best interest to remove this suffering, please do so. *But* if it fulfills *your* purpose, that's what I want, too."

Genuine surrender says, "Father, if this problem, pain, sickness, or circumstance is needed to fulfill your purpose and glory in my life or in another's, please *don't* take it away." This level of maturity does not come easy. In Jesus' case, he agonized so much over God's plan that he sweat drops of blood. Surrender is hard work. In our case, it is intense warfare against our self-centered nature.

The blessing of surrender. The Bible is crystal clear about how you benefit when you fully surrender your life to God. First, you experience peace: *"Stop quarreling with God! If you agree with him, you will have peace at last, and things will go well for you."*[17] Next, you experience freedom: *"Offer yourselves to the ways of God and the freedom never quits.... [his] commands set you free to live openly in his freedom!"*[18] Third, you experience God's power in your life. Stubborn temptations and overwhelming problems can be defeated by Christ when given to him.

As Joshua approached the biggest battle of his life,[19] he encountered God, fell in worship before him, and surrendered his plans. That surrender led to a stunning victory at Jericho. This is the paradox: Victory comes through surrender. Surrender doesn't weaken you; it strengthens you. Surrendered to God, you don't have to fear or surrender to anything else. William Booth, founder of the Salvation Army, said, "The greatness of a man's power is in the measure of his surrender."

Surrendered people are the ones God uses. God chose Mary to be the mother of Jesus, not because she was talented or wealthy or beautiful, but because she was totally surrendered to him. When the angel explained God's improbable plan, she calmly responded, *"I am the Lord's servant, and I am willing to accept whatever he wants."*[20] Nothing is more powerful than a surrendered life in the hands of God. *"So give yourselves completely to God."*[21]

The best way to live. Everybody eventually surrenders to something or someone. If not to God, you will surrender to the opinions or expectations of others, to money, to resentment, to fear, or to your own pride, lusts, or ego. You were designed to worship God — and if you fail to worship him, you will create other things (idols) to give your life to. You are free to choose what you surrender to, but you are not free from the consequences of that choice. E. Stanley Jones said, "If you don't surrender to Christ, you surrender to chaos."

Surrender is not the *best* way to live; it is the *only* way to live. Nothing else works. All other approaches lead to frustration, disappointment, and self-destruction. The King James Version calls surrender "your *reasonable* service."[22] Another version translates it "the most *sensible* way to serve God."[23] Surrendering your life is not a foolish emotional impulse but a rational, intelligent act, the most responsible and sensible thing you can do with your life. That is why Paul said, *"So we make it our goal to please him."*[24] Your wisest moments will be those when you say yes to God.

Sometimes it takes years, but eventually you discover that the greatest hindrance to God's blessing in your life is not others, it is yourself — your self-will, stubborn pride, and personal ambition. You cannot fulfill God's purposes for your life while focusing on your own plans.

> *Surrender is not the best way to live; it is the only way to live. Nothing else works.*

If God is going to do his deepest work in you, it will begin with this. So give it all to God: your past regrets, your present problems, your future ambitions, your fears, dreams, weaknesses, habits, hurts, and hang-ups. Put Jesus Christ in the driver's seat of your life and take your hands off the steering wheel. Don't be afraid; nothing under his control can ever be out of control. Mastered by

Christ, you can handle anything. You will be like Paul: *"I am ready for anything and equal to anything through Him who infuses inner strength into me, that is, I am self-sufficient in Christ's sufficiency."*[25]

Paul's moment of surrender occurred on the Damascus road after he was knocked down by a blinding light. For others, God gets our attention with less drastic methods. Regardless, surrendering is never just a one-time event. Paul said, "I die *daily*."[26] There is a *moment* of surrender, and there is the *practice* of surrender, which is moment-by-moment and lifelong. The problem with a *living* sacrifice is that it can crawl off the altar, so you may have to resurrender your life fifty times a day. You must make it a daily habit. Jesus said, *"If people want to follow me, they must give up the things they want. They must be willing to give up their lives daily to follow me."*[27]

Let me warn you: When you decide to live a totally surrendered life, that decision will be tested. Sometimes it will mean doing inconvenient, unpopular, costly, or seemingly impossible tasks. It will often mean doing the opposite of what you feel like doing.

One of the great Christian leaders of the twentieth century was Bill Bright, the founder of Campus Crusade for Christ. Through Crusade staff around the world, the Four Spiritual Laws tract, and the *Jesus* film (seen by over four billion people), more than 150 million people have come to Christ and will spend eternity in heaven.

I once asked Bill, "Why did God use and bless your life

so much?" He said, "When I was a young man, I made a contract with God. I literally wrote it out and signed my name at the bottom. It said, 'From this day forward, I am a slave of Jesus Christ.'"

Have you ever signed a contract like that with God? Or are you still arguing and struggling with God over his right to do with your life as he pleases? Now is your time to surrender — to God's grace, love, and wisdom.

DAY 10

Thinking about My Purpose

POINT TO PONDER: The heart of worship is surrender.

VERSE TO REMEMBER: *"Surrender your whole being to him to be used for righteous purposes."* ROMANS 6:13B (TEV)

QUESTION TO CONSIDER: What area of my life am I holding back from God?

MESSAGE TO HEAR: *www.purposedriven.com/day10*

DAY 11

Becoming Best Friends with God

Since we were restored to friendship with God by the death of his Son while we were still his enemies, we will certainly be delivered from eternal punishment by his life.

ROMANS 5:10 (NLT)

purposedriven.com/
day11

GOD WANTS TO BE YOUR BEST FRIEND.

Your relationship to God has many different aspects: God is your Creator and Maker, Lord and Master, Judge, Redeemer, Father, Savior, and much more.[1] But the most shocking truth is this: Almighty God yearns to be your Friend!

In Eden we see God's ideal relationship with us: Adam and Eve enjoyed an intimate friendship with God. There were no rituals, ceremonies, or religion — just a simple loving relationship between God and the people he created. Unhindered by guilt or fear, Adam and Eve delighted in God, and he delighted in them.

We were made to live in God's continual presence, but after the Fall, that ideal relationship was lost. Only a few people in Old Testament times had the privilege of friendship with God. Moses and Abraham were called "friends of God," David was called "a man after [God's] own heart," and Job, Enoch, and Noah had intimate friendships with God.[2] But fear of God, not friendship, was more common in the Old Testament.

Then Jesus changed the situation. When he paid for our sins on the cross, the veil in the temple that symbolized our separation from God was split from top to bottom, indicating that direct access to God was once again available.

Unlike the Old Testament priests who had to spend hours preparing to meet him, we can now approach God anytime. The Bible says, *"Now we can rejoice in our wonderful new relationship with God — all because of what our Lord Jesus Christ has done for us in making us friends of God."*[3]

Friendship with God is possible only because of the grace of God and the sacrifice of Jesus. *"All this is done by God, who through Christ changed us from enemies into his friends."*[4] The old hymn says, "What a friend we have in Jesus," but actually, God invites us to enjoy friendship and fellowship with all three persons of the Trinity: our Father,[5] the Son,[6] and the Holy Spirit.[7]

Jesus said, *"I no longer call you servants, because a servant does not know his master's business. Instead, I have called you friends, for everything that I learned from my Father I have made known to you."*[8] The word for *friend* in this verse does not mean a casual acquaintance but a close, trusted relationship. The same word is used to refer to the best man at a wedding[9] and a king's inner circle of intimate, trusted friends. In royal courts, servants must keep their distance from the king, but the inner circle of trusted friends enjoy close contact, direct access, and confidential information.

That God would want me for a close friend is hard to understand, but the Bible says, *"He is a God who is passionate about his relationship with you."*[10]

God deeply desires that we know him intimately. In fact, he planned the universe and orchestrated history, including the details of our lives, so that we could become his friends. The Bible says, *"He made the entire human race and made the earth hospitable, with plenty of time and space for living so we could seek after God, and not just grope around in the dark but actually* find *him."*[11]

> *Knowing and loving God is our greatest privilege, and being known and loved is God's greatest pleasure.*

Knowing and loving God is our greatest privilege, and being known and loved is God's greatest pleasure. God says, *"If any want to boast, they should boast that they know and understand me.... These are the things that please me."*[12]

It's difficult to imagine how an intimate friendship is possible between an omnipotent, invisible, perfect God and a finite, sinful human being. It's easier to understand a Master-servant relationship or a Creator-creation relationship or even Father-child. But what does it mean when God wants me as a friend? By looking at the lives of God's friends in the Bible, we learn six secrets of friendship with God. We will look at two secrets in this chapter and four more in the next.

Becoming a Best Friend of God

Through constant conversation. You will never grow a close relationship with God by just attending church once a week or even having a daily quiet time. Friendship with God is built by sharing *all* your life experiences with him.

Of course, it is important to establish the habit of a daily devotional time with God,[13] but he wants more than an appointment in your schedule. He wants to be included in *every* activity, every conversation, every problem, and even every thought. You can carry on a continuous, open-ended conversation with him throughout your day, talking with him about whatever you are doing or thinking *at that moment.* "Praying without ceasing"[14] means conversing with God while shopping, driving, working, or performing any other everyday tasks.

A common misconception is that "spending time with God" means being *alone* with him. Of course, as Jesus modeled, you need time alone with God, but that is only a fraction of your waking hours. *Everything* you do can be "spending time with God" if he is invited to be a part of it and you stay aware of his presence.

The classic book on learning how to develop a constant conversation with God is *Practicing the Presence of God.* It was written in the seventeenth century by Brother Lawrence, a humble cook in a French monastery. Brother Lawrence was able to turn even the most commonplace and menial tasks, like preparing meals and washing dishes, into acts of praise and communion with God. The key to friendship with God, he said, is not changing what you do, but changing *your attitude* toward what you do. What you normally do for yourself you begin doing for God, whether it is eating, bathing, working, relaxing, or taking out the trash.

Today we often feel we must "get away" from our daily routine in order to worship God, but that is only because we haven't learned to practice his presence all the time. Brother Lawrence found it easy to worship God through the common tasks of life; he didn't have to go away for special spiritual retreats.

This is God's ideal. In Eden, worship was not an event

to attend, but a perpetual attitude; Adam and Eve were in constant communion with God. Because God is with you all the time, no place is any closer to God than the place where you are right now. The Bible says, *"He rules everything and is everywhere and is in everything."*[15]

Another of Brother Lawrence's helpful ideas was to pray shorter conversational prayers *continually* through the day rather than trying to pray long sessions of complex prayers. To maintain focus and counteract wandering thoughts, he said, "I do not advise you to use a great multiplicity of words in prayer, since long discourses are often the occasions for wandering."[16] In an age of attention deficit, this 350-year-old suggestion to keep it simple seems to be particularly relevant.

> *Everything you do can be "spending time with God" if he is invited to be a part of it and you stay aware of his presence.*

The Bible tells us to *"pray all the time."*[17] How is it possible to do this? One way is to use "breath prayers" throughout the day, as many Christians have done for centuries. You choose a brief sentence or a simple phrase that can be repeated to Jesus in one breath: "You are with me." "I receive your grace." "I'm depending on you." "I want to know you." "I belong to you." "Help me trust you." You can also use a short phrase of Scripture: "For me to live is Christ." "You will never leave me." "You are my

God." Pray it as often as possible so it is rooted deep in your heart. Just be sure that your motive is to honor God, not control him.

Practicing the presence of God is a skill, a habit you can develop. Just as musicians practice scales every day in order to play beautiful music with ease, you must force yourself to think about God at different times in your day. You must train your mind to remember God.

At first you will need to create reminders to regularly bring your thoughts back to the awareness that God is with you in that moment. Begin by placing visual reminders around you. You might post little notes that say, *"God is with me and for me right now!"* Benedictine monks use the hourly chimes of a clock to remind them to pause and pray "the hour prayer." If you have a watch or cell phone with an alarm, you could do the same. Sometimes you will sense God's presence; other times you won't.

If you are seeking an *experience* of his presence through all of this, you have missed the point. We don't praise God to feel good, but to *do* good. Your goal is not a feeling, but a continual awareness of the *reality* that God is always present. That is the lifestyle of worship.

Through continual meditation. A second way to establish a friendship with God is by thinking about his Word throughout your day. This is called meditation, and the Bible repeatedly urges us to meditate on who God is, what he has done, and what he has said.[18]

It is impossible to be God's friend apart from *knowing what he says*. You can't love God unless you know him, and you can't know him without knowing his Word. The Bible says God *"revealed himself to Samuel through his word."*[19] God still uses that method today.

While you cannot spend all day studying the Bible, you can *think* about it throughout the day, recalling verses you have read or memorized and mulling them over in your mind.

DAY 11:

Becoming Best Friends with God

Meditation is often misunderstood as some difficult, mysterious ritual practiced by isolated monks and mystics. But meditation is simply focused thinking — a skill anyone can learn and use anywhere.

When you think about a problem over and over in your mind, that's called worry. When you think about God's Word over and over in your mind, that's meditation. If you know how to worry, you already know how to meditate! You just need to switch your attention from your problems to Bible verses. The more you meditate on God's Word, the less you will have to worry about.

The reason God considered Job and David his close friends was that they valued his Word above everything else, and they thought about it continually throughout the day. Job admitted, *"I have treasured the words of his mouth more than my daily bread."*[20] David said, *"Oh, how I love your law! I meditate on it all day long."*[21] *"They are constantly in my thoughts. I cannot stop thinking about them.*"[22]

Friends share secrets, and God will share his secrets with you if you develop the habit of thinking about his Word throughout the day. God told Abraham his secrets, and he did the same with Daniel, Paul, the disciples, and other friends.[23]

When you read your Bible or hear a sermon or listen to a tape, don't just forget it and walk away. Develop the practice of reviewing the truth in your mind, thinking about it over and over. The more time you spend reviewing what God has said, the more you will understand the "secrets" of this life that most people miss. The Bible says, *"Friendship with God is reserved for those who reverence him. With them alone he shares the secrets of his promises."*[24]

In the next chapter we will see four more secrets of cultivating a friendship with God, but don't wait until tomorrow. Start today by practicing constant conversation with God and continual meditation on his Word. Prayer lets you speak to God; meditation lets God speak to you. Both are essential to becoming a friend of God.

DAY 11

Thinking about My Purpose

POINT TO PONDER: God wants to be my best friend.

VERSE TO REMEMBER: *"Friendship with God is reserved for those who reverence him."* PSALM 25:14A (LB)

QUESTION TO CONSIDER: What can I do to remind myself to think about God and talk to him more often throughout the day?

MESSAGE TO HEAR: *www.purposedriven.com/day11*

DAY 12

Developing Your Friendship with God

He offers his friendship to the godly.

PROVERBS 3:32 (NLT)

purposedriven.com/
day12

*Draw close to God, and
God will draw close to you.*

JAMES 4:8 (NLT)

YOU ARE AS CLOSE TO GOD AS YOU CHOOSE TO BE.

Like any friendship, you must work at developing your friendship with God. It won't happen by accident. It takes desire, time, and energy. If you want a deeper, more intimate connection with God you must learn to honestly share your feelings with him, trust him when he asks you to do something, learn to care about what he cares about, and desire his friendship more than anything else.

I must choose to be honest with God. The first building block of a deeper friendship with God is complete honesty — about your faults and your feelings.

God doesn't expect you to be perfect, but he does insist on complete honesty. None of God's friends in the Bible were perfect. If perfection was a requirement for friendship with God, we would never be able to be his friends. Fortunately, because of God's grace, Jesus is still the *"friend of sinners."*[1]

> God doesn't expect you to be perfect, but he does insist on complete honesty.

In the Bible, the friends of God were honest about their feelings, often complaining, second-guessing, accusing, and arguing with their Creator. God, however, didn't seem to be bothered by this frankness; in fact, he encouraged it.

God allowed Abraham to question and challenge him over the destruction of the city of Sodom. Abraham pestered God over what it would take to spare the city, negotiating God down from fifty righteous people to only ten.

God also listened patiently to David's many accusations of unfairness, betrayal, and abandonment. God did not slay Jeremiah when he claimed that God had tricked him. Job was allowed to vent his bitterness during his ordeal, and in the end, God defended Job for being honest, and he rebuked Job's friends for being inauthentic. God told them, *"You haven't been honest either with me or about me — not the way my friend Job has.... My friend Job will now pray for you and I will accept his prayer."*[2]

In one startling example of frank friendship,[3]

God honestly expressed his total disgust with Israel's disobedience. He told Moses he would keep his promise to give the Israelites the Promised Land, *but* he wasn't going one step farther with them in the desert! God was fed up, and he let Moses know exactly how he felt.

Moses, speaking as a "friend" of God, responded with equal candor: *"Look, you tell me to lead this people but you don't let me know whom you're going to send with me.... If I'm so special to you, let me in on your plans.... Don't forget, this is YOUR people, your responsibility.... If your presence doesn't take the lead here, call this trip off right now! How else will I know that you're with me in this, with me and your people? Are you traveling with us or not?...' God said to Moses, 'All right. Just as you say; this also I will do, for I know you well and you are special to me.'"*[4]

Can God handle that kind of frank, intense honesty from you? Absolutely! Genuine friendship is built on disclosure. What may appear as *audacity* God views as *authenticity*. God listens to the passionate words of his friends; he is bored with predictable, pious clichés. To be God's friend, you must be honest to God, sharing your true feeling, not what you think you ought to feel or say.

It is likely that you need to confess some hidden anger and resentment at God for certain areas of your life where you have felt cheated or disappointed. Until we mature enough to understand that God uses *everything* for good in our lives, we harbor resentment toward God over our appearance, background, unanswered prayers, past hurts, and other things we would change if we were God. People often blame God for hurts caused by others. This creates what William Backus calls "your hidden rift with God."

Bitterness is the greatest barrier to friendship with God: Why would I want to be God's friend if he allowed *this?* The antidote, of course, is to realize that God *always* acts in your best interest, even when it is painful and you don't understand it. But releasing your resentment and revealing your feeling is the first step to healing. As so many people in the Bible did, tell God exactly how you feel.[5]

> Bitterness is the greatest barrier to friendship with God.

To instruct us in candid honesty, God gave us the book of Psalms — a worship manual, full of ranting, raving, doubts, fears, resentments, and deep passions combined with thanksgiving, praise, and statements of faith. Every possible emotion is catalogued in the Psalms. When you read the emotional confessions of David and others, realize this is how God wants *you* to worship him — holding back nothing of what you feel. You can pray like David: *"I pour out my complaints before him and tell him all my troubles. For I am overwhelmed."*[6]

It's encouraging to know that all of God's closest friends — Moses, David, Abraham, Job, and others — had bouts with doubt. But instead of masking their misgivings with pious clichés, they candidly voiced them openly and publicly. Expressing doubt is sometimes the first step toward the next level of intimacy with God.

I must choose to obey God in faith. Every time you trust God's wisdom and do whatever he says, even when you don't understand it, you deepen your friendship with God. We don't normally think of obedience as a characteristic of friendship; that's reserved for relationships with a parent or the boss or a superior officer, not a friend. However, Jesus made it clear that obedience is a condition of intimacy with God. He said, *"You are my friends if you do what I command."*[7]

In the last chapter I pointed out that the word Jesus used when he called us "friends" could refer to the "friends of the king" in a royal court. While these close companions had special privileges, they were still subject to the king and had to obey his commands. We are friends with God, but we are not his equals. He is our loving leader, and we follow him.

DAY 12:
Developing Your Friendship with God

We obey God, not out of duty or fear or compulsion, but because we *love* him and trust that he knows what is best for us. We *want* to follow Christ out of gratitude for all he has done for us, and the closer we follow him, the deeper our friendship becomes.

Unbelievers often think Christians obey out of obligation or guilt or fear of punishment, but the opposite is true. Because we have been forgiven and set free, we

obey out of love — and our obedience brings great joy! Jesus said, *"I have loved you even as the Father has loved me. Remain in my love. When you obey me, you remain in my love, just as I obey my Father and remain in his love. I have told you this so that you will be filled with my joy. Yes, your joy will overflow!"*[8]

Notice that Jesus expects us to do only what he did with the Father. His relationship with his Father is the model for our friendship with him. Jesus did whatever the Father asked him to do — out of love.

True friendship isn't passive; it acts. When Jesus asks us to love others, help the needy, share our resources, keep our lives clean, offer forgiveness, and bring others to him, love motivates us to obey immediately.

We are often challenged to do *"great things"* for God. Actually, God is more pleased when we do small things for him out of loving obedience. They may be unnoticed by others, but God notices them and considers them acts of worship.

Great opportunities may come once in a lifetime, but small opportunities surround us every day. Even through such simple acts as telling the truth, being kind, and encouraging others, we bring a smile to God's face. God treasures simple acts of obedience more than our prayers, praise, or offerings. The Bible tells us, *"What pleases the LORD more: burnt offerings and sacrifices or obedience to his voice? It is better to obey than to sacrifice."*[9]

Jesus began his public ministry at age thirty by being

baptized by John. At that event God spoke from heaven: *"This is my beloved Son, and I am fully pleased with him."*[10] What had Jesus been doing for thirty years that gave God so much pleasure? The Bible says nothing about those hidden years except for a single phrase in Luke 2:51: *"He went back to Nazareth with them, and lived obediently with them"* (MSG). Thirty years of pleasing God were summed up in two words: *"lived obediently"*!

I must choose to value what God values. This is what friends do — they care about what is important to the other person. The more you become God's friend, the more you will care about the things he cares about, grieve over the things he grieves over, and rejoice over the things that bring pleasure to him.

Paul is the best example of this. God's agenda was his agenda, and God's passion was his: *"The thing that has me so upset is that I care about you so much — this is the passion of God burning inside me!"*[11] David felt the same way: *"Passion for your house burns within me, so those who insult you are also insulting me."*[12]

What does God care about most? The redemption of his people. He wants all his lost children found! That's the whole reason Jesus came to earth. The dearest thing to the heart of God is the death of his Son. The second dearest thing is when his children share that news with others. To be a friend of God, you must care about all the people around you whom God cares about. Friends of God tell their friends about God.

I must desire friendship with God more than anything else. The Psalms are filled with examples of this desire. David passionately desired to know God above all else; he used words like *longing, yearning, thirsting, hungering*. He craved God. He said, *"The thing I seek most of all is the privilege of meditating in his Temple, living in his presence every day of my life, delighting in his incomparable perfections and glory."*[13] In another psalm he said, *"Your love means more than life to me."*[14]

Jacob's passion for God's blessing on his life was so intense that he wrestled in the dirt all night with God, saying, *"I will not let you go unless you bless me."*[15] The amazing part of that story is that God, who is all powerful, let Jacob win! God isn't offended when we "wrestle" with him, because wrestling requires personal contact and brings us close to him! It is also a passionate activity, and God loves it when we are passionate with him.

> The more you become God's friend, the more you will care about the things he cares about.

Paul was another man passionate for friendship with God. Nothing mattered more; it was the first priority, total focus, and ultimate goal of his life. This is the reason God used Paul in such a great way. The Amplified translation expresses the full force of Paul's passion: *"My determined purpose is that I may know Him — that I may progressively become more deeply and intimately acquainted with Him, perceiving and recognizing and understanding the wonders of His Person more strongly and more clearly.*"[16]

The truth is—you are as close to God *as you choose to be.* Intimate friendship with God is a choice, not an accident. You must intentionally seek it. Do you really want it—more than anything? What is it worth to you? Is it worth giving up other things? Is it worth the effort of developing the habits and skills required?

You may have been passionate about God in the past but you've lost that desire. That was the problem of the Christians in Ephesus—they had left their first love. They did all the right things, but out of duty, not love. If you have just been going through the motions spiritually, don't be surprised when God allows pain in your life.

Pain is the fuel of passion—it energizes us with an intensity to change that we don't normally possess. C. S. Lewis said, "Pain is God's megaphone." It is God's way of arousing us from spiritual lethargy. Your problems are not punishment; they are wake-up calls from a loving God. God is not mad at you; he's mad *about* you, and he will do whatever it takes to bring you back into fellowship with him. But there is an easier way to reignite your passion for God: Start asking God to give it to you, and keep on asking until you have it. Pray this throughout your day: "Dear Jesus, more than anything else, I want to get to know you intimately." God told the captives in Babylon, *"When you get serious about finding me and want it more than anything else, I'll make sure you won't be disappointed."*[17]

Your Most Important Relationship

There is nothing—absolutely nothing—more important than developing a friendship with God. It's a relationship that will last forever. Paul told Timothy, *"Some of these people have missed the most important thing in life— they don't know God."*[18] Have you been missing out on the most important thing in life? You can do something about it starting now. Remember, it's your choice. You are as close to God as you choose to be.

DAY 12

Thinking about My Purpose

POINT TO PONDER: I'm as close to God as I choose to be.

VERSE TO REMEMBER: *"Draw close to God, and God will draw close to you."* JAMES 4:8A (NLT)

QUESTION TO CONSIDER: What practical choices will I make today in order to grow closer to God?

MESSAGE TO HEAR: *www.purposedriven.com/day12*

DAY 13

Worship That Pleases God

Love the Lord your God
with all your heart and
with all your soul and
with all your mind and
with all your strength.

MARK 12:30 (NIV)

purposedriven.com/
day13

GOD WANTS ALL OF YOU.

God doesn't want a part of your life. He asks for
all your heart, *all* your soul, *all* your mind, and *all*
your strength. God is not interested in halfhearted
commitment, partial obedience, and the leftovers of your
time and money. He desires your full devotion, not little
bits of your life.

A Samaritan woman once tried to debate Jesus on the
best time, place, and style for worship. Jesus replied that
these external issues are irrelevant. Where you worship
is not as important as *why* you worship and *how much*

of yourself you offer to God when you worship. There is a right and wrong way to worship. The Bible says, *"Let us be grateful and worship God in a way that will please him."*[1] The kind of worship that pleases God has four characteristics:

God is pleased when our worship is accurate. People often say, "I like to think of God as...," and then they share their idea of the kind of God they would like to worship. But we cannot just create our own comfortable or politically correct image of God and worship it. That is idolatry.

Worship must be based on the truth of Scripture, not our opinions about God. Jesus told the Samaritan woman, *"True worshipers will worship the Father in spirit and truth, for they are the kind of worshipers the Father seeks."*[2]

> God-pleasing worship is deeply emotional and deeply doctrinal. We use both our hearts and our heads.

To "worship in truth" means to worship God as he is truly revealed in the Bible.

God is pleased when our worship is authentic. When Jesus said you must *"worship in spirit,"* he wasn't referring to the Holy Spirit, but to *your* spirit. Made in God's image, you are a spirit that resides in a body, and God designed your spirit to communicate with him. Worship is your spirit responding to God's Spirit.

When Jesus said, *"Love God with all your heart*

and soul" he meant that worship must be genuine and heartfelt. It is not just a matter of saying the right words; you must mean what you say. Heartless praise is not praise at all! It is worthless, an insult to God.

When we worship, God looks past our words to see the attitude of our hearts. The Bible says, *"Man looks at the outward appearance, but the* LORD *looks at the heart."*[3]

Since worship involves delighting in God, it engages your emotions. God gave you emotions so you could worship him with deep feeling — but those emotions must be genuine, not faked. God hates hypocrisy. He doesn't want showmanship or pretense or phoniness in worship. He wants your honest, real love. We can worship God imperfectly, but we cannot worship him *insincerely.*

Of course, sincerity alone is not enough; you can be sincerely wrong. That's why both spirit and truth are required. Worship must be both accurate and authentic. God-pleasing worship is deeply emotional and deeply doctrinal. We use both our hearts and our heads.

Today many equate being emotionally moved by music as being moved by the Spirit, but these are not the same. Real worship happens when your spirit responds to God, not to some musical tone. In fact, some sentimental, introspective songs *hinder* worship because they take the spotlight off God and focus on our feelings. Your biggest distraction in worship is yourself — your interests and your worries over what others think about you.

Christians often differ on the most appropriate or authentic way to express praise to God, but these arguments usually just reflect personality and background differences. Many forms of praise are mentioned in the Bible, among them confessing, singing, shouting, standing in honor, kneeling, dancing, making a joyful noise, testifying, playing musical instruments, and raising hands.[4] The best style of worship is the one that most authentically represents your love for God, based on the background and personality God gave you.

My friend Gary Thomas noticed that many Christians seem *stuck* in a worship rut — an unsatisfying routine — instead of having a vibrant friendship with God, because they force themselves to use devotional methods or worship styles that don't fit the way God uniquely shaped them.

Gary wondered, *If God intentionally made us all different, why should everyone be expected to love God in the same way?* As he read Christian classics and interviewed mature believers, Gary discovered that Christians have used many different paths for 2,000 years to enjoy intimacy with God: being outdoors, studying, singing, reading, dancing, creating art, serving others, having solitude, enjoying fellowship, and participating in dozens of other activities.

> *The best style of worship is the one that most authentically represents your love for God.*

In his book *Sacred Pathways,* Gary identifies nine of the ways people draw near to God: *Naturalists* are most inspired to love God out-of-doors, in natural settings. *Sensates* love God with their senses and appreciate beautiful worship services that involve their sight, taste, smell, and touch, not just their ears. *Traditionalists* draw closer to God through rituals, liturgies, symbols, and unchanging structures. *Ascetics* prefer to love God in solitude and simplicity. *Activists* love God through confronting evil, battling injustice, and working to make the world a better place. *Caregivers* love God by loving others and meeting their needs. *Enthusiasts* love God through celebration. *Contemplatives* love God through adoration. *Intellectuals* love God by studying with their minds.[5]

DAY 13:

Worship that Pleases God

There is no "one-size-fits-all" approach to worship and friendship with God. One thing is certain: You don't bring glory to God by trying to be someone he never intended you to be. God wants you to be yourself. *"That's the kind of people the Father is out looking for: those who are simply and honestly* themselves *before him in their worship."*[6]

God is pleased when our worship is thoughtful. Jesus' command to *"love God with all your mind"* is repeated four times in the New Testament. God is not pleased with thoughtless singing of hymns, perfunctory praying of clichés, or careless exclamations of "Praise the Lord," because we can't think of anything else to say at that moment. If worship is mindless, it is meaningless. You must engage your mind.

Jesus called thoughtless worship "vain repetitions."[7] Even biblical terms can become tired clichés from overuse, and we stop thinking about the meaning. It is so much easier to offer clichés in worship instead of making the effort to honor God with fresh words and ways. This is why I encourage you to read Scripture in different translations and paraphrases. It will expand your expressions of worship.

Try praising God without using the words *praise, hallelujah, thanks,* or *amen.* Instead of saying, "We just want to praise you," make a list of synonyms and use fresh words like *admire, respect, value, revere, honor,* and *appreciate.*

Also, *be specific.* If someone approached you and repeated, "I praise you!" ten times, you would probably think, *For what?* You would rather receive two specific compliments than twenty vague generalities. So would God.

Another idea is to make a list of the different names of God and focus on them. God's names are not arbitrary; they tell us about different aspects of his character. In the Old Testament, God gradually revealed himself to Israel by introducing new names for himself, and he commands us to praise his name.[8]

God wants our corporate worship gatherings to be thoughtful, too. Paul devotes an entire chapter to this in

1 Corinthians 14 and concludes, *"Everything should be done in a fitting and orderly way."*[9]

Related to this, God insists that our worship services be understandable to unbelievers when they are present in our worship gatherings. Paul observed, *"Suppose some strangers are in your worship service, when you are praising God with your spirit. If they don't understand you, how will they know to say, 'Amen'? You may be worshiping God in a wonderful way, but no one else will be helped."*[10] Being sensitive to unbelievers who visit your worship gatherings is a biblical command. To ignore this command is to be both disobedient and unloving. For a full explanation of this, see the chapter on "Worship Can Be a Witness" in *The Purpose Driven Church.*

God is pleased when our worship is practical. The Bible says, *"Offer your bodies as living sacrifices, holy and pleasing to God—this is your spiritual act of worship."*[11] Why does God want your body? Why doesn't he say, "Offer your spirit"? Because without your body you can't do anything on this planet. In eternity you will receive a new, improved, upgraded body, but while you're here on earth, God says, "Give me what you've got!" He's just being practical about worship.

You have heard people say, "I can't make it to the meeting tonight, but I'll be with you in *spirit.*" Do you know what that means? Nothing. It's worthless! As long as you're on earth, your spirit can only be where your body is. If your body isn't there, neither are you.

In worship we are to "offer our bodies as *living* sacrifices." Now, we usually associate the concept of "sacrifice" with something dead, but God wants you to be a living sacrifice. He wants you to *live* for him! However, the problem with a living sacrifice is that it can crawl off the altar, and we often do that. We sing, "Onward, Christian Soldiers" on Sunday, then go AWOL on Monday.

In the Old Testament, God took pleasure in the many sacrifices of worship because they foretold of Jesus' sacrifice for us on the cross. Now God is pleased with different sacrifices of worship: thanksgiving, praise, humility, repentance, offerings of money, prayer, serving others, and sharing with those in need.[12]

> *Real worship is rooted in the Word.*

Real worship costs. David knew this and said: *"I will not offer to the LORD my God sacrifices that have cost me nothing."*[13]

One thing worship costs us is our self-centeredness. You cannot exalt God and yourself at the same time. You don't worship to be seen by others or to please yourself. You deliberately shift the focus from yourself.

When Jesus said, *"Love God with all your strength,"* he pointed out that worship takes effort and energy. It is not always convenient or comfortable, and sometimes worship is a sheer act of the will — a willing sacrifice. Passive worship is an oxymoron.

When you praise God even when you don't feel like it, when you get out of bed to worship when you're tired, or when you help others when you are worn out, you are offering a sacrifice of worship to God. That pleases God.

Matt Redman, a worship leader in England, tells how his pastor taught his church the real meaning of worship. To show that worship is more than music, he banned all singing in their services for a period of time while they learned to worship in other ways. By the end of that time, Matt had written the classic song "Heart of Worship":

> I'll bring You more than a song,
> For a song itself
> Is not what You have required.
> You search much deeper within,
> Through the way things appear;
> You're looking into my heart.[14]

The heart of the matter is a matter of the heart.

DAY 13

Thinking about My Purpose

POINT TO PONDER: God wants *all* of me.

VERSE TO REMEMBER: *"Love the Lord your God with all your heart and with all your soul and with all your mind and with all your strength."* MARK 12:30 (NIV)

QUESTION TO CONSIDER: Which is more pleasing to God right now — my public worship or my private worship? What will I do about this?

MESSAGE TO HEAR: *www.purposedriven.com/day13*

DAY 14

When God Seems Distant

The Lord has hidden himself
from his people,
but I trust him and
place my hope in him.

ISAIAH 8:17 (TEV)

purposedriven.com/
day14

GOD IS REAL, NO MATTER HOW YOU FEEL.

It is easy to worship God when things are going great in your life — when he has provided food, friends, family, health, and happy situations. But circumstances are not always pleasant. How do you worship God then? What do you do when God seems a million miles away?

The deepest level of worship is praising God in spite of pain, thanking God during a trial, trusting him when tempted, surrendering while suffering, and loving him when he seems distant.

Friendships are often tested by separation and silence;

you are divided by physical distance or you are unable to talk. In your friendship with God, you won't always *feel* close to him. Philip Yancey has wisely noted, "Any relationship involves times of closeness and times of distance, and in a relationship with God, no matter how intimate, the pendulum will swing from one side to the other."[1] That's when worship gets difficult.

To mature your friendship, God will test it with periods of *seeming* separation — times when it feels as if he has abandoned or forgotten you. God feels a million miles away. St. John of the Cross referred to these days of spiritual dryness, doubt, and estrangement from God as "the dark night of the soul." Henri Nouwen called them "the ministry of absence." A. W. Tozer called them "the ministry of the night." Others refer to "the winter of the heart."

Besides Jesus, David probably had the closest friendship with God of anyone. God took pleasure in calling him "a man after my own heart."[2] Yet David frequently complained of God's apparent absence: *"Lord, why are you standing aloof and far away? Why do you hide when I need you the most?"*[3] *"Why have you forsaken me? Why do you remain so distant? Why do you ignore my cries for help?"*[4] *"Why have you abandoned me?"*[5]

Of course, God hadn't really left David, and he doesn't leave you. He has promised repeatedly, "I will *never* leave you nor forsake you."[6] But God has *not* promised "you will always *feel* my presence." In fact, God admits that sometimes he hides his face from us.[7] There are times when he appears to be *MIA*, missing-in-action, in your life.

Floyd McClung describes it: "You wake up one morning and all your spiritual feelings are gone. You pray, but nothing happens. You rebuke the devil, but it doesn't change anything. You go through spiritual exercises ... you have your friends pray for you ... you confess every sin you can imagine, then go around asking forgiveness of everyone you know. You fast ... still nothing. You begin to wonder how long this spiritual gloom might last. Days? Weeks? Months? Will it ever end? ... It feels as if your prayers simply bounce off the ceiling. In utter desperation, you cry out, 'What's the matter with me?'"[8]

The truth is, there's nothing wrong with you! This is a normal part of the testing and maturing of your friendship with God. *Every* Christian goes through it at least once, and usually several times. It is painful and disconcerting, but it is absolutely vital for

DAY 14:

When God Seems Distant

the development of your faith. Knowing this gave Job hope when he could not feel God's presence in his life. He said, *"I go east, but he is not there. I go west, but I cannot find him. I do not see him in the north, for he is hidden. I turn to the south, but I cannot find him. But he knows where I am going. And when he has tested me like gold in a fire, he will pronounce me innocent."*[9]

When God seems distant, you may feel that he is

angry with you or is disciplining you for some sin. In fact, sin *does* disconnect us from intimate fellowship with God. We grieve God's Spirit and quench our fellowship with him by disobedience, conflict with others, busyness, friendship with the world, and other sins.[10]

But often this feeling of abandonment or estrangement from God has nothing to do with sin. It is a test of faith — one we all must face: Will you continue to love, trust, obey, and worship God, even when you have no sense of his presence or visible evidence of his work in your life?

> *God admits that sometimes he hides his face from us.*

The most common mistake Christians make in worship today is seeking an *experience* rather than seeking God. They look for a feeling, and if it happens, they conclude that they have worshiped. Wrong! In fact, God often removes our feelings so we won't depend on them. Seeking a feeling, even the feeling of closeness to Christ, is not worship.

When you are a baby Christian, God gives you a lot of confirming emotions and often answers the most immature, self-centered prayers — so you'll know he exists. But as you grow in faith, he will wean you of these dependencies.

God's omnipresence and the manifestation of his presence are two different things. One is a fact; the other is often a feeling. God is always present, even when you are unaware of him, and his presence is too profound to be measured by mere emotion.

Yes, he wants you to sense his presence, but he's more concerned that you *trust* him than that you *feel* him.

Faith, not feelings, pleases God.

The situations that will stretch your faith most will be those times when life falls apart and God is nowhere to be found. This happened to Job. On a single day he lost *everything*—his family, his business, his health, and everything he owned. Most discouraging—for thirty-seven chapters, God said nothing!

> The most common mistake Christians make in worship today is seeking an experience rather than seeking God.

How do you praise God when you don't understand what's happening in your life and God is silent? How do you stay connected in a crisis without communication? How do you keep your eyes on Jesus when they're full of tears? You do what Job did: *"Then he fell to the ground in worship and said: 'Naked I came from my mother's womb, and naked I will depart. The LORD gave and the LORD has taken away; may the name of the LORD be praised.'"*[11]

Tell God exactly how you feel. Pour out your heart to God. Unload every emotion that you're feeling. Job did this when he said, *"I can't be quiet! I am angry and bitter. I have to speak!"*[12] He cried out when God seemed distant: *"Oh, for the days when I was in my prime, when God's intimate friendship blessed my house."*[13] God can handle your doubt, anger, fear, grief, confusion, and questions.

Did you know that admitting your hopelessness to God can be a statement of faith? Trusting God but feeling despair at the same time, David wrote, *"I believed, so I said, 'I am completely ruined!'"*[14] This sounds like a contradiction: I trust God, but I'm wiped out! David's frankness actually reveals deep faith: First, he believed in God. Second, he believed God would listen to his prayer. Third, he believed God would let him say what he felt and still love him.

Focus on who God is — his unchanging nature. Regardless of circumstances and how you feel, hang on to God's unchanging character. Remind yourself what you know to be eternally true about God: He is good, he loves me, he is with me, he knows what I'm going through, he cares, and he has a good plan for my life. V. Raymond Edman said, "Never doubt in the dark what God told you in the light."

When Job's life fell apart, and God was silent, Job still found things he could praise God for:

- That he is good and loving.[15]
- That he is all-powerful.[16]
- That he notices every detail of my life.[17]
- That he is in control.[18]
- That he has a plan for my life.[19]
- That he will save me.[20]

Trust God to keep his promises. During times of spiritual dryness you must patiently rely on the promises of God, not your emotions, and realize that he is taking you to a deeper level of maturity. A friendship based on emotion is shallow indeed.

So don't be troubled by trouble. Circumstances cannot change the character of God. God's grace is still in full force; he is still *for* you, even when you don't feel it. In the absence of confirming circumstances, Job held on to God's Word. He said, *"I have not departed from the commands of his lips; I have treasured the words of his mouth more than my daily bread."*[21]

This trust in God's Word caused Job to remain faithful even though nothing made sense. His faith was strong in the midst of pain: *"God may kill me, but still I will trust him."*[22]

When you feel abandoned by God yet continue to trust him in spite of your feelings, you worship him in the deepest way.

Remember what God has already done for you. If God never did anything else for you, he would still deserve your continual praise for the rest of your life because of what Jesus did for you on the cross. *God's Son died for you!* This is the greatest reason for worship.

Unfortunately, we forget the cruel details of the agonizing sacrifice God made on our behalf. Familiarity breeds complacency. Even before his crucifixion, the Son of God was stripped naked, beaten until almost unrecognizable, whipped, scorned and mocked, crowned with thorns, and spit on contemptuously. Abused and ridiculed by heartless men, he was treated worse than an animal.

Then, nearly unconscious from blood loss, he was forced to drag a cumbersome cross up a hill, was nailed to it, and was left to die the slow, excruciating torture of death by crucifixion. While his lifeblood drained out, hecklers stood by and shouted insults, making fun of his pain and challenging his claim to be God.

> When you feel abandoned by God yet continue to trust him, you worship him in the deepest way.

Next, as Jesus took all of mankind's sin and guilt on himself, God looked away from that ugly sight, and Jesus cried out in total desperation, "My God, my God, why have *you* forsaken me?" Jesus could have saved himself—but then he could not have saved you.

Words cannot describe the darkness of that moment. Why did God allow and endure such ghastly, evil mistreatment? Why? So *you* could be spared from eternity in hell, and so *you* could share in his glory forever! The Bible says, *"Christ was without sin, but for our sake God made him share our sin in order that in union with him we might share the righteousness of God."*[23]

Jesus gave up everything so you could have everything. He died so you could live forever. *That alone* is worthy of your continual thanks and praise. Never again should you wonder what you have to be thankful for.

DAY 14

Thinking about My Purpose

POINT TO PONDER: God is real, no matter how I feel.

VERSE TO REMEMBER: *"For God has said, 'I will never leave you; I will never abandon you.'"* HEBREWS 13:5 (TEV)

QUESTION TO CONSIDER: How can I stay focused on God's presence, especially when he feels distant?

MESSAGE TO HEAR: *www.purposedriven.com/day14*

YOU WERE FORMED FOR GOD'S FAMILY

I am the vine, and you are the branches.

JOHN 15:5 (CEV)

Christ makes us one body . . .
connected to each other.

ROMANS 12:5 (GWT)

Formed for God's Family

God is the One who made all things,
and all things are for his glory. He wanted
to have many children share his glory.

HEBREWS 2:10A (NCV)

See how very much our heavenly Father
loves us, for he allows us to be called
his children, and we really are!

1 JOHN 3:1 (NLT)

purposedriven.com/
day15

YOU WERE FORMED FOR GOD'S FAMILY.

God wants a family, and he created you to be a part
of it. This is God's second purpose for your life, which
he planned before you were born. The entire Bible is the
story of God building a family who will love him, honor
him, and reign with him forever. It says, *"His unchanging*
plan has always been to adopt us into his own family by
bringing us to himself through Jesus Christ. And this gave
him great pleasure."[1]

Because God is love, he treasures relationships. His
very nature is relational, and he identifies himself in

151

family terms: Father, Son, and Spirit. The Trinity is God's relationship to himself. It's the perfect pattern for relational harmony, and we should study its implications.

God has always existed in loving relationship to himself, so he has never been lonely. He didn't *need* a family — he desired one, so he devised a plan to create us, bring us into his family, and share with us all he has. This gives God great pleasure. The Bible says, *"It was a happy day for him when he gave us our new lives, through the truth of his Word, and we became, as it were, the first children in his new family."*[2]

When we place our faith in Christ, God becomes our Father, we become his children, other believers become our brothers and sisters, and the church becomes our spiritual family. The family of God includes all believers in the past, the present, and the future.

Every human being was *created* by God, but not everyone is a *child* of God. The only way to get into God's family is by being born again into it. You became part of the human family by your first birth, but you become a member of God's family by your second birth. God *"has given us the privilege of being born again, so that we are now members of God's own family."*[3]

The invitation to be part of God's family is universal,[4] but there is one condition: faith in Jesus. The Bible says, *"You are all children of God through faith in Christ Jesus."*[5]

Your spiritual family is even more important than your physical family because it will last forever. Our families on earth are wonderful gifts from God, but they are temporary and fragile, often broken by divorce, distance, growing old, and inevitably, death. On the other hand, our spiritual family — our relationship to other believers — will continue throughout eternity. It is a much stronger union, a more permanent bond, than blood relationships. Whenever Paul would stop to consider God's eternal purpose for us together, he would break out into praise: *"When I think of the wisdom and scope of his plan I fall down on my knees and pray to the Father of all the great family of God — some of them already in heaven and some down here on earth."*[6]

Benefits of Being in God's Family

The moment you were spiritually born into God's family, you were given some astounding birthday gifts: the family name, the family likeness, family privileges, family intimate access, and the family inheritance![7] The Bible says, *"Since you are his child, everything he has belongs to you."*[8]

> *Your spiritual family is even more important than your physical family because it will last forever.*

The New Testament gives great emphasis to our rich "inheritance." It tells us, *"My God will meet all your needs according to his glorious riches in Christ Jesus."*[9] As children of God we get to share in the family fortune.

Here on earth we are given *"the riches … of his grace … kindness … patience … glory … wisdom … power … and mercy."*[10] But in eternity we will inherit even more.

Paul said, *"I want you to realize what a rich and glorious inheritance he has given to his people."*[11] What exactly does that inheritance include? First, we will get to be with God forever.[12] Second, we will be completely changed to be like Christ.[13] Third, we will be freed from all pain, death, and suffering.[14] Fourth, we will be rewarded and reassigned positions of service.[15] Fifth, we will get to share in Christ's glory.[16] What an inheritance!

You are far richer than you realize.

DAY 15:

Formed for
God's Family

The Bible says, *"God has reserved a priceless inheritance for his children. It is kept in heaven for you, pure and undefiled, beyond the reach of change and decay."*[17] This means that your eternal inheritance is priceless, pure, permanent, and protected. No one can take it from you; it can't be destroyed by war, a poor economy, or a natural disaster. This eternal inheritance, not retirement, is what you should be looking forward to and working for. Paul says, *"Whatever you do, work at it with all your heart, as working for the Lord, not for men, since you know that you will receive an inheritance from the Lord as a reward."*[18] Retirement is a short-sighted goal. You should be living in light of eternity.

Baptism: Identifying with God's Family

Healthy families have family pride; members are not ashamed to be recognized as a part of the family. Sadly, I have met many believers who have never publicly identified themselves with their spiritual family as Jesus commanded — by being baptized.

Baptism is not an optional ritual, to be delayed or postponed. It signifies your inclusion in God's family. It publicly announces to the world, "I am not ashamed to be a part of God's family." Have you been baptized? Jesus commanded this beautiful act for all in his family. He told us to *"go and make disciples of all the nations, baptizing them in the name of the Father and the Son and the Holy Spirit."*[19]

For years I wondered why Jesus' Great Commission gives the same prominence to baptism as it does to the great tasks of evangelism and edification. Why is baptism so important? Then I realized it is because it symbolizes God's second purpose for your life: participating in the fellowship of God's eternal family.

Baptism is pregnant with meaning. Your baptism declares your faith, shares Christ's burial and resurrection, symbolizes your death to your old life, and announces your new life in Christ. It is also a celebration of your inclusion in God's family.

Your baptism is a physical picture of a spiritual truth. It represents what happened the moment God brought you into his family: *"Some of us are Jews, some are Gentiles, some are slaves, and some are free. But we have all been baptized into Christ's body by one Spirit, and we have all received the same Spirit."*[20]

Being included in God's family is the highest honor and the greatest privilege you will ever receive.

Baptism doesn't *make* you a member of God's family; only faith in Christ does that. Baptism *shows* you are part of God's family. Like a wedding ring, it is a visible reminder of an inward commitment made in your heart. It is an act of *initiation,* not something you put off until you are spiritually mature. The only biblical condition is that you believe.[21]

In the New Testament, people were baptized as soon as they believed. At Pentecost, 3,000 were baptized the *same day* they accepted Christ. Elsewhere, an Ethiopian leader was baptized *on the spot* when he was converted, and Paul and Silas baptized a Philippian jailer and his family *at midnight.* There are no delayed baptisms in the New Testament. If you haven't been baptized as an expression of your faith in Christ, do so as soon as possible, as Jesus commanded.

Life's Greatest Privilege

The Bible says, *"Jesus and the people he makes holy all belong to the same family. That is why he isn't ashamed to call them his brothers and sisters."*[22] Let that amazing truth sink in. You are a part of God's family, and because Jesus makes you holy, God is proud of you! The words of Jesus are unmistakable: *"[Jesus] pointed to his disciples and said, 'These are my mother and brothers. Anyone who does the will of my Father in heaven is my brother and sister and mother!'"*[23] Being included in God's family is the highest honor and the greatest privilege you will ever receive. Nothing else comes close. Whenever you feel unimportant, unloved, or insecure, remember to whom you belong.

DAY 15

Thinking about My Purpose

POINT TO PONDER: I was formed for God's family.

VERSE TO REMEMBER: *"His unchanging plan has always been to adopt us into his own family by bringing us to himself through Jesus Christ."* EPHESIANS 1:5A (NLT)

QUESTION TO CONSIDER: How can I start treating other believers like members of my own family?

MESSAGE TO HEAR: *www.purposedriven.com/day15*

DAY 16

What Matters Most

No matter what I say, what I believe, and what I do, I'm bankrupt without love.

1 CORINTHIANS 13:3B (MSG)

purposedriven.com/
day16

Love means living the way God commanded us to live. As you have heard from the beginning, his command is this: Live a life of love.

2 JOHN 1:6 (NCV)

LIFE IS ALL ABOUT LOVE.

Because God is love, the most important lesson he wants you to learn on earth is how to love. It is in loving that we are most like him, so love is the foundation of every command he has given us: *"The whole Law can be summed up in this one command: 'Love others as you love yourself.'"*[1]

Learning to love unselfishly is not an easy task. It runs counter to our self-centered nature. That's why we're given a lifetime to learn it. Of course, God wants us to love everyone, but he is *particularly* concerned that we learn to love others in his family. As we have already seen, this is the second purpose for your life. Peter tells us, *"Show special love for God's people."*[2] Paul echoes this sentiment: *"When we have the opportunity to help anyone, we should do it. But we should give special attention to those who are in the family of believers."*[3]

Why does God insist that we give special love and attention to other believers? Why do they get priority in loving? Because God wants his family to be known for its love more than anything else. Jesus said our love *for each other* — not our doctrinal beliefs — is our greatest witness to the world. He said, *"Your strong love for each other will prove to the world that you are my disciples."*[4]

In heaven we will enjoy God's family forever, but first we have some tough work to do here on earth to prepare ourselves for an eternity of loving. God trains us by giving us "family responsibilities," and the foremost of these is to practice loving each other.

God wants you to be in regular, close fellowship with other believers so you can develop the skill of loving. Love cannot be learned in isolation. You have to be around people — irritating, imperfect, frustrating people. Through fellowship we learn three important truths.

The Best Use of Life Is Love

Love should be your top priority, primary objective, and greatest ambition. Love is not a *good* part of your life; it's the *most important* part. The Bible says, *"Let love be your greatest aim."*[5]

It's not enough to say, *"One* of the things I want in life is to be loving," as if it's on your top ten list. Relationships must have priority in your life above everything else. Why?

Life without love is really worthless. Paul makes this point: *"No matter what I say, what I believe, and what I do, I'm bankrupt without love."*[6]

Often we act as if relationships are something to be squeezed into our schedule. We talk about *finding* time for our children or *making* time for people in our lives. That gives the impression that relationships are just a part of our lives along with many other tasks. But God says relationships are what life is all about.

Four of the Ten Commandments deal with our relationship to God while the other six deal with our relationships with people. But all ten are about relationships! Later, Jesus summarized what matters most to God in two statements: love God and love people. He said, *"'You must love the Lord your God with all your heart....' This is the first and greatest commandment. A second is equally important: 'Love your neighbor as yourself.' All the other commandments and all the demands of the prophets are based on these two commandments."*[7] After learning to love God (worship), learning to love others is the second purpose of your life.

Relationships, not achievements or the acquisition of

things, are what matters most in life. So why do we allow our relationships to get the short end of the stick? When our schedules become overloaded, we start skimming relationally, cutting back on giving the time, energy, and attention that loving relationships require. What's most important to God is displaced by what's urgent.

Busyness is a great enemy of relationships. We become preoccupied with making a living, doing our work, paying bills, and accomplishing goals as if these tasks are the point of life. They are not. The point of life is learning to love — God and people. Life minus love equals zero.

Love will last forever. Another reason God tells us to make love our top priority is that it is eternal: *"These three things continue forever: faith, hope, and love. And the greatest of these is love."*[8]

Love leaves a legacy. How you treated other people, not your wealth or accomplishments, is the most enduring impact you can leave on earth. As Mother Teresa said, "It's not what you do, but how much love you put into it that matters." Love is the secret of a lasting heritage.

I have been at the bedside of many people in their final moments, when they stand on the edge of eternity, and I have never heard anyone say, "Bring me my diplomas! I want to look at them one more time. Show me my awards, my medals, that gold watch I was given." When life on earth is ending, people don't surround themselves with objects. What we want around us is people — people we love and have relationships with.

In our final moments we all realize that relationships are what life is all about. Wisdom is learning that truth sooner rather than later. Don't wait until you're on your deathbed to figure out that nothing matters more.

We will be evaluated on our love. The third reason to make learning to love the goal of your life is that it is what we will be evaluated on in eternity. One of the ways God measures spiritual maturity is by the quality of your relationships. In heaven God won't say, "Tell me about your career, your bank account, and your hobbies." Instead he will review how you treated other people, particularly those in need.[9] Jesus said the way to love him is to love his family and care for their practical needs: *"Truly I tell you, just as you did it to one of the least of these who are members of my family, you did it to me."*[10]

When you transfer into eternity, you will leave everything else behind. All you're taking with you is your character. That's why the Bible says, *"The only thing that counts is faith expressing itself through love."*[11]

Knowing this, I suggest that when you wake up every morning, you kneel by your bed, or sit on the edge of it, and pray this: "God, whether I get anything else done today, I want to make sure that I spend time loving you and loving other people — because that's what life is all about. I don't want to waste this day." Why should God give you another day if you're going to waste it?

The Best Expression of Love Is Time

The importance of things can be measured by how much time we are willing to invest in them. The more time you give to something, the more you reveal its importance and value to you. If you want to know a person's priorities, just look at how they use their time.

Time is your most precious gift because you only have a set amount of it. You can make more money, but you can't make more time. When you give someone your time, you are giving them a portion of your life that you will never get back. Your time is your life. That is why the greatest gift you can give someone is your time.

It is not enough just to *say* relationships are important; we must prove it by investing time in them. Words alone are worthless. *"My children, our love should not be just words and talk; it must be true love, which shows itself in action."*[12] Relationships take time and effort, and the best way to spell love is "T – I – M – E."

> The greatest gift you can give someone is your time.

The essence of love is not what we think or do or provide for others, but how much we give *of ourselves*. Men, in particular, often don't understand this. Many have said to me, "I don't understand my wife and kids. I provide everything they need. What more could they want?" They want you! Your eyes, your ears, your time, your attention, your presence, your focus — your time. Nothing can take the place of that.

The most desired gift of love is not diamonds or roses or chocolate. It is *focused attention*. Love concentrates so intently on another that you forget yourself at that moment. Attention says, "I value you enough to give you my most precious asset — my time." Whenever you give your time, you are making a sacrifice, and sacrifice is the essence of love. Jesus modeled this: *"Be full of love for others, following the example of Christ who loved you and gave Himself to God as a sacrifice to take away your sins."*[13]

You can give without loving, but you cannot love without giving. *"God so loved the world that he gave...."*[14] Love means giving up — yielding my preferences, comfort, goals, security, money, energy, or time for the benefit of someone else.

The Best Time to Love Is Now

Sometimes procrastination is a legitimate response to a trivial task. But because love is what matters most, it takes top priority. The Bible stresses this repeatedly. It says, *"Whenever we have the opportunity, we should do good to everyone."*[15] *"Use every chance you have for doing good."*[16] *"Whenever you possibly can, do good to those who need it. Never tell your neighbor to wait until tomorrow if you can help them now."*[17]

Why is now the best time to express love? Because you don't know how long you will have the opportunity. Circumstances change. People die. Children grow up. You have no guarantee of tomorrow. If you want to express love, you had better do it now.

Knowing that one day you will stand before God, here are some questions you need to consider: How will you explain those times when projects or things were more important to you than people? Who do you need to start spending more time with? What do you need to cut out of your schedule to make that possible? What sacrifices do you need to make?

The best use of life is love. The best expression of love is time. The best time to love is now.

DAY 16

Thinking about My Purpose

POINT TO PONDER: Life is all about love.

VERSE TO REMEMBER: *"The entire law is summed up in a single command: 'Love your neighbor as yourself.'"* GALATIANS 5:14 (NIV)

QUESTION TO CONSIDER: Honestly, are relationships my first priority? How can I ensure that they are?

MESSAGE TO HEAR: *www.purposedriven.com/day16*

DAY 17

A Place to Belong

You are members of God's very own family, citizens of God's country, and you belong in God's household with every other Christian.

EPHESIANS 2:19B (LB)

purposedriven.com/
day17

God's family is the church of the living God, the pillar and foundation of the truth.

1 TIMOTHY 3:15B (GWT)

YOU ARE CALLED TO BELONG, NOT JUST BELIEVE.

Even in the perfect, sinless environment of Eden, God said, *"It is not good for man to be alone."*[1] We are created for community, fashioned for fellowship, and formed for a family, and none of us can fulfill God's purposes by ourselves.

The Bible knows nothing of solitary saints or spiritual hermits isolated from other believers and deprived of fellowship. The Bible says we are *put together, joined together, built together, members together, heirs together, fitted together,* and *held together* and *will be caught up together.*[2] You're not on your own anymore.

While your relationship to Christ is personal, God never intends it to be private. In God's family you are connected to every other believer, and we will belong to each other *for eternity.* The Bible says, *"In Christ we who are many form one body, and each member belongs to all the others."*[3]

Following Christ includes *belonging,* not just believing. We are *members* of his Body — the church. C. S. Lewis noted that the word *membership* is of Christian origin, but the world has emptied it of its original meaning. Stores offer discounts to "members," and advertisers use member names to create mailing lists. In churches, membership is often reduced to simply adding your name to a roll, with no requirements or expectations.

To Paul, being a "member" of the church meant being a vital organ of a living body, an indispensable, interconnected part of the Body of Christ.[4] We need to recover and practice the biblical meaning of membership. The church is a body, not a building; an organism, not an organization.

For the organs of your body to fulfill their purpose, they must be connected to your body. The same is true for you as a part of Christ's Body. You were created for a specific role, but you will miss this second purpose of your life if you're not attached to a living, local church. You discover your role in life through your relationships with others. The Bible tells us, *"Each part gets its meaning from the body as a whole, not the other way around. The body we're talking about is Christ's body of chosen people. Each of us finds our meaning and function as a part of his body. But as a chopped-off finger or cut-off toe we wouldn't amount to much, would we?"*[5]

If an organ is somehow severed from its body, it will shrivel and die. It cannot exist on its own, and neither can you. Disconnected and cut off from the lifeblood of a local body, your spiritual life will wither and eventually cease to exist.[6] This is why the first symptom of spiritual decline is usually inconsistent attendance at worship services and other gatherings of believers. Whenever we become careless about fellowship, everything else begins to slide, too.

We discover our role in life through our relationships with others.

Membership in the family of God is neither inconsequential nor something to be casually ignored. The church is God's agenda for the world. Jesus said, *"I will build my church, and all the powers of hell will not conquer it."*[7] The church is indestructible and will exist for eternity. It will outlive this universe, and so will your role in it. The person who says, "I don't need the church," is either arrogant or ignorant. The church is so significant that Jesus died on the cross for it. *"Christ loved the church and gave his life for it."*[8]

The Bible calls the church *"the bride of Christ"* and

"the body of Christ."[9] I can't imagine saying to Jesus, "I love you, but I dislike your wife." Or "I accept you, but I reject your body." But we do this whenever we dismiss or demean or complain about the church. Instead, God commands us to love the church as much as Jesus does. The Bible says, *"Love your spiritual family."*[10] Sadly, many Christians *use* the church but don't love it.

Your Local Fellowship

Except for a few important instances referring to all believers throughout history, almost every time the word *church* is used in the Bible it refers to a local, visible congregation. The New Testament assumes membership in a local congregation. The only Christians not members of a local fellowship were those under church discipline who had been removed from the fellowship because of gross public sin.[11]

The Bible says a Christian without a church home is like an organ without a body, a sheep without a flock, or a child without a family. It is an unnatural state. The Bible says, *"You belong in God's household with every other Christian."*[12]

Today's culture of independent individualism has created many spiritual orphans — "bunny believers" who hop around from one church to another without any identity, accountability, or commitment. Many believe one can be a "good Christian" without joining (or even attending) a local church, but God would strongly disagree. The Bible offers many compelling reasons for being committed and active in a local fellowship.

Why You Need a Church Family

A church family identifies you as a genuine believer. I can't claim to be following Christ if I'm not committed to any specific group of disciples.

The church will outlive this universe, and so will your role in it.

Jesus said, *"Your love for one another will prove to the world that you are my disciples."*[13]

When we come together in love as a church family from different backgrounds, race, and social status, it is a powerful witness to the world.[14] You are not the Body of Christ on your own. You need others to express that. *Together,* not separated, we are his Body.[15]

A church family moves you out of self-centered isolation. The local church is the classroom for learning how to get along in God's family. It is a lab for practicing unselfish, sympathetic love. As a participating member you learn to care about others and share the experiences of others: *"If one part of the body suffers, all the other parts suffer with it. Or if one part of our body is honored, all the other parts share its honor."*[16] Only in regular contact with ordinary, imperfect believers can we learn real fellowship and experience the New Testament truth of being connected and dependent on each other.[17]

Biblical fellowship is being as committed to each other as we are to Jesus Christ. God expects us to give our lives for each other. Many Christians who know John 3:16 are unaware of 1 John 3:16: *"Jesus Christ laid down his life for us. And we ought to lay down our lives for our brothers."*[18] This is the kind of sacrificial love God expects you to show other believers — a willingness to love them in the same way Jesus loves you.

A church family helps you develop spiritual muscle. You will never grow to maturity just by attending worship services and being a passive spectator. Only participation in the full life of a local church builds spiritual muscle. The Bible says, *"As each part does its own special work, it helps the other parts grow, so that the whole body is healthy and growing and full of love."*[19]

Over fifty times in the New Testament the phrase "one another" or "each other" is used. We are commanded to *love* each other, *pray* for each other, *encourage* each other, *admonish* each other, *greet* each other, *serve* each other, *teach* each other, *accept* each other, *honor* each other, *bear each other's burdens, forgive* each other, *submit* to each other, be *devoted* to each other, and many other mutual tasks. This is biblical membership! These are your "family responsibilities" that God expects you to fulfill through a local fellowship. *Who* are you doing these with?

It may seem easier to be holy when no one else is

around to frustrate your preferences, but that is a false, untested holiness. Isolation breeds deceitfulness; it is easy to fool ourselves into thinking we are mature if there is no one to challenge us. Real maturity shows up in relationships.

We need more than the Bible in order to grow; we need other believers. We grow faster and stronger by learning from each other and being accountable to each other. When others share what God is teaching them, I learn and grow, too.

The Body of Christ needs you. God has a unique role for you to play in his family. This is called your "ministry," and God has gifted you for this assignment: *"A spiritual gift is given to each of us as a means of helping the entire church."*[20]

Your local fellowship is the place God designed for you to discover, develop, and use your gifts. You may also have a wider ministry, but that is *in addition* to your service in a local body. Jesus has not promised to build your ministry; he has promised to build *his* church.

You will share in Christ's mission in the world. When Jesus walked the earth, God worked through the physical body of Christ; today he uses his spiritual body. The church is God's instrument on earth. We are not just to model God's love by loving each other; we are to carry it together to the rest of the world. This is an incredible privilege we have been given together. As members of Christ's body, *we* are his hands, his feet, his eyes, and his heart. He works through us in the world. We each have a contribution to make. Paul tells us, *"He creates each of us by Christ Jesus to join him in the work he does, the good work he has gotten ready for us to do, work we had better be doing."*[21]

A church family will help keep you from backsliding. None of us are immune to temptation. Given the right situation, you and I are capable of any sin.[22] God knows this, so he has assigned us as individuals the responsibility of keeping each other on track. The Bible says, *"Encourage one another daily ... so that none of you may be hardened by sin's deceitfulness."*[23] "Mind your own business" is not a Christian phrase. We are called and commanded to be involved in each other's lives. If you know someone who is wavering spiritually right now, it is your responsibility to go after them

> *Jesus has not promised to build your ministry; he has promised to build his church.*

and bring them back into the fellowship. James tells us, *"If you know people who have wandered off from God's truth, don't write them off. Go after them. Get them back."*[24]

A related benefit of a local church is that it also provides the spiritual protection of godly leaders. God gives shepherd leaders the responsibility to guard, protect, defend, and care for the spiritual welfare of his flock.[25] We are told, *"Their work is to watch over your souls, and they know they are accountable to God."*[26]

Satan loves detached believers, unplugged from the life of the Body, isolated from God's family, and unaccountable to spiritual leaders, because he knows they are defenseless and powerless against his tactics.

It's All in the Church

In my book *The Purpose Driven Church,* I explain how being part of a healthy church is essential to living a healthy life. I hope you will read that book, too, because it will help you understand how God designed his church specifically to help you fulfill the five purposes he has for your life. He created the church to meet your five deepest needs: a purpose to live for, people to live with, principles to live by, a profession to live out, and power to live on. There is no other place on earth where you can find all five of these benefits in one place.

God's purposes for his church are identical to his five purposes for you. Worship helps you *focus on God;* fellowship helps you *face life's problems;* discipleship helps *fortify your faith;* ministry helps *find your talents;* evangelism helps *fulfill your mission.* There is nothing else on earth like the church!

Your Choice

Whenever a child is born, he or she automatically becomes a part of the universal family of human beings.

But that child also needs to become a member of a specific family to receive nurture and care and grow up healthy and strong. The same is true spiritually. When you were born again, you automatically became a part of God's universal family, but you also need to become a member of a local expression of God's family.

The difference between being a church *attender* and a church *member* is commitment. Attenders are spectators from the sidelines; members get involved in the ministry. Attenders are consumers; members are contributors. Attenders want the benefits of a church without sharing the responsibility. They are like couples who want to live together without committing to a marriage.

Why is it important to join a local church family? Because it proves you are committed to your spiritual brothers and sisters in reality, not just in theory. God wants you to love *real* people, not *ideal* people. You can spend a lifetime searching for the perfect church, but you will never find it. You are called to love imperfect sinners, just as God does.

DAY 17: A Place to Belong

In Acts, the Christians in Jerusalem were very specific in their commitment to each other. They were devoted to fellowship. The Bible says, *"They committed themselves to the teaching of the apostles, the life together, the common meal, and the prayers."*[27] God expects you to commit to the same things today.

The Christian life is more than just commitment to

Christ; it includes a commitment to other Christians. The Christians in Macedonia understood this. Paul said, *"First they gave themselves to the Lord; and then, by God's will, they gave themselves to us as well."* Joining the membership of a local church is the natural next step once you have become a child of God. You become a Christian by committing yourself to Christ, but you become a *church member* by committing yourself to a specific group of believers. The first decision brings salvation; the second brings fellowship.

DAY 17

Thinking about My Purpose

POINT TO PONDER: I am called to belong, not just believe.

VERSE TO REMEMBER: *"In Christ we who are many form one body, and each member belongs to all the others."* ROMANS 12:5 (NIV)

QUESTION TO CONSIDER: Does my level of involvement in my local church demonstrate that I love and am committed to God's family?

MESSAGE TO HEAR: *www.purposedriven.com/day17*

Experiencing Life Together

Each one of you is part of the body of Christ, and you were chosen to live together in peace.

COLOSSIANS 3:15 (CEV)

How wonderful it is, how pleasant, for God's people to live together in harmony!

PSALM 133:1 (TEV)

purposedriven.com/
day18

LIFE IS MEANT TO BE SHARED.

God intends for us to experience life together. The Bible calls this shared experience *fellowship.* Today, however, the word has lost most of its biblical meaning. "Fellowship" now usually refers to casual conversation, socializing, food, and fun. The question, "Where do you fellowship?" means "Where do you attend church?" "Stay after for fellowship" usually means "Wait for refreshments."

Real fellowship is so much more than just showing up at services. It is *experiencing life together.* It includes unselfish loving, honest sharing, practical serving, sacrificial giving, sympathetic comforting, and all the other "one another" commands found in the New Testament.

When it comes to fellowship, size matters: *Smaller is better.* You can worship with a crowd, but you can't fellowship with one. Once a group becomes larger than about ten people, someone stops participating — usually the quietest person — and a few people will dominate the group.

Jesus ministered in the context of a small group of disciples. He could have chosen more, but he knew twelve is about the maximum size you can have in a small group if everyone is to participate.

The Body of Christ, like your own body, is really a collection of many small cells. The life of the Body of Christ, like your body, is contained in the cells. For this reason, every Christian needs to be involved in a small group within their church, whether it is a home fellowship group, a Sunday school class, or a Bible study. This is where real community takes place, not in the big gatherings. If you think of your church as a ship, the small groups are the lifeboats attached to it.

God has made an incredible promise about small groups of believers: *"For where two or three have gathered together in My name, I am there in their midst."*[1] Unfortunately, even being in a small group does not guarantee you will experience real community. Many

Sunday school classes and small groups are stuck in superficiality and have no clue as to what it's like to experience genuine fellowship. What is the difference between real and fake fellowship?

In real fellowship people experience authenticity. Authentic fellowship is not superficial, surface-level chit-chat. It is genuine, heart-to-heart, sometimes gut-level, sharing. It happens when people get honest about who they are and what is happening in their lives. They share their hurts, reveal their feelings, confess their failures, disclose their doubts, admit their fears, acknowledge their weaknesses, and ask for help and prayer.

Authenticity is the exact opposite of what you find in some churches. Instead of an atmosphere of honesty and humility, there is pretending, role-playing, politicking, and superficial politeness but shallow conversation. People wear masks, keep their guard up, and act as if everything is rosy in their lives. These attitudes are the death of real fellowship.

> *Real fellowship happens when people get honest about who they are and what is happening in their lives.*

It is only as we become open about our lives that we experience real fellowship. The Bible says, *"If we live in the light, as God is in the light, we can share fellowship with each other.... If we say we have no sin, we are fooling ourselves."*[2] The world thinks intimacy occurs in the dark, but God says it happens in the light. Darkness is used to hide our hurts, faults, fears, failures, and flaws. But in the light, we bring them all out into the open and admit who we really are.

Of course, being authentic requires both courage and humility. It means facing our fear of exposure, rejection, and being hurt again. Why would anyone take such a risk? Because it is the only way to grow spiritually and be emotionally healthy. The Bible says, *"Make this your common practice: Confess your sins to each other and pray for each other so that you can live together whole and healed."*[3] We only grow by taking risks, and the most difficult risk of all is to be honest with ourselves and with others.

In real fellowship people experience mutuality. Mutuality is the art of giving and receiving. It's depending on each other. The Bible says, *"The way God designed our bodies is a model for understanding our lives together as a church: every part dependent on every other part."*[4] Mutuality is the heart of fellowship: building reciprocal relationships, sharing responsibilities, and helping each other. Paul said, *"I want us to help each other with the faith we have. Your faith will help me, and my faith will help you."*[5]

All of us are more consistent in our faith when others walk with us and encourage us. The Bible commands mutual accountability, mutual encouragement, mutual serving, and mutual honoring.[6] Over fifty times in the New Testament we are commanded to do different tasks to "one another" and "each other." The Bible says, *"Make every effort to do what leads to peace and to mutual edification."*[7]

You are not responsible *for* everyone in the Body of Christ, but you are responsible *to* them. God expects you to do whatever you can to help them.

In real fellowship people experience sympathy. Sympathy is not giving advice or offering quick, cosmetic help; sympathy is entering in and sharing the pain of others. Sympathy says, "I understand what you're going through, and what you feel is neither strange nor crazy." Today some call this "empathy," but the biblical word is "sympathy." The Bible says, *"As holy people ... be sympathetic, kind, humble, gentle, and patient."*[8]

Sympathy meets two fundamental human needs: the need to be understood and the need to have your feelings validated. Every time you understand and affirm someone's feelings, you build fellowship. The problem is that we are often in so much of a hurry to fix things that we don't have time to sympathize with people. Or we're preoccupied with our own hurts. Self-pity dries up sympathy for others.

> *Every time you understand and affirm someone's feelings, you build fellowship.*

There are different levels of fellowship, and each is appropriate at different times. The simplest levels of fellowship are the *fellowship of sharing* and the *fellowship of studying* God's Word together.

A deeper level is the *fellowship of serving,* as when we minister together on mission trips or mercy projects. The deepest, most intense level is the *fellowship of suffering,*[9] where we enter into each other's pain and grief and carry each other's burdens. The Christians who understand this level best are those around the world who are being persecuted, despised, and often martyred for their faith.

The Bible commands: *"Share each other's troubles and problems, and in this way obey the law of Christ."*[10] It is in the times of deep crisis, grief, and doubt that we need each other most. When circumstances crush us to the point that our faith falters, that's when we need believing friends the most. We need a small group of friends to have faith in God *for* us and to pull us through. In a small group, the Body of Christ is real and tangible even when God seems distant. This is what Job desperately needed during his suffering. He cried out, *"A despairing man should have the devotion of his friends, even though he forsakes the fear of the Almighty."*[11]

In real fellowship people experience mercy. Fellowship is a place of grace, where mistakes aren't rubbed in but rubbed out. Fellowship happens when mercy wins over justice.

We all need mercy, because we all stumble and fall and require help getting back on track. We need to offer mercy to each other and be willing to receive it from each other. God says, *"When people sin, you should forgive and comfort them, so they won't give up in despair."*[12]

You can't have fellowship without forgiveness. God warns, *"Never hold grudges,"*[13] because bitterness and resentment always destroy fellowship. Because we're imperfect, sinful people, we inevitably hurt each other when we're together for a long enough time. Sometimes we hurt each other intentionally and sometimes unintentionally, but either way, it takes massive amounts of mercy and grace to create and maintain fellowship. The Bible says, *"You must make allowance for each other's faults and forgive the person who offends you. Remember, the Lord forgave you, so you must forgive others."*[14]

God's mercy to us is the motivation for showing mercy to others. Remember, you will never be asked to forgive someone else more than God has already forgiven you. Whenever you are hurt by someone, you have a choice to make: Will I use my energy and emotions for *retaliation* or for *resolution*? You can't do both.

Many people are reluctant to show mercy because they don't understand the difference between trust and forgiveness. Forgiveness is letting go of the past. Trust has to do with future behavior.

Forgiveness must be immediate, whether or not a person asks for it. Trust must be rebuilt over time. Trust requires a track record. If someone hurts you repeatedly, you are commanded by God to forgive them instantly, but you are not expected to trust them immediately, and you are not expected to continue allowing them to hurt you. They must prove they have changed over time. The best place to restore trust is within the supportive context of a small group that offers both encouragement and accountability.

There are many other benefits you will experience in being a part of a small group committed to real fellowship. It is an essential part of your Christian life that you cannot overlook. For over 2,000 years Christians have regularly gathered in small groups for fellowship. If you have never been a part of a group or class like this, you really don't know what you're missing.

In the next chapter we will look at what it takes to create this kind of community with other believers, but I hope this chapter has made you hungry to experience the authenticity, mutuality, sympathy, and mercy of real fellowship. You were created for community.

DAY 18

Thinking about My Purpose

POINT TO PONDER: I need others in my life.

VERSE TO REMEMBER: *"Share each other's troubles and problems, and in this way obey the law of Christ."* GALATIANS 6:2 (NLT)

QUESTION TO CONSIDER: What one step can I take today to connect with another believer at a more genuine, heart-to-heart level?

MESSAGE TO HEAR: *www.purposedriven.com/day18*

DAY 19

Cultivating Community

You can develop a healthy, robust community that lives right with God and enjoy its results only if you do the hard work of getting along with each other, treating each other with dignity and honor.

JAMES 3:18 (MSG)

purposedriven.com/
day19

They committed themselves to the teaching of the apostles, the life together, the common meal, and the prayers.

ACTS 2:42 (MSG)

COMMUNITY REQUIRES COMMITMENT.

Only the Holy Spirit can create real fellowship between believers, but he cultivates it with the choices and commitments we make. Paul points out this dual responsibility when he says, *"You are joined together with peace through the Spirit, so make every effort to continue together in this way."*[1] It takes both God's power and our effort to produce a loving Christian community.

Unfortunately, many people grow up in families with unhealthy relationships, so they lack the relational skills needed for real fellowship. They must be taught how to get along with and relate to others in God's family. Fortunately, the New Testament is filled with instruction on how to share life together. Paul wrote, *"I am writing these things to you ... [so] you will know how to live in the family of God. That family is the church."*[2]

If you're tired of fake fellowship and you would like to cultivate real fellowship and a loving community in your small group, Sunday school class, and church, you'll need to make some tough choices and take some risks.

Cultivating community takes honesty. You will have to care enough to lovingly speak the truth, even when you would rather gloss over a problem or ignore an issue. While it is much easier to remain silent when others around us are harming themselves or others with a sinful pattern, it is not the loving thing to do. Most people have no one in their lives who loves them enough to tell them the truth (even when it's painful), so they continue in self-destructive ways. Often we *know* what needs to be said to someone, but our fears prevent us from saying anything. Many fellowships have been sabotaged by fear: No one had the courage to speak up in the group while a member's life fell apart.

The Bible tells us to *"speak the truth in love"*[3] because we can't have community without candor. Solomon said, *"An honest answer is a sign of true friendship."*[4] Sometimes this means caring enough to lovingly confront one who is sinning or is being tempted to sin. Paul says,

"Brothers and sisters, if someone in your group does something wrong, you who are spiritual should go to that person and gently help make him right again."[5]

Many church fellowships and small groups remain superficial because they are afraid of conflict. Whenever an issue pops up that might cause tension or discomfort, it is immediately glossed over in order to preserve a false sense of peace. *Mr. "Don't Rock the Boat"* jumps in and tries to smooth everyone's ruffled feathers, the issue is never resolved, and everyone lives with an underlying frustration. Everyone knows about the problem, but no one talks about it openly. This creates a sick environment of secrets where gossip thrives. Paul's solution was straightforward: *"No more lies, no more pretense. Tell your neighbor the truth. In Christ's body we're all connected to each other, after all. When you lie to others, you end up lying to yourself."*[6]

Real fellowship, whether in a marriage, a friendship, or your church, depends on frankness. In fact, the tunnel of conflict is the passageway to intimacy in any relationship. Until you care enough to confront and resolve the underlying barriers, you will never grow close to each other. When conflict is handled correctly, we grow closer to each other by facing and resolving our differences. The Bible says, *"In the end, people appreciate frankness more than flattery."*[7]

Frankness is not a license to say anything you want, wherever and whenever you want. It is not rudeness. The

Bible tells us there is a right time and a right way to do everything.[8] Thoughtless words leave lasting wounds. God tells us to speak to each other in the church as loving family members: *"Never use harsh words when you correct an older man, but talk to him as if he were your father. Talk to younger men as if they were your brothers, older women as if they were your mothers, and younger women as if they were your sisters."*[9]

Sadly, thousands of fellowships have been destroyed by a lack of honesty. Paul had to rebuke the Corinthian church for their passive code of silence in allowing immorality in their fellowship. Since no one had the courage to confront it, he said, *"You must not simply look the other way and hope it goes away on its own. Bring it out in the open and deal with it.... Better devastation and embarrassment than damnation.... You pass it off as a small thing, but it's anything but that.... you shouldn't act as if everything is just fine when one of your Christian companions is promiscuous or crooked, is flip with God or rude to friends, gets drunk or becomes greedy and predatory. You can't just go along with this, treating it as acceptable behavior. I'm not responsible for what the* outsiders *do, but don't we have some responsibility for those within our community of believers?"*[10]

> When conflict is handled correctly, we grow closer to each other.

Cultivating community takes humility. Self-importance, smugness, and stubborn pride destroy fellowship faster than anything else. Pride builds walls between people; humility builds bridges. Humility is the oil that smooths and soothes relationships. That's why the Bible says, *"Clothe yourselves with humility toward one another."*[11] The proper dress for fellowship is a humble attitude.

The rest of that verse says, *"... because, God opposes the proud but gives grace to the humble."*[12] This is the other reason we need to be humble: Pride blocks God's grace in our lives, which we must have in order to grow, change, heal, and help others. We receive God's grace by humbly admitting that we need it. The Bible says anytime we are prideful, we are living in *opposition* to God! That is a foolish and dangerous way to live.

> Humility is not thinking less of yourself; it is thinking of yourself less.

You can develop humility in very practical ways: by admitting your weaknesses, by being patient with others' weaknesses, by being open to correction, and by pointing the spotlight on others. Paul advised, *"Live in harmony with each other. Don't try to act important, but enjoy the company of ordinary people. And don't think you know it all!"*[13] To the Christians in Philippi he wrote, *"Give more honor to others than to yourselves. Do not be interested only in your own life, but be interested in the lives of others."*[14]

Humility is not thinking less of yourself; it is thinking

of yourself less. Humility is thinking more of others. Humble people are so focused on serving others, they don't think of themselves.

Cultivating community takes courtesy. Courtesy is respecting our differences, being considerate of each other's feelings, and being patient with people who irritate us. The Bible says, *"We must bear the 'burden' of being considerate of the doubts and fears of others."*[15] Paul told Titus, *"God's people should be bighearted and courteous."*[16]

In every church and in every small group, there is always at least one "difficult" person, usually more than one. These people may have special emotional needs, deep insecurities, irritating mannerisms, or poor social skills. You might call them *EGR* people — "Extra Grace Required."

God put these people in our midst for both their benefit and ours. They are an opportunity for growth and a test of fellowship: Will we love them as brothers and sisters and treat them with dignity?

In a family, acceptance isn't based on how smart or beautiful or talented you are. It's based on the fact that we belong to each other. We defend and protect family. A family member may be a little goofy, but she's one of us. In the same way, the Bible says, *"Be devoted to each other like a loving family. Excel in showing respect for each other."*[17]

The truth is, we all have quirks and annoying traits.

But community has nothing to do with compatibility. The basis for our fellowship is our relationship to God: We're family.

One key to courtesy is to understand where people are coming from. Discover their history. When you know what they've been through, you will be more understanding. Instead of thinking about how far they still have to go, think about how far they have come in spite of their hurts.

Another part of courtesy is not downplaying other people's doubts. Just because you don't fear something doesn't make it an invalid feeling. Real community happens when people know it is safe enough to share their doubts and fears without being judged.

Cultivating community takes confidentiality. Only in the safe environment of warm acceptance and trusted confidentiality will people open up and share their deepest hurts, needs, and mistakes. Confidentiality does not mean keeping silent while your brother or sister sins. It means that what is shared in your group needs to stay in your group, and the group needs to deal with it, not gossip to others about it.

The fellowship of the church is more important than any individual.

God hates gossip, especially when it is thinly disguised as a "prayer request" for someone else. God says, *"Gossip is spread by wicked people; they stir up trouble and break up friendships."*[18]

Gossip always causes hurt and divisions, and it destroys fellowship, and God is very clear that we are to confront those who cause division among Christians.[19] They may get mad and leave your group or church if you confront them about their divisive actions, but the fellowship of the church is more important than any individual.

Cultivating community takes frequency. You *must* have frequent, regular contact with your group in order to build genuine fellowship. Relationships take time. The Bible tells us, *"Let us not give up the habit of meeting together, as some are doing. Instead, let us encourage one another."*[20] We are to develop the *habit* of meeting together. A habit is something you do with frequency, not occasionally. You have to spend time with people —*a lot of time*—to build deep relationships. This is why fellowship is so shallow in many churches; we don't spend enough time together, and the time we do spend is usually listening to one person speak.

Community is built not on convenience ("we'll get together when I feel like it") but on the conviction that I need it for spiritual health. If you want to cultivate real fellowship, it will mean meeting together even when you don't feel like it, because you believe it is important. The first Christians met together every day! *"They worshiped together regularly at the Temple each day, met in small groups in homes for Communion, and shared their meals with great joy and thankfulness."*[21] Fellowship requires an investment of time.

If you are a member of a small group or class, I urge you to make a group covenant that includes the nine characteristics of biblical fellowship: We will share our true feelings (authenticity), encourage each other (mutuality), support each other (sympathy), forgive each other (mercy), speak the truth in love (honesty), admit our weaknesses (humility), respect our differences (courtesy), not gossip (confidentiality), and make group a priority (frequency).

DAY 19:
Cultivating
Community

When you look at the list of characteristics, it is obvious why genuine fellowship is so rare. It means giving up our self-centeredness and independence in order to become interdependent. But the benefits of sharing life together far outweigh the costs, and it prepares us for heaven.

DAY 19

Thinking about My Purpose

POINT TO PONDER: Community requires commitment.

VERSE TO REMEMBER: *"We understand what love is when we realize that Christ gave his life for us. That means we must give our lives for other believers."* 1 JOHN 3:16 (GWT)

QUESTION TO CONSIDER: How can I help cultivate today the characteristics of real community in my small group and my church?

MESSAGE TO HEAR: *www.purposedriven.com/day19*

DAY 20

Restoring Broken Fellowship

purposedriven.com/
day20

*[God] has restored our relationship
with him through Christ,
and has given us this ministry
of restoring relationships.*

2 CORINTHIANS 5:18 (GWT)

RELATIONSHIPS ARE ALWAYS WORTH RESTORING.
Because life is all about learning how to love, God
wants us to value relationships and make the effort to
maintain them instead of discarding them whenever
there is a rift, a hurt, or a conflict. In fact, the Bible
tells us that God has given us the ministry of restoring
relationships.[1] For this reason a significant amount of
the New Testament is devoted to teaching us how to
get along with one another. Paul wrote, *"If you've gotten
anything at all out of following Christ, if his love has made
any difference in your life, if being in a community of the*

Spirit means anything to you,... Agree with each other, love each other, be deep-spirited friends."[2] Paul taught that our ability to get along with others is a mark of spiritual maturity.[3]

Since Christ wants his family to be known for our love for each other,[4] broken fellowship is a disgraceful testimony to unbelievers. This is why Paul was so embarrassed that the members of the church in Corinth were splitting into warring factions and even taking each other to court. He wrote, *"Shame on you! Surely there is at least one wise person in your fellowship who can settle a dispute between fellow Christians."*[5] He was shocked that no one in the church was mature enough to resolve the conflict peaceably. In the same letter, he said, *"I'll put it as urgently as I can: You must get along with each other."*[6]

If you want God's blessing on your life and you want to be known as a child of God, you must learn to be a peacemaker. Jesus said, *"God blesses those who work for peace, for they will be called the children of God."*[7] Notice Jesus didn't say, "Blessed are the peace lovers," because everyone *loves* peace. Neither did he say, "Blessed are the peaceable," who are never disturbed by anything. Jesus said, "Blessed are those who *work* for peace" — those who actively seek to resolve conflict. Peacemakers are rare because peacemaking is hard work.

Because you were formed to be a part of God's family and the second purpose of your life on earth is to learn how to love and relate to others, peacemaking is one of the most important skills you can develop. Unfortunately, most of us were never taught how to resolve conflict.

Peacemaking is not *avoiding conflict*. Running from a problem, pretending it doesn't exist, or being afraid to talk about it is actually cowardice. Jesus, the Prince of Peace, was never afraid of conflict. On occasion he *provoked* it for the good of everyone. Sometimes we need to avoid conflict, sometimes we need to create it, and sometimes we need to resolve it. That's why we must pray for the Holy Spirit's continual guidance.

Peacemaking is also not *appeasement.* Always giving in, acting like a doormat, and allowing others to always run over you is not what Jesus had in mind. He refused to back down on many issues, standing his ground in the face of evil opposition.

How to Restore a Relationship

As believers, God has *"called us to settle our relationships with each other."*[8] Here are seven biblical steps to restoring fellowship:

Talk to God before talking to the person. Discuss the problem with God. If you will pray about the conflict first instead of gossiping to a friend, you will often discover that either God changes your heart or he changes the other person without your help. All your relationships would go smoother if you would just pray more about them.

As David did with his psalms, use prayer to *ventilate vertically.* Tell God your frustrations. Cry out to him. He's never surprised or upset by your anger, hurt, insecurity, or any other emotions. So tell him exactly how you feel.

Most conflict is rooted in unmet needs. Some of these needs can only be met by God. When you expect anyone —a friend, spouse, boss, or family member—to meet a need that only God can fulfill, you are setting yourself up for disappointment and bitterness. *No one* can meet all of your needs except God.

The apostle James noted that many of our conflicts are caused by prayerlessness: *"What causes fights and quarrels among you?... You want something but don't get it.... You do not have, because you do not ask God."*[9] Instead of looking to God, we look to others to make us happy and then get angry when they fail us. God says, "Why don't you come to me first?"

Always take the initiative. It doesn't matter whether you are the offender or the offended: God expects you to make the first move. Don't wait for the other party. Go to them first. Restoring broken fellowship is so important, Jesus commanded that it even takes priority over group worship. He said, *"If you enter your place of worship and, about to make an offering, you suddenly remember a grudge a friend has against you, abandon your offering, leave immediately, go to this friend and make things right.*

Then and only then, come back and work things out with God."[10]

When fellowship is strained or broken, plan a peace conference immediately. Don't procrastinate, make excuses, or promise "I'll get around to it someday." Schedule a face-to-face meeting as soon as possible. Delay only deepens resentment and makes matters worse. In conflict, time heals nothing; it causes hurts to fester.

Acting quickly also reduces the spiritual damage to you. The Bible says sin, including unresolved conflict, blocks our fellowship with God and keeps our prayers from being answered,[11] besides making us miserable. Job's friends reminded him, *"To worry yourself to death with resentment would be a foolish, senseless thing to do"* and *"You are only hurting yourself with your anger."*[12]

God expects you to make the first move.

The success of a peace conference often depends on choosing the right time and place to meet. Don't meet when either of you are tired or rushed or will be interrupted. The best time is when you both are at your best.

Sympathize with their feelings. Use your ears more than your mouth. Before attempting to solve any disagreement you must first listen to people's feelings. Paul advised, *"Look out for one another's interests, not just for your own."*[13] The phrase "look out for" is the Greek word *skopos,* from which we form our words *telescope* and *microscope.* It means pay close attention! Focus on their feelings, not the facts. Begin with sympathy, not solutions.

Don't try to talk people out of how they feel at first. Just listen and let them unload emotionally without being defensive. Nod that you understand even when you don't agree. Feelings are not always true or logical. In fact, resentment makes us act and think in foolish ways. The psalmist admitted, *"When my thoughts were bitter and my feelings were hurt, I was as stupid as an animal."*[14] We all act beastly when hurt.

In contrast, the Bible says, *"A man's wisdom gives him patience; it is to his glory to overlook an offense."*[15] Patience comes from wisdom, and wisdom comes from hearing the perspective of others. Listening says, "I value your opinion, I care about our relationship, and you matter to me." The cliché is true: People don't care what we know until they know we care.

To restore fellowship *"we must bear the 'burden' of being considerate of the doubts and fears of others.... Let's please the other fellow, not ourselves, and do what is for his good."*[16] It is a sacrifice to patiently absorb the anger of others, especially if it's unfounded. But remember, this is what Jesus did for you. He endured unfounded, malicious anger in order to save you: *"Christ did not indulge his own feelings ... as scripture says:* The insults of those who insult you fall on me."[17]

Confess your part of the conflict. If you are serious

about restoring a relationship, you should begin with admitting your own mistakes or sin. Jesus said it's the way to see things more clearly: *"First get rid of the log from your own eye; then perhaps you will see well enough to deal with the speck in your friend's eye."*[18]

Since we all have blind spots, you may need to ask a third party to help you evaluate your own actions before meeting with the person with whom you have a conflict. Also ask God to show you how much of the problem is your fault. Ask, "Am I the problem? Am I being unrealistic, insensitive, or too sensitive?" The Bible says, *"If we claim that we're free of sin, we're only fooling ourselves."*[19]

In resolving conflict, how you say it is as important as what you say.

Confession is a powerful tool for reconciliation. Often the way we handle a conflict creates a bigger hurt than the original problem itself. When you begin by humbly admitting your mistakes, it defuses the other person's anger and disarms their attack because they were probably expecting you to be defensive. Don't make excuses or shift the blame; just honestly own up to any part you have played in the conflict. Accept responsibility for your mistakes and ask for forgiveness.

Attack the problem, not the person. You cannot fix the problem if you're consumed with fixing the blame. You must choose between the two. The Bible says, *"A gentle response defuses anger, but a sharp tongue kindles* *a temper-fire.*"[20] You will never get your point across by being cross, so choose your words wisely. A soft answer is always better than a sarcastic one.

In resolving conflict, *how* you say it is as important as *what* you say. If you say it offensively, it will be received defensively. God tells us, *"A wise, mature person is known for his understanding. The more pleasant his words, the more persuasive he is."*[21] Nagging never works. You are never persuasive when you're abrasive.

During the Cold War, both sides agreed that some weapons were so destructive they should never be used. Today chemical and biological weapons are banned, and the stockpiles of nuclear weapons are being reduced and destroyed. For the sake of fellowship, you must destroy your arsenal of relational nuclear weapons, including condemning, belittling, comparing, labeling, insulting, condescending, and being sarcastic. Paul sums it up this way: *"Do not use harmful words, but only helpful words, the kind that build up and provide what is needed, so that what you say will do good to those who hear you."*[22]

Cooperate as much as possible. Paul said, *"Do everything possible on your part to live in peace with everybody."*[23] Peace always has a price tag. Sometimes it costs our pride; it often costs our self-centeredness. For the sake of fellowship, do your best to compromise, adjust to others, and show preference to what they need.[24] A paraphrase of Jesus' seventh beatitude says, *"You're blessed when you can show people how to cooperate instead of* *compete or fight. That's when you discover who you really are, and your place in God's family."*[25]

Emphasize reconciliation, not resolution. It is unrealistic to expect everyone to agree about everything. Reconciliation focuses on the relationship, while resolution focuses on the problem. When we focus on reconciliation, the problem loses significance and often becomes irrelevant.

We can reestablish a relationship even when we are unable to resolve our differences. Christians often have legitimate, honest disagreements and differing opinions, but we can disagree without being disagreeable. The same diamond looks different from different angles. God expects unity, not uniformity, and we can walk arm-in-arm without seeing eye-to-eye on every issue.

> *Reconciliation focuses on the relationship, while resolution focuses on the problem.*

This doesn't mean you give up on finding a solution. You may need to continue discussing and even debating — but you do it in a spirit of harmony. Reconciliation means you bury the hatchet, not necessarily the issue.

Who do you need to contact as a result of this chapter? With whom do you need to restore fellowship? Don't delay another second. Pause right now and talk to God about that person. Then pick up the phone and begin the process. These seven steps are simple, but they are not easy. It takes a lot of effort to restore a relationship. That's why Peter urged, *"Work hard at living in peace with others."*[26] But when you work for peace, you are doing what God would do. That's why God calls peacemakers his children.[27]

DAY 20

Thinking about My Purpose

POINT TO PONDER: Relationships are always worth restoring.

VERSE TO REMEMBER: *"Do everything possible on your part to live in peace with everybody."* ROMANS 12:18 (TEV)

QUESTION TO CONSIDER: Who do I need to restore a broken relationship with today?

MESSAGE TO HEAR: *www.purposedriven.com/day20*

DAY 21

Protecting Your Church

You are joined together with peace through the Spirit, so make every effort to continue together in this way.

EPHESIANS 4:3 (NCV)

purposedriven.com/
day21

Most of all, let love guide your life, for then the whole church will stay together in perfect harmony.

COLOSSIANS 3:14 (LB)

IT IS YOUR JOB TO PROTECT THE UNITY OF YOUR church.

Unity in the church is so important that the New Testament gives more attention to it than to either heaven or hell. God deeply desires that we experience *oneness* and harmony with each other.

Unity is the soul of fellowship. Destroy it, and you rip the heart out of Christ's Body. It is the essence, the core, of how God intends for us to experience life together in his church. Our supreme model for unity is the Trinity. The Father, Son, and Holy Spirit are completely unified as one. God himself is the highest example of sacrificial love, humble other-centeredness, and perfect harmony.

Just like every parent, our heavenly Father enjoys watching his children get along with each other. In his final moments before being arrested, Jesus prayed passionately for our unity.[1] It was our unity that was uppermost in his mind during those agonizing hours. That shows how significant this subject is.

Nothing on earth is more valuable to God than his church. He paid the highest price for it, and he wants it protected, especially from the devastating damage that is caused by division, conflict, and disharmony. If you are a part of God's family, it is your responsibility to protect the unity where you fellowship. You are commissioned by Jesus Christ to do everything possible to preserve the unity, protect the fellowship, and promote harmony in your church family and among all believers. The Bible says, *"Make every effort to keep the unity of the Spirit through the bond of peace."*[2] How are we to do this? The Bible gives us practical advice.

> Nothing on earth is more valuable to God than his church.

Focus on what we have in common, not our differences. Paul tells us, *"Let us concentrate on the things which make for harmony, and on the growth of one another's character."*[3] As believers we share one Lord, one body, one purpose, one Father, one Spirit, one hope, one faith, one baptism, and one love.[4] We share the same salvation, the same life, and the same future — factors far more important than any differences we could enumerate. These are the issues, not our personal differences, that we should concentrate on.

We must remember that it was God who chose to give us different personalities, backgrounds, races, and preferences, so we should value and enjoy those differences, not merely tolerate them. God wants unity, not uniformity. But for unity's sake we must never let differences divide us. We must stay focused on what matters most — learning to love each other as Christ has loved us, and fulfilling God's five purposes for each of us and his church.

Conflict is usually a sign that the focus has shifted to less important issues, things the Bible calls *"disputable matters."*[5] When we focus on personalities, preferences, interpretations, styles, or methods, division always happens. But if we concentrate on loving each other and fulfilling God's purposes, harmony results. Paul pleaded for this: *"Let there be real harmony so there won't be divisions in the church. I plead with you to be of one mind, united in thought and purpose."*[6]

Be realistic in your expectations. Once you discover what God intends *real* fellowship to be, it is easy to become discouraged by the gap between the *ideal* and the *real* in your church. Yet we must passionately love the church in spite of its imperfections. Longing for the ideal while criticizing the real is evidence of immaturity.

On the other hand, settling for the real without striving for the ideal is complacency. Maturity is living with the tension.

Other believers *will* disappoint you and let you down, but that's no excuse to stop fellowshiping with them. They are your family, even when they don't act like it, and you can't just walk out on them. Instead God tells us, *"Be patient with each other, making allowance for each other's faults because of your love."*[7]

People become disillusioned with the church for many understandable reasons. The list could be quite long: conflict, hurt, hypocrisy,

> We must passionately love the church in spite of its imperfections.

neglect, pettiness, legalism, and other sins. Rather than being shocked and surprised, we must remember that the church is made up of real sinners, including ourselves. Because we're sinners, we hurt each other, sometimes intentionally and sometimes unintentionally. But instead of leaving the church, we need to stay and work it out if at all possible. Reconciliation, not running away, is the road to stronger character and deeper fellowship.

Divorcing your church at the first sign of disappointment or disillusionment is a mark of immaturity. God has things he wants to teach you, and others, too. Besides, there is no perfect church to escape to. Every church has its own set of weaknesses and problems. You will soon be disappointed again.

Groucho Marx was famous for saying he wouldn't want to belong to any club that would let him in. If a church must be perfect to satisfy you, that same perfection will exclude you from membership, because you're not perfect!

Dietrich Bonhoeffer, the German pastor who was martyred for resisting Nazis, wrote a classic book on fellowship, *Life Together.* In it he suggests that disillusionment with our local church is a good thing because it destroys our false expectations of perfection. The sooner we give up the illusion that a church must be perfect in order to love it, the sooner we quit pretending and start admitting we're *all* imperfect and need grace. This is the beginning of real community.

Every church could put out a sign "No perfect people need apply. This is a place only for those who admit they are sinners, need grace, and want to grow."

Bonhoeffer said, "He who loves his dream of community more than the Christian community itself becomes a destroyer of the latter.... If we do not give thanks daily for the Christian fellowship in which we have been placed, even when there is no great experience, no discoverable riches, but much weakness, small faith, and difficulty; if on the contrary, we keep complaining that everything is paltry and petty, then we hinder God from letting our fellowship grow."[8]

Choose to encourage rather than criticize. It is always easier to stand on the sidelines and take shots at those who are serving than it is to get involved and make a contribution. God warns us over and over not to criticize, compare, or judge each other.[9] When you criticize what another believer is doing in faith and from sincere conviction, you are interfering with God's business: *"What right do you have to criticize someone else's servants? Only their Lord can decide if they are doing right."*[10]

Paul adds that we must not stand in judgment or look down on other believers whose convictions differ from our own: *"Why, then, criticise your brother's actions, why try to make him look small? We shall all be judged one day, not by each other's standards or even our own, but by the standard of Christ."*[11]

Whenever I judge another believer, four things instantly happen: I lose fellowship with God, I expose my own pride and insecurity, I set myself up to be judged by God, and I harm the fellowship of the church. A critical spirit is a costly vice.

The Bible calls Satan *"the accuser of our brothers."*[12] It's the Devil's job to blame, complain, and criticize members of God's family. Anytime we do the same, we're being duped into doing Satan's work for him. Remember, other Christians, no matter how much you disagree with them, are not the real enemy. Any time we spend comparing or criticizing other believers is time that should have been spent building the unity of our fellowship. The Bible says, *"Let's agree to use all our energy in getting along with each*

*other. Help others with encouraging words; don't drag
them down by finding fault.*"[13]

Refuse to listen to gossip. Gossip is passing on
information when you are neither part of the problem nor
part of the solution. You know spreading gossip is wrong,
but you should not *listen* to it, either, if you want to
protect your church. Listening to gossip is like accepting
stolen property, and it makes you just as guilty
of the crime.

DAY 21:

Protecting
Your Church

When someone begins to gossip to you,
have the courage to say, "Please stop. I don't
need to know this. Have you talked directly
to that person?" People who gossip *to* you will also gossip
about you. They cannot be trusted. If you listen to gossip,
God says you are a troublemaker.[14] *"Troublemakers
listen to troublemakers."*[15] *"These are the ones who split
churches, thinking only of themselves."*[16]

It is sad that in God's flock, the greatest wounds
usually come from other sheep, not wolves. Paul warned
about "cannibal Christians" who *"devour one another"*
and destroy the fellowship.[17] The Bible says these kind of
troublemakers should be avoided. *"A gossip reveals secrets;
therefore do not associate with a babbler."*[18] The fastest
way to end a church or small group conflict is to lovingly
confront those who are gossiping and insist they stop it.
Solomon pointed out, *"Fire goes out for lack of fuel, and
tensions disappear when gossip stops."*[19]

Practice God's method for conflict resolution. In

addition to the principles mentioned in the last chapter, Jesus gave the church a simple three-step process: *"If a fellow believer hurts you, go and tell him — work it out between the two of you. If he listens, you have made a friend. If he won't listen, take one or two others along so that the presence of witnesses will keep things honest, and try again. If he still won't listen, tell the church."*[20]

During conflict, it is tempting to complain to a third party rather than courageously speak the truth in love to the person you're upset with. This makes the matter worse. Instead, you should go directly to the person involved.

Private confrontation is always the first step, and you should take it as soon as possible. If you're unable to work things out between the two of you, the next step is to take one or two witnesses to help confirm the problem and reconcile the relationship. What should you do if the person is still stuck in stubbornness? Jesus says to take it to the church. If the person still refuses to listen after that, you should treat that person like an unbeliever.[21]

Support your pastor and leaders. There are no perfect leaders, but God gives leaders the responsibility and the authority to maintain the unity of the church. During interpersonal conflicts that is a thankless job. Pastors often have the unpleasant task of serving as mediator between hurt, conflicting, or immature members. They're also given the impossible task of trying to make *everyone* happy, which even Jesus could not do!

The Bible is clear about how we are to relate to those who serve us: *"Be responsive to your pastoral leaders. Listen to their counsel. They are alert to the condition of your lives and work under the strict supervision of God. Contribute to the joy of their leadership, not its drudgery. Why would you want to make things harder for them?"*[22]

Pastors will one day stand before God and give an account of how well they watched over you. *"They keep watch over you as men who must give an account."*[23] But you are accountable, too. You will give an account to God of how well you followed your leaders.

> We protect the fellowship when we honor those who serve us by leading.

The Bible gives pastors very specific instructions on how to deal with divisive people in the fellowship. They are to avoid arguing, gently teach the opposition while praying they will change, warn those who are argumentative, plead for harmony and unity, rebuke those who are disrespectful of leadership, and remove divisive people from the church if they ignore two warnings.[24]

We protect the fellowship when we honor those who serve us by leading. Pastors and elders need our prayers, encouragement, appreciation, and love. We are commanded, *"Honor those leaders who work so hard for you, who have been given the responsibility of urging and guiding you along in your obedience. Overwhelm them with appreciation and love!"*[25]

I challenge you to accept your responsibility to protect and promote the unity of your church. Put your full effort into it, and God will be pleased. It will not always be easy. Sometimes you will have to do what's best for the Body, not yourself, showing preference to others. That's one reason God puts us in a church family — to learn unselfishness. In community we learn to say "we" instead of "I," and "our" instead of "mine." God says, *"Don't think only of your own good. Think of other Christians and what is best for them."*[26]

God blesses churches that are unified. At Saddleback Church, every member signs a covenant that includes a promise to protect the unity of our fellowship. As a result, the church has never had a conflict that split the fellowship. Just as important, because it is a loving, unified fellowship, a lot of people *want* to be a part of it! In the past seven years, the church has baptized over 9,100 new believers. When God has a bunch of baby believers he wants to deliver, he looks for the warmest incubator church he can find.

What are you doing personally to make your church family more warm and loving? There are many people in your community who are looking for love and a place to belong. The truth is, *everyone* needs and wants to be loved, and when people find a church where members genuinely love and care for each other, you would have to lock the doors to keep them away.

DAY 21

Thinking about My Purpose

POINT TO PONDER: It is my responsibility to protect the unity of my church.

VERSE TO REMEMBER: *"Let us concentrate on the things which make for harmony and the growth of our fellowship together."* ROMANS 14:19 (PH)

QUESTION TO CONSIDER: What am I personally doing to protect unity in my church family right now?

MESSAGE TO HEAR: *www.purposedriven.com/day21*

YOU WERE CREATED TO BECOME LIKE CHRIST

*Let your roots grow down into Christ
and draw up nourishment from him.
See that you go on growing in the Lord, and
become strong and vigorous in the truth.*

COLOSSIANS 2:7 (LB)

Created to Become Like Christ

God knew what he was doing from the very beginning. He decided from the outset to shape the lives of those who love him along the same lines as the life of his Son.... We see the original and intended shape of our lives there in him.

ROMANS 8:29 (MSG)

purposedriven.com/
day22

We look at this Son and see God's original purpose in everything created.

COLOSSIANS 1:15 (MSG)

YOU WERE CREATED TO BECOME LIKE CHRIST.

From the very beginning, God's plan has been to make you like his Son, Jesus. This is your destiny and the third purpose of your life. God announced this intention at Creation: *"Then God said, 'Let us make human beings in our image and likeness.'"*[1]

In all of creation, only human beings are made "in God's image." This is a great privilege and gives us dignity. We don't know *all* this phrase covers, but we do

219

know some of the aspects it includes: Like God, we are *spiritual beings* — our spirits are immortal and will outlast our earthly bodies; we are *intellectual* — we can think, reason, and solve problems; like God, we are *relational* — we can give and receive real love; and we have a *moral consciousness* — we can discern right from wrong, which makes us accountable to God.

The Bible says that all people, not just believers, possess part of the image of God; that is why murder and abortion are wrong.[2] But the image is incomplete and has been damaged and distorted by sin. So God sent Jesus on a mission to restore the full image that we have lost.

What does the full "image and likeness" of God look like? It looks like Jesus Christ! The Bible says Jesus is *"the exact likeness of God," "the visible image of the invisible God,"* and *"the exact representation of his being."*[3]

People often use the phrase "like father, like son" to refer to family resemblance. When people see my likeness in my kids, it pleases me. God wants his children to bear his image and likeness, too. The Bible says, *"You were ... created to be like God, truly righteous and holy."*[4]

Let me be absolutely clear: You will never become God, or even *a* god. That prideful lie is Satan's oldest temptation. Satan promised Adam and Eve that if they followed his advice, *"ye shall be as gods."*[5] Many religions and New Age philosophies still promote this old lie that we are divine or can become gods.

This desire to be a god shows up every time we try

to control our circumstances, our future, and people around us. But as creatures, we will never be the *Creator.* God doesn't want you to become a god; he wants you to become *godly* — taking on his values, attitudes, and character. The Bible says, *"Take on an entirely new way of life — a God-fashioned life, a life renewed from the inside and working itself into your conduct as God accurately reproduces his character in you."*[6]

God's ultimate goal for your life on earth is not comfort, but character development. He wants you to grow up spiritually and become like Christ. Becoming like Christ does not mean losing your personality or becoming a mindless clone. God created your uniqueness, so he certainly doesn't want to destroy it. Christlikeness is all about transforming your character, not your personality.

> God's ultimate goal for your life on earth is not comfort, but character development.

God wants you to develop the kind of character described in the beatitudes of Jesus,[7] the fruit of the Spirit,[8] Paul's great chapter on love,[9] and Peter's list of the characteristics of an effective and productive life.[10] Every time you forget that character is one of God's purposes for your life, you will become frustrated by your circumstances. You'll wonder, "Why is this happening to me? Why am I having such a difficult time?" One answer is that life is *supposed* to be difficult! It's what enables us to grow. Remember, earth is not heaven!

Many Christians misinterpret Jesus' promise of the "abundant life"[11] to mean perfect health, a comfortable lifestyle, constant happiness, full realization of your dreams, and instant relief from problems through faith and prayer. In a word, they expect the Christian life to be easy. They expect heaven on earth.

This self-absorbed perspective treats God as a genie who simply exists to serve you in your selfish pursuit of personal fulfillment. But God is *not* your servant, and if you fall for the idea that life is supposed to be easy, either you will become severely disillusioned or you will live in denial of reality.

Never forget that life is not about you! You exist for God's purposes, not vice versa. Why would God provide *heaven on earth* when he's planned the real thing for you in eternity? God gives us our time on earth to build and strengthen our character for heaven.

God's Spirit Working in You

It is the Holy Spirit's job to produce Christlike character in you. The Bible says, *"As the Spirit of the Lord works within us, we become more and more like him and reflect his glory even more."*[12] This process of changing us to be more like Jesus is called *sanctification*, and it is the third purpose of your life on earth.

You cannot reproduce the character of Jesus on your own strength. New Year's resolutions, willpower, and best intentions are not enough. Only the Holy Spirit has the power to make the changes God wants to make in our lives. The Bible says, *"God is working in you, giving you the desire to obey him and the power to do what pleases him."*[13]

Mention "the power of the Holy Spirit," and many people think of miraculous demonstrations and intense emotions. But most of the time the Holy Spirit's power is released in your life in quiet, unassuming ways that you aren't even aware of or can't feel. He often nudges us with *"a gentle whisper."*[14]

> Your character is essentially the sum of your habits.

Christlikeness is not produced by imitation, but by inhabitation. We allow Christ to live *through* us. *"For this is the secret: Christ lives in you."*[15] How does this happen in real life? Through the choices we make. We choose to do the right thing in situations and then trust God's Spirit to give us his power, love, faith, and wisdom to do it. Since God's Spirit lives inside of us, these things are always available for the asking.

We must cooperate with the Holy Spirit's work. Throughout the Bible we see an important truth illustrated over and over: The Holy Spirit releases his power *the moment* you take a step of faith. When Joshua was faced with an impassible barrier, the floodwaters of the Jordan River receded only *after* the leaders stepped into the rushing current in obedience and faith.[16] Obedience unlocks God's power.

God waits for you to act first. Don't wait to feel powerful or confident. Move ahead in your weakness, doing the right thing in spite of your fears and feelings. This is how you cooperate with the Holy Spirit, and it is how your character develops.

The Bible compares spiritual growth to a seed, a building, and a child growing up. Each metaphor requires active participation: Seeds must be planted and cultivated, buildings must be built — they don't just appear — and children must eat and exercise to grow.

While effort has nothing to do with your salvation, it has much to do with your spiritual growth. At least eight times in the New Testament we are told to *"make every effort"*[17] in our growth toward becoming like Jesus. You don't just sit around and wait for it to happen.

Paul explains in Ephesians 4:22 — 24 our three responsibilities in becoming like Christ. First, we must choose to let go of old ways of acting. *"Everything ...*

DAY 22:
Created to Become
Like Christ

connected with that old way of life has to go. It's rotten through and through. Get rid of it!"[18]

Second, we must change the way we think. *"Let the Spirit change your way of thinking."*[19] The Bible says we are "transformed" by the renewing of our minds.[20] The Greek word for transformed, *metamorphosis* (used in Romans 12:2 and 2 Corinthians 3:18), is used today to describe the amazing change a caterpillar goes through in becoming a butterfly.

It is a beautiful picture of what happens to us spiritually when we allow God to direct our thoughts: We are changed from the inside out, we become more beautiful, and we are set free to soar to new heights.

Third, we must "put on" the character of Christ by developing new, godly habits. Your character is essentially the sum of your habits; it is how you *habitually* act. The Bible says, *"Put on the new self, created to be like God in true righteousness and holiness."*[21]

God uses his Word, people, and circumstances to mold us. All three are indispensable for character development. God's Word provides the *truth* we need to grow, God's people provide the *support* we need to grow, and circumstances provide the *environment* we need to practice Christlikeness. If you study and apply God's Word, connect regularly with other believers, and learn to trust God in difficult circumstances, I guarantee you will become more like Jesus. We will look at each of these growth ingredients in the chapters ahead.

Many people assume all that is needed for spiritual growth is Bible study and prayer. But some issues in life will *never* be changed by Bible study or prayer alone. God uses people. He usually prefers to work through people rather than perform miracles, so that we will depend on each other for fellowship. He wants us to grow together.

In many religions, the people considered to be the most spiritually mature and holy are those who isolate themselves from others in mountaintop monasteries, uninfected by contact with other people. But this is a gross misunderstanding. Spiritual maturity is not a solitary, individual pursuit! You cannot grow to Christlikeness in isolation. You must be around other people and interact with them. You need to be a part of a church and community. Why? Because true spiritual maturity is all about learning to love like Jesus, and you can't practice being like Jesus without being in relationship with other people. Remember, it's all about love — loving God and loving others.

Becoming like Christ is a long, slow process of growth. Spiritual maturity is neither instant nor automatic; it is a gradual, progressive development that will take the rest of your life. Referring to this process, Paul said, *"This will continue until we are … mature, just as Christ is, and we will be completely like him."*[22]

You are a work in progress. Your spiritual transformation in developing the character of Jesus will take the rest of your life, and even then it won't be completed here on earth. It will only be finished when you get to heaven or when Jesus returns. At that point, whatever unfinished work on your character is left will be wrapped up. The Bible says that when we are finally able to see Jesus perfectly, we will become perfectly like him: *"We can't even imagine what we will be like when Christ returns. But we do know that when he comes we will be like him, for we will see him as he really is."*[23]

Much confusion in the Christian life comes from

ignoring the simple truth that God is far more interested
in building your character than he is anything else. We
worry when God seems silent on specific issues such as
"What career should I choose?" The truth is, there are
many different careers that could be in God's will for
your life. What God cares about most is that whatever
you do, you do in a Christlike manner.[24]

God is far more interested in what you are than in
what you do. We are human *beings,* not human *doings.*
God is much more concerned about your character than
your career, because you will take your character into
eternity, but not your career.

The Bible warns, *"Don't become so well-adjusted
to your culture that you fit into
it without even thinking. Instead,
fix your attention on God. You'll
be changed from the inside out....
Unlike the culture around you, always
dragging you down to its level of
immaturity, God brings the best out
of you, develops well-formed maturity in you."*[25] You must
make a counter-culture decision to focus on becoming
more like Jesus. Otherwise, other forces like peers,
parents, coworkers, and culture will try to mold you into
their image.

> God is far more
> interested in what
> you are than in
> what you do.

Sadly, a quick review of many popular Christian
books reveals that many believers have abandoned
living for God's great purposes and settled for personal

fulfillment and emotional stability. That is narcissism, not discipleship. Jesus did not die on the cross just so we could live comfortable, well-adjusted lives. His purpose is far deeper: He wants to make us like himself before he takes us to heaven. This is our greatest privilege, our immediate responsibility, and our ultimate destiny.

DAY 22

Thinking about My Purpose

POINT TO PONDER: I was created to become like Christ.

VERSE TO REMEMBER: *"As the Spirit of the Lord works within us, we become more and more like him and reflect his glory even more."* 2 CORINTHIANS 3:18B (NLT)

QUESTION TO CONSIDER: In what area of my life do I need to ask for the Spirit's power to be like Christ today?

MESSAGE TO HEAR: *www.purposedriven.com/day22*

How We Grow

God wants us to grow up ...
like Christ in everything.

EPHESIANS 4:15A (MSG)

We are not meant to remain as children.

EPHESIANS 4:14A (PH)

purposedriven.com/
day23

GOD WANTS YOU TO GROW UP.

Your heavenly Father's goal is for you to mature and
develop the characteristics of Jesus Christ. Sadly, millions
of Christians *grow older* but never *grow up.* They are
stuck in perpetual spiritual infancy, remaining in diapers
and booties. The reason is that they never *intended* to
grow.

Spiritual growth is not automatic. It takes an
intentional commitment. You must *want* to grow, *decide*
to grow, *make an effort* to grow, and *persist* in growing.
Discipleship — the process of becoming like Christ —

229

always begins with a decision. Jesus calls us, and we respond: "*'Come, be my disciple,' Jesus said to him. So Matthew got up and followed him.*"[1]

When the first disciples chose to follow Jesus, they didn't understand all the implications of their decision. They simply responded to Jesus' invitation. That's all you need to get started: *Decide* to become a disciple.

Nothing shapes your life more than the commitments you choose to make. Your commitments can develop you or they can destroy you, but either way, they will define you. Tell me what you are committed to, and I'll tell you what you will be in twenty years. We become whatever we are committed to.

It is at this point of commitment that most people miss God's purpose for their lives. Many are afraid to commit to anything and just drift through life. Others make halfhearted commitments to competing values, which leads to frustration and mediocrity. Others make a full commitment to worldly goals, such as becoming wealthy or famous, and end up disappointed and bitter. Every choice has eternal consequences, so you had better choose wisely. Peter warns, "*Since everything around us is going to melt away, what holy, godly lives you should be living!*"[2]

God's part and your part. Christlikeness is the result of making Christlike choices and depending on his Spirit to help you fulfill those choices. Once you decide to get serious about becoming like Christ, you must begin to act in new ways. You will need to let go of some old routines, develop some new habits, and intentionally change the way you think. You can be certain that the Holy Spirit will help you with these changes. The Bible says, *"Continue to work out your salvation with fear and trembling, for it is God who works in you to will and to act according to his good purpose."*[3]

We become whatever we are committed to.

This verse shows the two parts of spiritual growth: *"work out"* and *"work in."* The *"work out"* is your responsibility, and the *"work in"* is God's role. Spiritual growth is a collaborative effort between you and the Holy Spirit. God's Spirit works *with* us, not just in us.

This verse, written to believers, is not about how to be saved, but how to grow. It does not say *"work for"* your salvation, because you can't add anything to what Jesus already did. During a physical "workout," you exercise to develop your body, not to get a body.

When you "work out" a puzzle, you already have all the pieces — your task is to put them together. Farmers "work" the land, not to *get* land, but to develop what they already have. God has given you a new life; now you are responsible to develop it *"with fear and trembling."* That means to take your spiritual growth seriously! When people are casual about their spiritual growth, it shows they don't understand the eternal implications (as we saw in chapters 4 and 5).

Changing your autopilot. To change your life, you must change the way you think. Behind everything you do is a thought. Every behavior is motivated by a belief, and every action is prompted by an attitude. God revealed this thousands of years before psychologists understood it: *"Be careful how you think; your life is shaped by your thoughts."*[4]

Imagine riding in a speedboat on a lake with an automatic pilot set to go east. If you decide to reverse and head west, you have two possible ways to change the boat's direction. One way is to grab the steering wheel and physically *force it* to head in the opposite direction from where the autopilot is programmed to go. By sheer willpower you could overcome the autopilot, but you would feel constant resistance. Your arms would eventually tire of the stress, you'd let go of the steering wheel, and the boat would instantly head back east, the way it was internally programmed.

This is what happens when you try to change your life with willpower: You say, "I'll *force* myself to eat less ... exercise more ... quit being disorganized and late." Yes, willpower *can* produce short-term change, but it creates constant internal stress because you haven't dealt with the root cause. The change doesn't feel natural, so eventually you give up, go off your diet, and quit exercising. You quickly revert to your old patterns.

There is a better and easier way: Change your autopilot — the way you think. The Bible says, *"Let God transform you into a new person by changing the way you think.*"[5] Your first step in spiritual growth is to start changing the way you think. Change always starts first in your mind. The way you *think* determines the way you *feel,* and the way you feel influences the way you *act.* Paul said, *"There must be a spiritual renewal of your thoughts and attitudes."*[6]

To be like Christ you must develop the mind of Christ. The New Testament calls this mental shift *repentance,* which in Greek literally means "to change your mind." You repent whenever you change the way you think by adopting how God thinks — about yourself, sin, God, other people, life, your future, and everything else. You take on Christ's outlook and perspective.

We are commanded to *"think the same way that Christ Jesus thought."*[7] There are two parts to doing this. The first half of this mental shift is to stop thinking *immature* thoughts, which are self-centered and self-seeking. The Bible says, *"Stop thinking like children. In regard to evil be infants, but in your thinking be adults."*[8] Babies by nature are completely selfish. They think only of themselves and their own needs. They are incapable of giving; they can only receive. That is immature thinking. Unfortunately, many people never grow beyond that kind of thinking. The Bible says that selfish thinking is the source of sinful behavior: *"Those who live following their sinful selves think only about things that their sinful selves want."*[9]

DAY 23:

How

We Grow

The second half of thinking like Jesus is to *start* thinking *maturely,* which focuses on others, not yourself. In his great chapter on what real love is, Paul concluded that thinking of others is the mark of maturity: *"When I was a child, I talked like a child, I thought like a child, I reasoned like a child. When I became a man, I put childish ways behind me."*[10]

The way you think determines the way you feel, and the way you feel determines the way you act.

Today many assume that spiritual maturity is measured by the amount of biblical information and doctrine you know. While knowledge is *one* measurement of maturity, it isn't the whole story. The Christian life is far more than creeds and convictions; it includes conduct and character. Our deeds must be consistent with our creeds, and our beliefs must be backed up with Christlike behavior.

Christianity is not a religion or a philosophy, but a relationship and a lifestyle. The core of that lifestyle is thinking of others, as Jesus did, instead of ourselves. The Bible says, *"We should think of their good and try to help them by doing what pleases them. Even Christ did not try to please himself."*[11]

Thinking of others is the heart of Christlikeness and the best evidence of spiritual growth. This kind of thinking is unnatural, counter-cultural, rare, and difficult. Fortunately we have help: *"God has given us his*

Spirit. That's why we don't think the same way that the people of this world think."[12] In the next few chapters we will look at the tools the Holy Spirit uses to help us grow.

DAY 23

Thinking about My Purpose

POINT TO PONDER: It is never too late to start growing.

VERSE TO REMEMBER: *"Let God transform you inwardly by a complete change of your mind. Then you will be able to know the will of God — what is good and is pleasing to him and is perfect."* ROMANS 12:2B (TEV)

QUESTION TO CONSIDER: What is one area where I need to stop thinking *my* way and start thinking *God's* way?

MESSAGE TO HEAR: *www.purposedriven.com/day23*

DAY 24

Transformed by Truth

*People need more than bread for their life;
they must feed on every word of God.*

MATTHEW 4:4 (NLT)

purposedriven.com/
day24

*God's ... gracious Word
can make you into what he wants
you to be and give you everything
you could possibly need.*

ACTS 20:32 (MSG)

THE TRUTH TRANSFORMS US.

Spiritual growth is the process of replacing lies with
truth. Jesus prayed, *"Sanctify them by the truth; your word
is truth."*[1] Sanctification requires revelation. The Spirit
of God uses the Word of God to make us like the Son of
God. To become like Jesus, we must fill our lives with
his Word. The Bible says, *"Through the Word we are put
together and shaped up for the tasks God has for us."*[2]

God's Word is unlike any other word. It is alive.[3] Jesus
said, *"The words that I have spoken to you are spirit and
are life."*[4] When God speaks, things change. Everything

around you — all of creation — exists because *"God said it."* He spoke it all into existence. Without God's Word you would not even be alive. James points out, *"God decided to give us life through the word of truth so we might be the most important of all the things he made."*[5]

The Bible is far more than a doctrinal guidebook. God's Word generates life, creates faith, produces change, frightens the Devil, causes miracles, heals hurts, builds character, transforms circumstances, imparts joy, overcomes adversity, defeats temptation, infuses hope, releases power, cleanses our minds, brings things into being, and guarantees our future forever! We cannot live without the Word of God! *Never* take it for granted. You should consider it as essential to your life as food. Job said, *"I have treasured the words of his mouth more than my daily bread."*[6]

God's Word is the spiritual nourishment you *must* have to fulfill your purpose. The Bible is called our milk, bread, solid food, and sweet dessert.[7] This four-course meal is the Spirit's menu for spiritual strength and growth. Peter advises us, *"Crave pure spiritual milk, so that by it you may grow up in your salvation."*[8]

Abiding in God's Word

There are more Bibles in print today than ever before, but a Bible on the shelf is worthless. Millions of believers are plagued with spiritual anorexia, starving to death

The Spirit of God uses the Word of God to make us like the Son of God.

from spiritual malnutrition. To be a healthy disciple of Jesus, feeding on God's Word must be your first priority. Jesus called it *"abiding."* He said, *"If you abide in My word, then you are truly disciples of Mine."*[9] In day-to-day living, abiding in God's Word includes three activities.

I must accept its authority. The Bible must become the authoritative standard for my life: the compass I rely on for direction, the counsel I listen to for making wise decisions, and the benchmark I use for evaluating everything. The Bible must always have the first and last word in my life.

Many of our troubles occur because we base our choices on unreliable authorities: culture ("everyone is doing it"), tradition ("we've always done it"), reason ("it seemed logical"), or emotion ("it just felt right"). All four of these are flawed by the Fall. What we need is a perfect standard that will never lead us in the wrong direction. Only God's Word meets that need. Solomon reminds us, *"Every word of God is flawless,"*[10] and Paul explains, *"Everything in the Scriptures is God's Word. All of it is useful for teaching and helping people and for correcting them and showing them how to live."*[11]

In the early years of his ministry, Billy Graham went through a time when he struggled with doubts about the accuracy and authority of the Bible. One moonlit night he dropped to his knees in tears and told God that, in spite of confusing passages he didn't understand, from that point on he would completely trust the Bible as the sole authority for his life and ministry. From that day forward, Billy's life was blessed with unusual power and effectiveness.

The most important decision you can make today is to settle this issue of what will be the ultimate authority for your life. Decide that regardless of culture, tradition, reason, or emotion, you choose the Bible as your final authority. Determine to first ask, "What does the Bible say?" when making decisions. Resolve that when God says to do something, you will trust God's Word and do it whether or not it makes sense or you feel like doing it. Adopt Paul's statement as your personal affirmation of faith: *"I believe everything that agrees with the Law and that is written in the Prophets."*[12]

I must assimilate its truth. It is not enough just to believe the Bible; I must fill my mind with it so that the Holy Spirit can transform me with the truth. There are five ways to do this: You can receive it, read it, research it, remember it, and reflect on it.

First, you *receive* God's Word when you listen and accept it with an open, receptive attitude. The parable of the sower illustrates how our receptiveness determines whether or not God's Word takes root in our lives and bears fruit. Jesus identified three unreceptive attitudes — a closed mind (hard soil), a superficial mind (shallow soil), and a distracted mind (soil with weeds) — and then he said, *"Consider carefully how you listen."*[13]

Anytime you feel you are not learning anything from a sermon or a Bible teacher, you should check your attitude, especially for pride, because God can speak through even the most boring teacher when you are humble and receptive. James advises, *"In a humble (gentle, modest) spirit, receive and welcome the Word which implanted and rooted in your hearts contains the power to save your souls."*[14]

Second, for most of the 2,000-year history of the church, only priests got to personally *read* the Bible, but now billions of us have access to it. In spite of this, many believers are more faithful to reading their daily newspaper than their Bibles. It's no wonder we don't grow. We can't watch television for three hours, then read the Bible for three minutes and expect to grow.

Many who claim to believe the Bible "from cover to cover" have never read it from cover to cover. But if you will read the Bible just fifteen minutes a day, you will read completely through it once a year. If you cut out one thirty-minute television program a day and read your Bible instead, you will read through the entire Bible twice a year.

Daily Bible reading will keep you in range of God's voice. This is why God instructed the kings of Israel to always keep a copy of his Word nearby: *"He should keep it with him all the time and read from it every day of his life.*"[15] But don't just keep it near you; read it regularly! A simple tool that is helpful for this is a daily Bible reading plan. It will prevent you from just skipping around the Bible arbitrarily and overlooking sections. If you would like a copy of my personal Bible reading plan, see appendix 2.

Third, *researching,* or studying, the Bible is another practical way to abide in the Word. The difference between reading and studying the Bible involves two additional activities: asking questions of the text and writing down your insights. You haven't really studied the Bible unless you've written your thoughts down on paper or computer.

Many who claim to believe the Bible "from cover to cover" have never read it from cover to cover.

Space does not allow me to explain the different methods of Bible study. Several helpful books on Bible study methods are available, including one I wrote over twenty years ago.[16] The secret of good Bible study is simply learning to ask the right questions. Different methods use different questions. You will discover far more if you pause and ask such simple questions as who? what? when? where? why? and how? The Bible says, *"Truly happy people are those who carefully study God's perfect law that makes people free, and they continue to study it. They do not forget what they heard, but they obey what God's teaching says. Those who do this will be made happy."*[17]

The fourth way to abide in God's Word is by *remembering* it. Your capacity to remember is a God-given gift. You may think you have a poor memory, but the truth is, you have millions of ideas, truths, facts, and figures memorized. You remember what is *important* to you. If God's Word is important, you will take the time to remember it.

There are enormous benefits to memorizing Bible verses. It will help you resist temptation, make wise decisions, reduce stress, build confidence, offer good advice, and share your faith with others.[18]

Your memory is like a muscle. The more you use it, the stronger it will become, and memorizing Scripture will become easier. You might begin by selecting a few Bible verses out of this book that have touched you and writing them down on a small card you can carry with you. Then review them *aloud* throughout your day. You can memorize Scripture anywhere: while working or exercising or driving or waiting or at bedtime. The three keys to memorizing Scripture are review, review, and review! The Bible says, *"Remember what Christ taught and let his words enrich your lives and make you wise."*[19]

DAY 24: Transformed by Truth

The fifth way to abide in God's Word is to *reflect* on it, which the Bible calls "meditation." For many, the idea of meditating conjures up images of putting your mind in neutral and letting it wander. This is the exact opposite of biblical meditation.

Meditation is *focused* thinking. It takes serious effort. You select a verse and reflect on it over and over in your mind.

As I mentioned in chapter 11, if you know how to worry, you already know how to meditate. Worry is focused thinking on something negative. Meditation is doing the same thing, only focusing on God's Word instead of your problem.

No other habit can do more to transform your life and make you more like Jesus than daily reflection on Scripture. As we take the time to contemplate God's truth, seriously reflecting on the example of Christ, we are *"transformed into his likeness with ever-increasing glory."*[20]

If you look up all the times God speaks about meditation in the Bible, you will be amazed at the benefits he has promised to those who take the time to reflect on his Word throughout the day. One of the reasons God called David *"a man after my own heart"*[21] is that David loved to reflect on God's Word. He said, *"How I love your teachings! I think about them all day long."*[22] Serious reflection on God's truth is a key to answered prayer and the secret to successful living.[23]

I must apply its principles. Receiving, reading, researching, remembering, and reflecting on the Word are all useless if we fail to put them into practice. We must become *"doers of the word."*[24] This is the hardest step of all, because Satan fights it so intensely. He doesn't mind you going to Bible studies as long as you don't do anything with what you learn.

We fool ourselves when we assume that just because we have heard or read or studied a truth, we have internalized it. Actually, you can be so busy going to the next class or seminar or Bible conference that you have no time to implement what you've learned. You forget it on the way to your next study. Without implementation, all our Bible studies are worthless. Jesus said, *"Everyone who hears these words of mine and puts them into practice is like a wise man who built his house on the rock."*[25] Jesus also pointed out that God's blessing comes from obeying the truth, not just knowing it. He said, *"Now that you know these things, you will be blessed if you do them."*[26]

> The truth will set you free, but first it may make you miserable!

Another reason we avoid personal application is that it can be difficult or even painful. The truth *will* set you free, but first it may make you miserable! God's Word exposes our motives, points out our faults, rebukes our sin, and expects us to change. It's human nature to resist change, so applying God's Word is hard work. This is why it is so important to discuss your personal applications with other people.

I cannot overstate the value of being a part of a small Bible study discussion group. We always learn from others truths we would never learn on our own. Other

people will help you see insights you would miss and help you apply God's truth in a practical way.

The best way to become a "doer of the Word" is to always write out an action step as a result of your reading or studying or reflecting on God's Word. Develop the habit of writing down exactly what you intend to do. This action step should be *personal* (involving *you*), *practical* (something you can *do*), and *provable* (with a *deadline* to do it). Every application will involve either your relationship to God, your relationship to others, or your personal character.

Before reading the next chapter, spend some time thinking about this question: What has God *already* told you to do in his Word that you haven't started doing yet? Then write down a few action statements that will help you act on what you know. You might tell a friend who can hold you accountable. As D. L. Moody said, "The Bible was not given to increase our knowledge but to change our lives."

DAY 24

Thinking about My Purpose

POINT TO PONDER: The truth transforms me.

VERSE TO REMEMBER: *"If ye continue in my word, then are ye my disciples indeed; and ye shall know the truth, and the truth shall make you free."* JOHN 8:31 — 32 (KJV)

QUESTION TO CONSIDER: What has God already told me in his Word that I haven't started doing yet?

MESSAGE TO HEAR: *www.purposedriven.com/day24*

Transformed by Trouble

*For our light and momentary troubles
are achieving for us an eternal glory
that far outweighs them all.*

2 CORINTHIANS 4:17 (NIV)

*It is the fire of suffering that
brings forth the gold of godliness.*

MADAME GUYON

purposedriven.com/
day25

GOD HAS A PURPOSE BEHIND EVERY PROBLEM.

He uses circumstances to develop our character. In fact, he depends more on circumstances to make us like Jesus than he depends on our reading the Bible. The reason is obvious: You face circumstances twenty-four hours a day.

Jesus warned us that we would have problems in the world.[1] No one is immune to pain or insulated from suffering, and no one gets to skate through life problem-free. Life is a series of problems. Every time you solve one, another is waiting to take its place. Not all of them are big, but all are significant in God's growth process for you. Peter assures us that problems are normal, saying, *"Don't be bewildered or surprised when you go through the fiery trials ahead, for this is no strange, unusual thing that is going to happen to you."*[2]

God uses problems to draw you closer to himself. The Bible says, *"The Lord is close to the brokenhearted; he rescues those who are crushed in spirit."*[3] Your most profound and intimate experiences of worship will likely be in your darkest days — when your heart is broken, when you feel abandoned, when you're out of options, when the pain is great — and you turn to God alone. It is during suffering that we learn to pray our most authentic, heartfelt, honest-to-God prayers. When we're in pain, we don't have the energy for superficial prayers.

Joni Eareckson Tada notes, "When life is rosy, we may slide by with knowing about Jesus, with imitating him and quoting him and speaking of him. But only in suffering will we *know* Jesus."[4] We learn things about God in suffering that we can't learn any other way.

God could have kept Joseph out of jail,[5] kept Daniel out of the lion's den,[6] kept Jeremiah from being tossed into a slimy pit,[7] kept Paul from being shipwrecked three times,[8] and kept the three Hebrew young men from being thrown into the blazing furnace[9] — but he didn't. He let those problems happen, and every one of those persons was drawn closer to God as a result.

Problems force us to look to God and depend on him

instead of ourselves. Paul testified to this benefit: *"We felt we were doomed to die and saw how powerless we were to help ourselves; but that was good, for then we put everything into the hands of God, who alone could save us."*[10] You will never know that God is all you need until God is all you've got.

> *Your most profound and intimate experiences of worship will likely be in your darkest days.*

Regardless of the cause, none of your problems could happen without God's permission. Everything that happens to a child of God is *Father-filtered*, and he intends to use it for good even when Satan and others mean it for bad.

Because God is sovereignly in control, accidents are just incidents in God's good plan for you. Because every day of your life was written on God's calendar before you were born,[11] *everything* that happens to you has spiritual significance. Everything! Romans 8:28 — 29 explains why: *"We know that God causes everything to work together for the good of those who love God and are called according to his purpose for them. For God knew his people in advance, and he chose them to become like his Son."*[12]

Understanding Romans 8:28–29

This is one of the most misquoted and misunderstood passages in the Bible. It doesn't say, "God causes everything to work out the way I want it to." Obviously that's not true. It also doesn't say, "God causes everything to work out to have a happy ending on earth." That is not true either. There are many unhappy endings on earth.

We live in a fallen world. Only in heaven is everything done perfectly the way God intends. That is why we are told to pray, *"Thy will be done in earth, as it is in heaven."*[13] To fully understand Romans 8:28 — 29 you must consider it phrase by phrase.

"We know": Our hope in difficult times is not based on positive thinking, wishful thinking, or natural optimism. It is a certainty based on the truths that God is in complete control of our universe and that he loves us.

"that God causes": There's a Grand Designer behind everything. Your life is not a result of random chance, fate, or luck. There is a master plan. History is *His story.* God is pulling the strings. *We* make mistakes, but God never does. God *cannot* make a mistake — because he is God.

"everything": God's plan for your life involves *all* that happens to you — including your mistakes, your sins, and your hurts. It includes illness, debt, disasters, divorce, and death of loved ones. God can bring good out of the worst evil. He did at Calvary.

"to work together": Not separately or independently. The events in your life work *together* in God's plan. They are not isolated acts, but interdependent parts of the process to make you like Christ. To bake a cake you must use flour, salt, raw eggs, sugar, and oil. Eaten individually, each is pretty distasteful or even bitter. But bake them together and they become delicious. If you will give God all your distasteful, unpleasant experiences, he will blend them together for good.

"for the good": This does not say that everything in life is good. Much of what happens in our world is evil and bad, but God specializes in bringing good out of it. In the official family tree of Jesus Christ,[14] four women are listed: Tamar, Rahab, Ruth, and Bathsheba. Tamar seduced her father-in-law to get pregnant. Rahab was a prostitute. Ruth was not even Jewish and broke the law by marrying a Jewish man. Bathsheba committed adultery with David, which resulted in her husband's murder. These were not exactly sterling reputations, but God brought good out of bad, and Jesus came through their lineage. God's purpose is greater than our problems, our pain, and even our sin.

"of those who love God and are called": This promise is only for God's children. It is not for everyone. All things work *for bad* for those living in opposition to God who insist on having their own way.

Everything that happens to you has spiritual significance.

"according to his purpose": What is that purpose? It is that we **"become like his Son."** Everything God allows to happen in your life is permitted for that purpose!

Building Christlike Character

We are like jewels, shaped with the hammer and chisel of adversity. If a jeweler's hammer isn't strong enough to chip off our rough edges, God will use a sledgehammer. If we're really stubborn, he uses a jackhammer. He will use whatever it takes.

Every problem is a character-building opportunity, and the more difficult it is, the greater the potential for building spiritual muscle and moral fiber. Paul said, *"We know that these troubles produce patience. And patience produces character."*[15] What happens outwardly in your life is not as important as what happens *inside* you. Your circumstances are temporary, but your character will last forever.

The Bible often compares trials to a metal refiner's fire that burns away the impurities. Peter said, *"These troubles come to prove that your faith is pure. This purity of faith is worth more than gold."*[16] A silversmith was asked, "How do you know when the silver is pure?" He replied, "When I see my reflection in it." When you have been refined by trials, people can see Jesus' reflection in you. James said, *"Under pressure, your faith-life is forced into the open and shows its true colors."*[17]

> What happens outwardly in your life is not as important as what happens inside you.

Since God intends to make you like Jesus, he will take

you through the same experiences Jesus went through. That includes loneliness, temptation, stress, criticism, rejection, and many other problems. The Bible says Jesus *"learned obedience through suffering"* and *"was made perfect through suffering."*[18] Why would God exempt us from what he allowed his own Son to experience? Paul said, *"We go through exactly what Christ goes through. If we go through the hard times with him, then we're certainly going to go through the good times with him!"*[19]

Responding to Problems as Jesus Would

Problems don't automatically produce what God intends. Many people become bitter, rather than better, and never grow up. You have to respond the way Jesus would.

Remember that God's plan is good. God knows what is best for you and has your best interests at heart. God told Jeremiah, *"The plans I have for you [are] plans to prosper you and not to harm you, plans to give you hope and a future."*[20] Joseph understood this truth when he told his brothers who had sold him into slavery, *"You intended to harm me, but God intended it for good."*[21] Hezekiah echoed the same sentiment about his life-threatening illness: *"It was for my own good that I had such hard times."*[22] Whenever God says no to your request for relief, remember, *"God is doing what is best for us, training us to live God's holy best."*[23]

It is vital that you stay focused on God's plan, not your

pain or problem. That is how Jesus endured the pain of the cross, and we are urged to follow his example: *"Keep your eyes on Jesus, our leader and instructor. He was willing to die a shameful death on the cross because of the joy he knew would be his afterwards."*[24] Corrie ten Boom, who suffered in a Nazi death camp, explained the power of focus: "If you look at the world, you'll be distressed. If you look within, you'll be depressed. But if you look at Christ, you'll be at rest!"[25] Your focus will determine your feelings.

The secret of endurance is to remember that your pain is temporary but your reward will be eternal. Moses endured a life of problems *"because he was looking ahead to his reward."*[26] Paul endured hardship the same way. He said, *"Our present troubles are quite small and won't last very long. Yet they produce for us an immeasurably great glory that will last forever!"*[27]

DAY 25:
Transformed by Trouble

Don't give in to short-term thinking. Stay focused on the end result: *"If we are to share his glory, we must also share his suffering. What we suffer now is nothing compared to the glory he will give us later."*[28]

Rejoice and give thanks. The Bible tells us to *"give thanks in all circumstances, for this is God's will for you in Christ Jesus."*[29] How is this possible? Notice that God tells us to give thanks *"in* all circumstances" not *"for* all circumstances." God doesn't expect you to be thankful *for* evil, *for* sin, *for* suffering, or for their painful consequences in the world. Instead, God wants you to thank him that he will use your problems to fulfill his purposes.

The Bible says, *"Rejoice in the Lord always."*[30] It doesn't say, "Rejoice over your pain." That's masochism. You rejoice *"in the Lord."* No matter what's happening, you can rejoice in God's love, care, wisdom, power, and faithfulness. Jesus said, *"Be full of joy at that time, because you have a great reward waiting for you in heaven."*[31]

We can also rejoice in knowing that God is going through the pain with us. We do not serve a distant and detached God who spouts encouraging clichés safely from the sideline. Instead, he enters into our suffering. Jesus did it in the Incarnation, and his Spirit does it in us now. God will never leave us on our own.

Refuse to give up. Be patient and persistent. The Bible says, *"Let the process go on until your endurance is fully developed, and you will find that you have become men of mature character ... with no weak spots."*[32]

Character building is a slow process. Whenever we try to avoid or escape the difficulties in life, we short-circuit the process, delay our growth, and actually end up with a worse kind of pain — the worthless type that accompanies denial and avoidance. When you grasp the eternal consequences of your character development, you will pray fewer *"Comfort me"* prayers ("Help me feel good") and more *"Conform me"* prayers ("Use this to make me more like you").

You know you are maturing when you begin to see the hand of God in the random, baffling, and seemingly pointless circumstances of life.

If you are facing trouble right now, don't ask, "Why me?" Instead ask, "What do you want me to learn?" Then trust God and keep on doing what's right. *"You need to stick it out, staying with God's plan so you'll be there for the promised completion."*[33] Don't give up — grow up!

DAY 25

Thinking about My Purpose

POINT TO PONDER: There is a purpose behind every problem.

VERSE TO REMEMBER: *"And we know that in all things God works for the good of those who love him, who have been called according to his purpose."* ROMANS 8:28 (NIV)

QUESTION TO CONSIDER: What problem in my life has caused the greatest growth in me?

MESSAGE TO HEAR: *www.purposedriven.com/day25*

Growing through Temptation

*Happy is the man who doesn't give
in and do wrong when he is tempted,
for afterwards he will get as his reward
the crown of life that God has
promised those who love him.*

JAMES 1:12 (LB)

*My temptations have been
my masters in divinity.*

MARTIN LUTHER

purposedriven.com/
day26

EVERY TEMPTATION IS AN OPPORTUNITY TO DO GOOD.
On the path to spiritual maturity, even temptation
becomes a stepping-stone rather than a stumbling block
when you realize that it is just as much an occasion to do
the right thing as it is to do the wrong thing. Temptation
simply provides the choice. While temptation is Satan's
primary weapon to destroy you, God wants to use it to
develop you. Every time you choose to do good instead
of sin, you are growing in the character of Christ.

To understand this, you must first identify the

character qualities of Jesus. One of the most concise descriptions of his character is the fruit of the Spirit: *"When the Holy Spirit controls our lives, he will produce this kind of fruit in us: love, joy, peace, patience, kindness, goodness, faithfulness, gentleness, and self-control."*[1]

These nine qualities are an expansion of the Great Commandment and portray a beautiful description of Jesus Christ. Jesus is *perfect* love, joy, peace, patience, and all the other fruit embodied in a single person. To have the fruit of the Spirit is to be like Christ.

How, then, does the Holy Spirit produce these nine fruit in your life? Does he create them instantly? Will you wake up one day and be suddenly filled with these characteristics fully developed? No. Fruit always matures and ripens *slowly*.

This next sentence is one of the most important spiritual truths you will ever learn: God develops the fruit of the Spirit in your life by allowing you to experience circumstances in which you're tempted to express *the exact opposite quality!* Character development always involves a choice, and temptation provides that opportunity.

> *God develops the fruit of the Spirit in your life by allowing you to experience circumstances in which you're tempted to express the exact opposite quality!*

For instance, God teaches us *love* by putting some *unlovely* people around us. It takes no character to love people who are lovely and loving to you. God teaches us real *joy* in the midst of sorrow, when we turn to him. Happiness depends on external circumstances, but joy is based on your relationship to God.

God develops real *peace* within us, not by making things go the way we planned, but by allowing times of chaos and confusion. Anyone can be peaceful watching a beautiful sunset or relaxing on vacation. We learn real peace by choosing to trust God in circumstances in which we are tempted to worry or be afraid. Likewise, *patience* is developed in circumstances in which we're forced to wait and are tempted to be angry or have a short fuse.

God uses the opposite situation of each fruit to allow us a choice. You can't claim to be good if you have never been tempted to be bad. You can't claim to be faithful if you have never had the opportunity to be unfaithful. Integrity is built by defeating the temptation to be dishonest; humility grows when we refuse to be prideful; and endurance develops every time you reject the temptation to give up. Every time you defeat a temptation, you become more like Jesus!

How Temptation Works

It helps to know that Satan is entirely predictable. He has used the same strategy and old tricks since Creation. All temptations follow the same pattern. That's why Paul said, *"We are very familiar with his evil schemes."*[2] From the Bible we learn that temptation follows a four-step process, which Satan used both on Adam and Eve and on Jesus.

In step one, Satan identifies a *desire* inside of you. It may be a sinful desire, like the desire to get revenge or to control others, or it may be a legitimate, normal desire, like the desire to be loved and valued or to feel pleasure. Temptation starts when Satan suggests (with a thought) that you give in to an evil desire, or that you fulfill a legitimate desire in a wrong way or at the wrong time. Always beware of shortcuts. They are often temptations! Satan whispers, "You deserve it! You should have it now! It will be exciting … comforting … or make you feel better."

We think temptation lies around us, but God says it begins *within* us. If you didn't have the internal desire, the temptation could not attract you. Temptation always starts in your mind, not in circumstances. Jesus said, *"For from within, out of a person's heart, come evil thoughts, sexual immorality, theft, murder, adultery, greed, wickedness, deceit, eagerness for lustful pleasure, envy, slander, pride, and foolishness. All these vile things come from within."*[3] James tells us that there is *"a whole army of evil desires within you."*[4]

Step two is *doubt.* Satan tries to get you to doubt what God has said about the sin: Is it really wrong? Did God really say not to do it? Didn't God mean this prohibition for someone else or some other time? Doesn't God want me to be happy? The Bible warns, *"Watch out! Don't let evil thoughts or doubts make any of you turn from the living God."*[5]

Step three is *deception.* Satan is incapable of telling the truth and is called *"the Father of lies."*[6] Anything he tells you will be untrue or just half-true. Satan offers his lie to replace what God has already said in his Word. Satan says, "You will not die. You'll be wiser like God. You can get away with it. No one will ever know. It will solve your problem. Besides, everyone else is doing it. It is only a little sin." But a little sin is like being a little pregnant: It will eventually show itself.

> We think temptation lies around us, but God says it begins within us.

Step four is *disobedience.* You finally act on the thought you have been toying with in your mind. What began as an idea gets birthed into behavior. You give in to whatever got your attention. You believe Satan's lies and fall into the trap that James warns about: *"We are tempted when we are drawn away and trapped by our own evil desires. Then our evil desires conceive and give birth to sin; and sin, when it is full-grown, gives birth to death. Do not be deceived, my dear friends!"*[7]

Overcoming Temptation

Understanding how temptation works is in itself helpful, but there are specific steps you need to take to overcome it.

Refuse to be intimidated. Many Christians are frightened and demoralized by tempting thoughts, feeling guilty that they aren't "beyond" temptation. They feel ashamed just for being tempted. This is a misunderstanding of maturity. You will *never* outgrow temptation.

In one sense you can consider temptation a compliment. Satan does not have to tempt those who are already doing his evil will; they are already his. Temptation is a sign that Satan hates you, not a sign of weakness or worldliness. It is also a normal part of being human and living in a fallen world. Don't be surprised or shocked or discouraged by it. Be realistic about the inevitability of temptation; you will never be able to avoid it completely. The Bible says, "*When* you're tempted,..." not *if.* Paul advises, "*Remember that the temptations that come into your life are no different from what others experience.*"[8]

It is not a sin to be tempted. Jesus was tempted, yet he never sinned.[9] Temptation only becomes a sin when you give in to it. Martin Luther said, "You cannot keep birds from flying over your head but you can keep them from building a nest in your hair." You can't keep the Devil from suggesting thoughts, but you *can* choose not to dwell or act on them.

For example, many people don't know the difference between physical attraction or sexual arousal, and lust. They are *not* the same. God made every one of us a sexual being, and that is good. Attraction and arousal are the natural, spontaneous, God-given responses to physical beauty, while lust is *a deliberate act of the will.* Lust is a choice to commit in your mind what you'd like to do with your body. You can be attracted or even aroused without choosing to sin by lusting. Many people, especially Christian men, feel guilty that their God-given hormones are working. When they automatically notice an attractive woman, they assume it is lust and feel ashamed and condemned. But attraction is not lust until you begin to dwell on it.

Actually, the closer you grow to God, the more Satan will try to tempt

> Temptation is a sign that Satan hates you, not a sign of weakness or worldliness.

you. The moment you became God's child, Satan, like a mobster hit man, put out a "contract" on you. You are his enemy, and he's plotting your downfall.

Sometimes while you are praying, Satan will suggest a bizarre or evil thought just to distract you and shame you. Don't be alarmed or ashamed by this, but realize that Satan fears your prayers and will try anything to stop them. Instead of condemning yourself with "How could I think such a thought?" treat it as a distraction from Satan and immediately refocus on God.

Recognize your pattern of temptation and be prepared for it. There are certain situations that make you more vulnerable to temptation than others.

Some circumstances will cause you to stumble almost immediately, while others don't bother you much. These situations are unique to your weaknesses, and you need to identify them because Satan surely knows them! He knows *exactly* what trips you up, and he is constantly working to get you into those circumstances. Peter warns, *"Stay alert. The Devil is poised to pounce, and would like nothing better than to catch you napping."*[10]

DAY 26:
Growing through Temptation

Ask yourself, *"When* am I most tempted? What day of the week? What time of day?"* Ask, *"Where* am I most tempted? At work? At home? At a neighbor's house? At a sports bar? In an airport or motel out of town?"

Ask, *"Who is with me* when I'm most tempted? Friends? Coworkers? A crowd of strangers? When I'm alone?"* Also ask, *"How do I usually feel* when I am most tempted?"* It may be when you are tired or lonely or bored or depressed or under stress. It may be when you have been hurt or angry or worried, or after a big success or spiritual high.

You should identify your typical pattern of temptation and then prepare to avoid those situations as much as possible. The Bible tells us repeatedly to anticipate and be ready to face temptation.[11] Paul said, *"Don't give the Devil a chance."*[12] Wise planning reduces temptation. Follow the advice of Proverbs: *"Plan carefully what you do.... Avoid evil and walk straight ahead. Don't go one step off* the right way."[13] *"God's people avoid evil ways, and they protect themselves by watching where they go."*[14]

Request God's help. Heaven has a twenty-four-hour emergency hotline. God wants you to ask him for assistance in overcoming temptation. He says, *"Call on me in times of trouble. I will rescue you, and you will honor me."*[15]

I call this a "microwave" prayer because it is quick and to the point: Help! SOS! Mayday! When temptation strikes, you don't have time for a long conversation with God; you simply cry out. David, Daniel, Peter, Paul, and millions of others have prayed this kind of instant prayer for help in trouble.

The Bible guarantees that our cry for help will be heard because Jesus is sympathetic to our struggle. He faced the same temptations we do. He *"understands our weaknesses, for he faced all of the same temptations we do, yet he did not sin."*[16]

If God is waiting to help us defeat temptation, why don't we turn to him more often? Honestly, sometimes we don't *want* to be helped! We *want* to give in to temptation even though we know it's wrong. At that moment we think we know what's best for us more than God does.

At other times we're embarrassed to ask God for help because we keep giving in to the same temptation over and over. But God never gets irritated, bored, or impatient when we keep coming back to him. The Bible says, *"Let us have confidence, then, and approach God's throne, where there is grace. There we will receive mercy and find grace to help us just when we need it.*"[17]

God's love is everlasting, and his patience endures forever. If you have to cry out for God's help two hundred times a day to defeat a particular temptation, he will still be eager to give mercy and grace, so come boldly. Ask him for the power to do the right thing and then expect him to provide it.

Temptations keep us dependent upon God. Just as the roots grow stronger when wind blows against a tree, so every time you stand up to a temptation you become more like Jesus. When you stumble — which you will — it is not fatal. Instead of giving in or giving up, look up to God, expect him to help you, and remember the reward that is waiting for you: *"When people are tempted and still continue strong, they should be happy. After they have proved their faith, God will reward them with life forever."*[18]

DAY 26

Thinking about My Purpose

POINT TO PONDER: Every temptation is an opportunity to do good.

VERSE TO REMEMBER: *"God blesses the people who patiently endure testing. Afterward they will receive the crown of life that God has promised to those who love him."* JAMES 1:12 (NLT)

QUESTION TO CONSIDER: What Christlike character quality can I develop by defeating the most common temptation I face?

MESSAGE TO HEAR: *www.purposedriven.com/day26*

DAY 27

Defeating Temptation

Run from anything that gives you the evil thoughts ... but stay close to anything that makes you want to do right.

2 TIMOTHY 2:22 (LB)

purposedriven.com/
day27

Remember that the temptations that come into your life are no different from what others experience. And God is faithful. He will keep the temptation from becoming so strong that you can't stand up against it. When you are tempted, he will show you a way out so that you will not give in to it.

1 CORINTHIANS 10:13 (NLT)

THERE IS ALWAYS A WAY OUT.

You may sometimes feel that a temptation is too overpowering for you to bear, but that's a lie from Satan. God has promised never to allow more *on* you than he puts *within* you to handle it. He will not permit any temptation that you could not overcome. However, you must do your part too by practicing four biblical keys to defeating temptation.

Refocus your attention on something else. It may surprise you that *nowhere* in the Bible are we told to "resist temptation." We are told to *"resist the devil,"*[1] but that is *very* different, as I'll explain later. Instead, we are advised to refocus our attention because resisting a thought doesn't work. It only intensifies our focus on the wrong thing and strengthens its allure. Let me explain:

Every time you try to block a thought out of your mind, you drive it deeper into your memory. By resisting it, you actually reinforce it. This is especially true with temptation. You don't defeat temptation by fighting the feeling of it. The more you fight a feeling, the more it consumes and controls you. You strengthen it every time you think it.

Since temptation always begins with a thought, the quickest way to neutralize its allure is to turn your attention to something else. Don't fight the thought, just change the channel of your mind and get interested in another idea. This is the first step in defeating temptation.

> The battle for sin is won or lost in your mind. Whatever gets your attention will get you.

The battle for sin is won or lost in your mind. Whatever gets your attention will get you. That's why Job said, *"I made a covenant with my eyes not to look with lust upon a young woman."*[2] And David prayed, *"Keep me from paying attention to what is worthless."*[3]

Have you ever watched a food advertisement on television and suddenly felt you were hungry? Have you ever heard someone cough and immediately felt the need to clear your throat? Ever watched someone release a big yawn and felt the urge to yawn yourself? (You may be yawning right now as you read this!) That is the power of suggestion. We naturally move toward whatever we focus our attention on. The more you think about something, the stronger it takes hold of you.

That is why repeating "I must stop eating too much … or stop smoking … or stop lusting" is a self-defeating strategy. It keeps you focused on what you don't want. It's like announcing, "I'm never going to do what my mom did." You are setting yourself up to repeat it.

Most diets don't work because they keep you thinking about food all the time, guaranteeing that you'll be hungry. In the same way, a speaker who keeps repeating to herself, "Don't be nervous!" sets herself up to be nervous! Instead she should focus on anything except her feelings — on God, on the importance of her speech, or on the needs of those listening.

Temptation begins by capturing your attention. What gets your attention arouses your emotions. Then your emotions activate your behavior, and you act on what you felt. The more you focus on "I don't want to do this," the stronger it draws you into its web.

Ignoring a temptation is far more effective than fighting it. Once your mind is on something else, the temptation loses its power. So when temptation calls you on the phone, don't argue with it, just hang up!

Sometimes this means physically leaving a tempting situation. This is one time it is okay to run away. Get up and turn off the television set. Walk away from a group that is gossiping. Leave the theater in the middle of the movie. To avoid being stung, stay away from the bees. Do whatever is necessary to turn your attention to something else.

Spiritually, your mind is your most vulnerable organ. To reduce temptation, keep your mind occupied with God's Word and other good thoughts. You defeat bad thoughts by thinking of something better. This is the principle of replacement. You overcome evil with good.[4] Satan can't get your attention when your mind is preoccupied with something else. That's why the Bible repeatedly tells us to keep our minds focused: *"Fix your thoughts on Jesus."*[5] *"Always think about Jesus Christ."*[6]

"Fill your minds with those things that are good and that deserve praise: things that are true, noble, right, pure, lovely, and honorable."[7]

If you're serious about defeating temptation you must manage your mind and monitor your media intake. The wisest man who ever lived warned, *"Be careful how you think; your life is shaped by your thoughts."*[8] Don't allow trash into your mind indiscriminately. Be selective. Choose carefully what you think about. Follow Paul's model: *"We capture every thought and make it give up and obey Christ."*[9] This takes a lifetime of practice, but with the help of the Holy Spirit you can reprogram the way you think.

Reveal your struggle to a godly friend or support group. You don't have to broadcast it to the whole world, but you need at least one person you can honestly share your struggles with. The Bible says, *"You are better off to have a friend than to be all alone.... If you fall, your friend can help you up. But if you fall without having a friend nearby, you are really in trouble."*[10]

Let me be clear: If you're losing the battle against a persistent bad habit, an addiction, or a temptation, and you're stuck in a repeating cycle of good intention-failure-guilt, you will not get better on your own! You need the help of other people. Some temptations are only overcome with the help of a partner who prays for you, encourages you, and holds you accountable.

God's plan for your growth and freedom includes other Christians. Authentic, honest fellowship is the antidote to your lonely struggle against those sins that won't budge. God says it is the only way you're going to break free: *"Confess your sins to each other and pray for each other so that you may be healed."*[11]

> *The truth is, whatever you can't talk about is already out of control in your life.*

Do you really want to be healed of that persistent

temptation that keeps defeating you over and over? God's solution is plain: Don't repress it; confess it! Don't conceal it; reveal it. Revealing your feeling is the beginning of healing.

Hiding your hurt only intensifies it. Problems grow in the dark and become bigger and bigger, but when exposed to the light of truth, they shrink. You are only as sick as your secrets. So take off your mask, stop pretending you're perfect, and walk into freedom.

At Saddleback Church we have seen the awesome power of this principle to break the grip of seemingly hopeless addictions and persistent temptations through a program we developed called Celebrate Recovery. It is a biblical, eight-step recovery process based on the Beatitudes of Jesus and built around small support groups. In the past ten years over 5,000 lives have been set free from all kinds of habits, hurts, and addictions. Today the program is used in thousands of churches. I highly recommend it for your church.

Satan wants you to think that your sin and temptation are unique so you must keep them a secret. The truth is, we're all in the same boat. We all fight the same temptations,[12] and *"all of us have sinned."*[13] Millions have felt what you're feeling and have faced the same struggles you're facing right now.

The reason we hide our faults is pride. We want others to think we have everything "under control." The truth is, whatever you can't talk about is already out of control in your life: problems with your finances, marriage, kids, thoughts, sexuality, secret habits, or anything else. If you could handle it on your own, you would have already done so. But you can't. Willpower and personal resolutions aren't enough.

Some problems are too ingrained, too habitual, and too big to solve on your own. You need a small group or an accountability partner who will encourage you, support you, pray for you, love you unconditionally, and hold you accountable. Then you can do the same for them.

Whenever someone confides to me, "I've never told this to anyone until now," I get excited for that person because I know they are about to experience great relief and liberation. The pressure valve is going to be released, and for the first time they are going to see a glimmer of hope for their future. It always happens when we do what God tells us to do by admitting our struggles to a godly friend.

Let me ask you a tough question: What are you pretending isn't a problem in your life? What are you afraid to talk about? You're not going to solve it on your own. Yes, it is humbling to admit our weaknesses to others, but lack of humility is the very thing that is keeping you from getting better. The Bible says, *"God sets himself against the proud, but he shows favor to the humble. So humble yourselves before God."*[14]

Resist the Devil. After we have humbled ourselves

and submitted to God, we are then told to defy the Devil. The rest of James 4:7 says, *"Resist the Devil and he will flee from you."* We don't passively resign ourselves to his attacks. We are to fight back.

The New Testament often describes the Christian life as a spiritual battle against evil forces, using war terms such as fight, conquer, strive, and overcome. Christians are often compared to soldiers serving in enemy territory.

How can we resist the Devil? Paul tells us, *"Put on salvation as your helmet, and take the sword of the Spirit, which is the word of God."*[15] The first step is to accept God's salvation. You won't be able to say no to the Devil unless you have said yes to Christ. Without Christ we are defenseless against the Devil, but with "the helmet of salvation" our minds are protected by God. Remember this: If you are a believer, Satan cannot force you to do anything. He can only suggest.

> *Don't ever try to argue with the Devil. He's better at arguing than you are, having had thousands of years to practice.*

Second, you must use the Word of God as your weapon against Satan. Jesus modeled this when he was tempted in the wilderness. Every time Satan suggested a temptation, Jesus countered by quoting Scripture. He didn't argue with Satan. He didn't say, "I'm not hungry," when tempted to use his power to meet a personal need. He simply quoted Scripture from memory. We must do the same. There is power in God's Word, and Satan fears it.

Don't ever try to argue with the Devil. He's better at arguing than you are, having had thousands of years to practice. You can't bluff Satan with logic or your opinion, but you can use the weapon that makes him tremble — the truth of God. This is why memorizing Scripture is absolutely essential to defeating temptation. You have quick access to it whenever you're tempted. Like Jesus, you have the truth stored in your heart, ready to be remembered.

If you don't have any Bible verses memorized, you've got no bullets in your gun! I challenge you to memorize one verse a week for the rest of your life. Imagine how much stronger you'll be.

Realize your vulnerability. God warns us never to get cocky and overconfident; that is the recipe for disaster. Jeremiah said, *"The heart is deceitful above all things and beyond cure."*[16] That means we are good at fooling ourselves. Given the right circumstances, any of us are capable of any sin. We must never let down our guard and think we're beyond temptation.

Don't carelessly place yourself in tempting situations. Avoid them.[17] Remember that it is easier to stay out of temptation than to get out of it. The Bible says, *"Don't be so naive and self-confident. You're not exempt. You could fall flat on your face as easily as anyone else. Forget about self-confidence; it's useless. Cultivate God-confidence."*[18]

DAY 27

Thinking about My Purpose

POINT TO PONDER: There is always a way out.

VERSE TO REMEMBER: *"God is faithful. He will keep the temptation from becoming so strong that you can't stand up against it. When you are tempted, he will show you a way out so that you will not give in to it."* 1 CORINTHIANS 10:13B (NLT)

QUESTION TO CONSIDER: Who could I ask to be a spiritual partner to help me defeat a persistent temptation by praying for me?

MESSAGE TO HEAR: *www.purposedriven.com/day27*

It Takes Time

Everything on earth has its own time and its own season.

ECCLESIASTES 3:1 (CEV)

I am sure that God who began the good work within you will keep right on helping you grow in his grace until his task within you is finally finished on that day when Jesus Christ returns.

PHILIPPIANS 1:6 (LB)

purposedriven.com/
day28

THERE ARE NO SHORTCUTS TO MATURITY.

It takes years for us to grow to adulthood, and it takes a full season for fruit to mature and ripen. The same is true for the fruit of the Spirit. The development of Christlike character cannot be rushed. Spiritual growth, like physical growth, takes time.

When you try to ripen fruit quickly, it loses its flavor. In America, tomatoes are usually picked unripened so they won't bruise during shipping to the stores. Then, before they are sold, these green tomatoes are sprayed with CO_2 gas to turn them red instantly. Gassed tomatoes

278

are edible, but they are no match to the flavor of a vine-ripened tomato that is allowed to mature slowly.

While we worry about *how fast* we grow, God is concerned about *how strong* we grow. God views our lives *from* and *for* eternity, so he is never in a hurry.

Pastor-evangelist Lane Adams once compared the process of spiritual growth to the strategy the Allies used in World War II to liberate islands in the South Pacific. First they would "soften up" an island, weakening the resistance by shelling the enemy strongholds with bombs from offshore ships. Next, a small group of Marines would invade the island and establish a "beachhead" — a tiny fragment of the island that they could control. Once the beachhead was secured, they would begin the long process of liberating the rest of the island, one bit of territory at a time. Eventually the entire island would be brought under control, but not without some costly battles.

> *While we worry about how fast we grow, God is concerned about how strong we grow.*

Adams drew this parallel: Before Christ invades our lives at conversion, he sometimes has to "soften us up" by allowing problems we can't handle. While some open their lives to Christ the first time he knocks on the door, most of us are resistant and defensive. Our pre-conversion experience is Jesus saying, *"Behold I stand at the door and bomb!"*

The moment you open yourself to Christ, God gets a "beachhead" in your life. You may think you have surrendered *all* your life to him, but the truth is, there is a lot to your life that you aren't even aware of. You can only give God as much of you as you understand at that moment. That's okay. Once Christ is given a beachhead, he begins the campaign to take over more and more territory until all of your life is completely his. There will be struggles and battles, but the outcome will never be in doubt. God has promised that *"he who began a good work in you will carry it on to completion."*[1]

Discipleship is the process of conforming to Christ. The Bible says, *"We arrive at real maturity — that measure of development which is meant by 'the fullness of Christ.'"*[2] Christlikeness is your eventual destination, but your journey will last a lifetime.

So far we have seen that this journey involves *believing* (through worship), *belonging* (through fellowship), and *becoming* (through discipleship). Every day God wants you to become a little more like him: *"You have begun to live the new life, in which you are being made new and are becoming like the One who made you."*[3]

> There is no growth without change, no change without fear or loss, and no loss without pain.

Today we're obsessed with speed, but God is more interested in strength and stability than swiftness. We want the quick fix, the shortcut, the on-the-spot solution.

We want a sermon, a seminar, or an experience that will instantly resolve all problems, remove all temptation, and release us from all growing pains. But real maturity is never the result of a single experience, no matter how powerful or moving. Growth is gradual. The Bible says, *"Our lives gradually becoming brighter and more beautiful as God enters our lives and we become like him."*[4]

Why Does It Take So Long?

Although God *could* instantly transform us, he has chosen to develop us slowly. Jesus is deliberate in developing his disciples. Just as God allowed the Israelites to take over the Promised Land *"little by little"*[5] so they wouldn't be overwhelmed, he prefers to work in incremental steps in our lives.

Why does it take so long to change and grow up? There are several reasons.

We are slow learners. We often have to relearn a lesson forty or fifty times to really get it. The problems keep recurring, and we think, "Not again! I've already learned that!" — but God knows better. The history of Israel illustrates how quickly we forget the lessons God teaches us and how soon we revert to our old patterns of behavior. We need repeated exposure.

We have a lot to unlearn. Many people go to a counselor with a personal or relational problem that took *years* to develop and say, "I need you to fix me.

I've got an hour." They naïvely expect a quick solution to a long-standing, deep-rooted difficulty. Since most of our problems — and all of our bad habits — didn't develop overnight, it's unrealistic to expect them to go away immediately. There is no pill, prayer, or principle that will instantly undo the damage of many years. It requires the hard work of removal and replacement. The Bible calls it *"taking off the old self"* and *"putting on the new self."*[6] While you were given a brand new nature at the moment of conversion, you still have old habits, patterns, and practices that need to be removed and replaced.

We are afraid to humbly face the truth about ourselves. I have already pointed out that the truth will set us free but it often makes us miserable first. The fear of what we might discover if we honestly faced our character defects keeps us living in the prison of denial. Only as God is allowed to shine the light of his truth on our faults, failures, and hang-ups can we begin to work on them. This is why you cannot grow without a humble, teachable attitude.

Growth is often painful and scary. There is no growth without change; there is no change without fear or loss; and there is no loss without pain. Every change involves a loss of some kind: You must let go of old ways in order to experience the new. We fear these losses, even if our old ways were self-defeating, because, like a worn out pair of shoes, they were at least comfortable and familiar.

People often build their identity around their defects. We say, "It's just like me to be …" and "It's just the way I am." The unconscious worry is that if I let go of my habit, my hurt, or my hang-up, who will I be? This fear can definitely slow down your growth.

Habits take time to develop. Remember that your character is the sum total of your habits. You can't claim to be kind unless you are *habitually* kind — you show kindness without even thinking about it. You can't claim to have integrity unless it is your *habit* to always be honest. A husband who is faithful to his wife *most* of the time is not faithful at all! Your habits define your character.

There is only one way to develop the habits of Christlike character: You must *practice* them — and that takes time! There are no *instant habits.* Paul urged Timothy, *"Practice these things. Devote your life to them so that everyone can see your progress."*[7]

If you practice something over time, you get good at it. Repetition is the mother of character and skill. These character-building habits are often called *"spiritual disciplines,"* and there are dozens of great books that can teach you how to do these. See appendix 2 for a recommended reading list of books for spiritual growth.

Don't Get in a Hurry

As you grow to spiritual maturity, there are several ways to cooperate with God in the process.

Believe God is working in your life even when you don't feel it. Spiritual growth is sometimes tedious work, one small step at a time. Expect gradual improvement. The Bible says, *"Everything on earth has its own time and its own season."*[8] There are seasons in your spiritual life, too. Sometimes you will have a short, intense burst of growth (springtime) followed by a period of stabilizing and testing (fall and winter).

What about those problems, habits, and hurts you would like miraculously removed? It's fine to pray for a miracle, but don't be disappointed if the answer comes through a gradual change. Over time, a slow, steady stream of water will erode the hardest rock and turn giant boulders into pebbles. Over time, a little sprout can turn into a giant redwood tree towering 350 feet tall.

Keep a notebook or journal of lessons learned. This is not a diary of events, but a record of what you are learning. Write down the insights and life lessons God teaches you about him, about yourself, about life, relationships, and everything else. Record these so you can review and remember them and pass them on to the next generation.[9] The reason we must relearn lessons is that we forget them. Reviewing your spiritual journal regularly can spare you a lot of unnecessary pain and heartache. The Bible says, *"It's crucial that we keep a firm grip on what we've heard so that we don't drift off."*[10]

Be patient with God and with yourself. One of life's frustrations is that God's timetable is rarely the same as ours. We are often in a hurry when God isn't. You may feel frustrated with the seemingly slow progress you're making in life. Remember that God is never in a hurry, but he is always on time. He will use your entire lifetime to prepare you for your role in eternity.

The Bible is filled with examples of how God uses a long process to develop character, especially in leaders. He took eighty years to prepare Moses, including forty in the wilderness. For 14,600 days Moses kept waiting and wondering, "Is it time yet?" But God kept saying, "Not yet."

Contrary to popular book titles, there are no *Easy Steps to Maturity* or *Secrets of Instant Sainthood.* When

> God is never in a hurry, but he is always on time.

God wants to make a mushroom, he does it overnight, but when he wants to make a giant oak, he takes a hundred years. Great souls are grown through struggles and storms and seasons of suffering. Be patient with the process. James advised, *"Don't try to get out of anything prematurely. Let it do its work so you become mature and well-developed."*[11]

Don't get discouraged. When Habakkuk became depressed because he didn't think God was acting quickly enough, God had this to say: *"These things I plan won't* *happen right away. Slowly, steadily, surely, the time approaches when the vision will be fulfilled. If it seems slow, do not despair, for these things will surely come to pass. Just be patient! They will not be overdue a single day!*"[12] A delay is not a denial from God.

Remember how far you've come, not just how far you have to go. You are not where you want to be, but neither are you where you used to be. Years ago people wore a popular button with the letters PBPGINFWMY. It stood for "Please Be Patient, God Is Not Finished With Me Yet." God isn't finished with you, either, so keep on moving forward. Even the snail reached the ark by persevering!

DAY 28

Thinking about My Purpose

POINT TO PONDER: There are no shortcuts to maturity.

VERSE TO REMEMBER: *"God began doing a good work in you, and I am sure he will continue it until it is finished when Jesus Christ comes again."*
PHILIPPIANS 1:6 (NCV)

QUESTION TO CONSIDER: In what area of my spiritual growth do I need to be more patient and persistent?

MESSAGE TO HEAR: *www.purposedriven.com/day28*

YOU WERE SHAPED FOR SERVING GOD

We are simply God's servants....
Each one of us does the work
which the Lord gave him to do:
I planted the seed,
Apollos watered the plant,
but it was God
who made the plant grow.
1 CORINTHIANS 3:5 – 6 (TEV)

Accepting Your Assignment

*It is God himself who has made us
what we are and given us new lives
from Christ Jesus; and long ages ago
he planned that we should spend
these lives in helping others.*

EPHESIANS 2:10 (LB)

purposedriven.com/
day29

*I glorified you on earth by
completing down to the last detail
what you assigned me to do.*

JOHN 17:4 (MSG)

YOU WERE PUT ON EARTH TO MAKE A CONTRIBUTION.
You weren't created just to consume resources — to
eat, breathe, and take up space. God designed you to
make a difference with your life. While many best-selling
books offer advice on how to *"get"* the most out of life,
that's not the reason God made you. You were created to
add to life on earth, not just take from it. God wants you
to give something back. This is God's fourth purpose for

289

your life, and it is called your "ministry," or service. The Bible gives us the details.

You were created to serve God. The Bible says, *"[God] has created us for a life of good deeds, which he has already prepared for us to do."*[1] These "good deeds" are your service. Whenever you serve others in any way, you are actually serving God[2] and fulfilling one of your purposes. In the next two chapters you will see how God has carefully *shaped* you for this purpose. What God told Jeremiah is also true for you: *"Before I made you in your mother's womb, I chose you. Before you were born, I set you apart for a special work."*[3] You were placed on this planet for a special assignment.

You were saved to serve God. The Bible says, *"It is he who saved us and chose us for his holy work, not because we deserved it but because that was his plan."*[4] God redeemed you so you could do his "holy work." You're not saved *by* service, but you are saved *for* service. In God's kingdom, you have a place, a purpose, a role, and a function to fulfill. This gives your life great significance and value.

It cost Jesus his own life to purchase your salvation. The Bible reminds us, *"God paid a great price for you. So use your body to honor God."*[5] We don't serve God out of guilt or fear or even duty, but out of joy, and deep gratitude for what he's done for us. We owe him our lives. Through salvation our past has been forgiven, our present is given meaning, and our future is secured. In light of these incredible benefits Paul concluded, *"Because of God's great mercy ... Offer yourselves as a living sacrifice to God, dedicated to his service."*[6]

The apostle John taught that our loving service to others shows that we are truly saved. He said, *"Our love for each other proves that we have gone from death to life."*[7] If I have no love for others, no desire to serve others, and I'm only concerned about my needs, I should question whether Christ is really in my life. A saved heart is one that wants to serve.

Another term for serving God that's misunderstood by most people is the word *ministry*. When most people hear "ministry," they think of pastors, priests, and professional clergy, but God says every member of his family is a minister. In the Bible, the words *servant* and *minister* are synonyms, as are *service* and *ministry*. If you are a Christian, you are a minister, and when you're serving, you're ministering.

> If I have no love for others, no desire to serve others, I should question whether Christ is really in my life.

When Peter's sick mother-in-law was healed by Jesus, she instantly *"stood up and began to serve Jesus,"*[8] using her new gift of health. This is what we're to do. We are healed to help others. We are blessed to be a blessing. We are saved to serve, not to sit around and wait for heaven.

Have you ever wondered why God doesn't just immediately take us to heaven the moment we accept his grace? Why does he leave us in a fallen world? He leaves us here to fulfill his purposes. Once you are saved, God intends to use you for his goals. God has a *ministry* for you in his church and a *mission* for you in the world.

You are called to serve God. Growing up, you may have thought that being "called" by God was something only missionaries, pastors, nuns, and other "full-time" church workers experienced, but the Bible says every Christian is called to service.[9] Your call to salvation included your call to service. They are the same. Regardless of your job or career, you are called to *full-time* Christian service. A "non-serving Christian" is a contradiction in terms.

The Bible says, *"He saved us and called us to be his own people, not because of what we have done, but because of his own purpose."*[10] Peter adds, *"You were chosen to tell about the excellent qualities of God, who called you."*[11] Anytime you use your God-given abilities to help others, you are fulfilling your calling.

DAY 29:
Accepting Your
Assignment

The Bible says, *"Now you belong to him ... in order that we might be useful in the service of God."*[12] How much of the time are you being useful in the service of God? In some churches in China, they welcome new believers by saying "Jesus now has a new pair of eyes to see with, new ears to listen with, new hands to help with, and a new heart to love others with."

One reason why you need to be connected to a church

family is to fulfill your calling to serve other believers in practical ways. The Bible says, *"All of you together are Christ's body, and each one of you is a separate and necessary part of it."*[13] Your service is desperately needed in the Body of Christ — just ask any local church. Each of us has a role to play, and every role is important. There is no small service to God; it all matters.

Likewise, there are no insignificant ministries in the church. Some are visible and some are behind the scenes, but all are valuable. Small or hidden ministries often make the biggest difference. In my home, the most important light is not the large chandelier in our dining room but the little night light that keeps me from stubbing my toe when I get up at night. There is no correlation between size and significance. Every ministry matters because we are all dependent on each other to function.

What happens when one part of your body fails to function? You get sick. The rest of your body suffers. Imagine if your liver decided to start living for itself: "I'm tired! I don't want to serve the body anymore! I want a year off just to be fed. I've got to do what's best for me! Let some other part take over." What would happen? Your body would die. Today thousands of local churches are dying because of Christians who are unwilling to serve. They sit on the sidelines as spectators, and the Body suffers.

You are commanded to serve God. Jesus was

unmistakable: *"Your attitude* must *be like my own, for I, the Messiah, did not come to be served, but to serve and to give my life."*[14] For Christians, service is not optional, something to be tacked onto our schedules if we can spare the time. It is the heart of the Christian life. Jesus came "to serve" and "to give" — and those two verbs should define your life on earth, too. Serving and giving sum up God's fourth purpose for your life. Mother Teresa once said, "Holy living consists in doing God's work with a smile."

> Spiritual maturity is never an end in itself. We grow up in order to give out.

Jesus taught that spiritual maturity is never an end in itself. Maturity is for ministry! We grow up in order to give out. It is not enough to keep learning more and more. We must act on what we know and practice what we claim to believe. *Impression* without *expression* causes *depression.* Study without service leads to spiritual stagnation. The old comparison between the Sea of Galilee and the Dead Sea is still true. Galilee is a lake full of life because it takes in water but also gives it out. In contrast, nothing lives in the Dead Sea because, with no outflow, the lake has stagnated.

The *last* thing many believers need today is to go to another Bible study. They already know far more than they are putting into practice. What they need are *serving* experiences in which they can exercise their spiritual muscles.

Serving is the opposite of our natural inclination. Most of the time we're more interested in *"serve us"* than *service.* We say, "I'm looking for a church that meets my needs and blesses me," not "I'm looking for a place to serve and *be* a blessing." We expect others to serve us, not vice versa. But as we mature in Christ, the focus of our lives should increasingly shift to living a life of service. The mature follower of Jesus stops asking, "Who's going to meet *my* needs?" and starts asking, "Whose needs can I meet?" Do you *ever* ask that question?

Preparing for Eternity

At the end of your life on earth you will stand before God, and he is going to evaluate how well you served others with your life. The Bible says, *"Each of us will have to give a personal account to God."*[15] Think about the implications of that. One day God will compare how much time and energy we spent on ourselves compared with what we invested in serving others.

At that point, all our excuses for self-centeredness will sound hollow: "I was too busy" or "I had my own goals" or "I was preoccupied with working, having fun, or preparing for retirement." To all excuses God will respond, "Sorry, wrong answer. I created, saved, and called you and commanded you to live a life of service. *What part* did you not understand?" The Bible warns unbelievers, *"He will pour out his anger and wrath on those who live for themselves,"*[16] but for Christians it will mean a loss of eternal rewards.

We are only fully alive when we're helping others. Jesus said, *"If you insist on saving your life, you will lose it. Only those who throw away their lives for my sake and for the sake of the Good News will ever know what it means to really live."*[17] This truth is so important that it is repeated five times in the Gospels. If you aren't serving, you're just existing, because life is meant for ministry. God wants you to learn to love and serve others unselfishly.

Service and Significance

You are going to give your life for something. What will it be — a career, a sport, a hobby, fame, wealth? None of these will have lasting significance. Service is the pathway to real significance. It is through ministry that we discover the meaning of our lives. The Bible says, *"Each of us finds our meaning and function as a part of his body."*[18] As we serve together in God's family, our lives take on eternal importance. Paul said, *"I want you to think about how all this makes you more significant, not less … because of what you are a part of."*[19]

God wants to use you to make a difference in his world. He wants to work through you. What matters is not the *duration* of your life, but the *donation* of it. Not *how long* you lived, but *how* you lived.

If you're not involved in any service or ministry,

what excuse have you been using? Abraham was old, Jacob was insecure, Leah was unattractive, Joseph was abused, Moses stuttered, Gideon was poor, Samson was codependent, Rahab was immoral, David had an affair and all kinds of family problems, Elijah was suicidal, Jeremiah was depressed, Jonah was reluctant, Naomi was a widow, John the Baptist was eccentric to say the least, Peter was impulsive and hot-tempered, Martha worried a lot, the Samaritan woman had several failed marriages, Zacchaeus was unpopular, Thomas had doubts, Paul had poor health, and Timothy was timid. That is quite a variety of misfits, but God used each of them in his service. He will use you, too, if you stop making excuses.

> *Service is the pathway to real significance.*

DAY 29

Thinking about My Purpose

POINT TO PONDER: Service is not optional.

VERSE TO REMEMBER: *"For we are God's workmanship, created in Christ Jesus to do good works, which God prepared in advance for us to do."* EPHESIANS 2:10 (NIV)

QUESTION TO CONSIDER: What is holding me back from accepting God's call to serve him?

MESSAGE TO HEAR: *www.purposedriven.com/day29*

Shaped for Serving God

*Your hands shaped me
and made me.*

JOB 10:8 (NIV)

*The people I have shaped for
myself will broadcast my praises.*

ISAIAH 43:21 (NJB)

purposedriven.com/
day30

YOU WERE SHAPED TO SERVE GOD.

God formed every creature on this planet with a special area of expertise. Some animals run, some hop, some swim, some burrow, and some fly. Each has a particular role to play, based on the way they were shaped by God. The same is true with humans. Each of us was uniquely designed, or *"shaped,"* to do certain things.

Before architects design any new building they first ask, "What will be its purpose? How will it be used?" The intended function always determines the form of the building. Before God created you, he decided what role he wanted you to play on earth. He planned exactly how he wanted you to serve him, and then he shaped you for those tasks. You are the way you are because you were made for a specific ministry.

The Bible says, *"We are God's workmanship, created in Christ Jesus to do good works."*[1] Our English word *poem* comes from the Greek word translated "workmanship." You are God's handcrafted work of art. You are not an assembly-line product, mass produced without thought. You are a custom-designed, one-of-a-kind, original masterpiece.

God deliberately shaped and formed you to serve him in a way that makes your ministry unique. He carefully mixed the DNA cocktail that created you. David praised God for this incredible personal attention to detail: *"You made all the delicate, inner parts of my body and knit me together in my mother's womb. Thank you for making me so wonderfully complex! Your workmanship is marvelous."*[2] As gospel singer Ethel Waters said, "God doesn't make junk."

_____

God never wastes anything.

_____

Not only did God shape you before your birth, he planned every day of your life to support his shaping process. David continues, *"Every day of my life was recorded in your book. Every moment was laid out before a single day had passed."*[3] This means that nothing that happens in your life is insignificant. God uses *all of it* to mold you for your ministry to others and shape you for your service to him.

God never wastes anything. He would not give you abilities, interests, talents, gifts, personality, and life experiences unless he intended to use them for his glory. By identifying and understanding these factors you can discover God's will for your life.

The Bible says you are *"wonderfully complex."* You are a combination of many different factors. To help you remember five of these factors, I have created a simple acrostic: SHAPE. In this chapter and the next we will look at these five factors, and following that, I will explain how to discover and use your shape.

How God Shapes You for Your Ministry

Whenever God gives us an assignment, he always equips us with what we need to accomplish it. This custom combination of capabilities is called your SHAPE:

> **S**piritual gifts
>
> **H**eart
>
> **A**bilities
>
> **P**ersonality
>
> **E**xperience

SHAPE: Unwrapping Your *Spiritual Gifts*

God gives every believer spiritual gifts to be used in ministry.[4] These are special God-empowered abilities for serving him that are given only to believers. The Bible says, *"Whoever does not have the Spirit cannot receive the gifts that come from God's Spirit."*[5]

You can't earn your spiritual gifts or deserve them —that's why they are called *gifts!* They are an expression of God's grace to you. *"Christ has generously divided out his gifts to us."*[6] Neither do you get to choose which gifts you'd like to have; God determines that. Paul explained, *"It is the one and only Holy Spirit who distributes these gifts. He alone decides which gift each person should have."*[7]

Because God loves variety and he wants us to be special, no single gift is given to everyone.[8] Also, no individual receives *all* the gifts. If you had them all, you'd have no need of anyone else, and that would defeat one of God's purposes — to teach us to love and depend on each other.

Your spiritual gifts were not given for your own benefit but for the benefit of *others*, just as other people were given gifts for your benefit. The Bible says, *"A spiritual gift is given to each of us as a means of helping the entire church."*[9] God planned it this way so we would need each other. When we use our gifts together, we all benefit. If others don't use their gifts, you get cheated, and if you don't use your gifts, they get cheated. This is why we're commanded to discover and develop our spiritual gifts. Have you taken the time to discover your spiritual gifts? An unopened gift is worthless.

An unopened gift is worthless.

Whenever we forget these basic truths about gifts, it always causes trouble in the church. Two common problems are *"gift-envy"* and *"gift-projection."* The first occurs when we compare our gifts with others', feel dissatisfied with what God gave us, and become resentful or jealous of how God uses others. The second problem happens when we expect everyone else to have our gifts, do what we are called to do, and feel as passionate about it as we do. The Bible says, *"There are different kinds of service in the church, but it is the same Lord we are serving."*[10]

Sometimes spiritual gifts are overemphasized to the neglect of the other factors God uses to shape you for service. Your gifts reveal one *key to discovering* God's will for your ministry, but your spiritual gifts are not the total picture. God has shaped you in four other ways, too.

SHAPE: Listening to Your *Heart*

The Bible uses the term *heart* to describe the bundle of desires, hopes, interests, ambitions, dreams, and affections you have. Your heart represents the source of all your motivations — what you love to do and what you care about most. Even today we still use the word in this way when we say, *"I love you with all my heart."*

The Bible says, *"As a face is reflected in water, so the heart reflects the person."*[11] Your heart reveals the *real* you — what you truly are, not what others *think* you are or what circumstances force you to be. Your heart determines why you *say* the things you do, why you *feel* the way you do, and why you *act* the way you do.[12]

Physically, each of us has a unique heartbeat. Just as we each have unique thumbprints, eye prints, and voice prints, our hearts beat in slightly different patterns. It's amazing that out of all the billions of people who have ever lived, no one has had a heartbeat exactly like yours.

In the same way, God has given each of us a unique *emotional* "heartbeat" that races when we think about the subjects, activities, or circumstances that interest us. We instinctively care about some things and not about others. These are clues to where you should be serving.

DAY 30:
Shaped for Serving God

Another word for heart is *passion*. There are certain subjects you feel passionate about and others you couldn't care less about. Some experiences turn you on and capture your attention while others turn you off or bore you to tears. These reveal the nature of your heart.

When you were growing up, you may have discovered that you were intensely interested in some subjects that no one else in your family cared about. Where did those interests come from? They came from God. God had a purpose in giving you these inborn interests. Your emotional heartbeat is the second key to understanding your shape for service. Don't ignore your interests. Consider how they might be used for God's glory. There is a reason that you love to do these things.

Repeatedly the Bible says to *"serve the Lord with all your heart."*[13] God wants you to serve him passionately, not dutifully. People rarely excel at tasks they don't enjoy doing or feel passionate about. God wants you to use your natural interests to serve him and others. Listening for inner promptings can point to the ministry God intends for you to have.

How do you know when you are serving God from your heart? The first telltale sign is *enthusiasm.* When you are doing what you *love* to do, no one has to motivate you or challenge you or check up on you. You do it for the sheer enjoyment. You don't need rewards or applause or payment, because you love serving in this way. The opposite is also true: When you don't have a heart for what you're doing, you are easily discouraged.

The second characteristic of serving God from your heart is *effectiveness.* Whenever you do what God wired you to *love* to do, you get good at it. Passion drives perfection. If you don't care about a task, it is unlikely that you will excel at it. In contrast, the highest achievers in any field are those who do it because of passion, not duty or profit.

> When you are doing what you love to do, no one has to motivate you.

We have all heard people say, "I took a job I hate in order to make a lot of money, so someday I can quit and do what I love to do." That's a big mistake. Don't waste your life in a job that doesn't express your heart.

Remember, the greatest things in life are not *things.*
Meaning is far more important than money. The richest
man in the world once said, *"A simple life in the fear-of-
God is better than a rich life with a ton of headaches."*[14]

Don't settle for just achieving "the good life," because
the good life is not good enough. Ultimately it doesn't
satisfy. You can have a lot to live *on* and still have nothing
to live *for.* Aim instead for *"the better life"* — serving God
in a way that expresses your heart. Figure out what you
love to do — what God gave you a heart to do — and then
do it for his glory.

DAY 30

Thinking about My Purpose

POINT TO PONDER: I was shaped for serving God.

VERSE TO REMEMBER: *"God works through different
men in different ways, but it is the same God
who achieves his purposes through them all."*
1 CORINTHIANS 12:6 (PH)

QUESTION TO CONSIDER: In what way can I see myself
passionately serving others and loving it?

MESSAGE TO HEAR: *www.purposedriven.com/day30*

Understanding Your Shape

You shaped me first inside, then out;
you formed me in my mother's womb.

PSALM 139:13 (MSG)

purposedriven.com/
day31

ONLY YOU CAN BE YOU.

God designed each of us so there would be no duplication in the world. No one has the exact same mix of factors that make you unique. That means no one else on earth will ever be able to play the role God planned for you. If you don't make your unique contribution to the Body of Christ, it won't be made. The Bible says, *"There are different kinds of spiritual gifts ... different ways of serving ... [and] different abilities to perform service."*[1] In the last chapter we looked at the first two of these: your spiritual gifts and your heart. Now we will look at the rest of your SHAPE for serving God.

SHAPE: Applying Your *Abilities*

Your abilities are the natural talents you were born with.
Some people have a natural ability with words: They
came out of the womb talking! Other people have natural
athletic abilities, excelling in physical coordination. Still
others are good at mathematics or music or mechanics.

When God wanted to create the Tabernacle and
all the utensils for worship, he provided artists and
craftsmen who were shaped with the *"skill, ability, and
knowledge in all kinds of crafts to make artistic designs ...
and to engage in all kinds of craftsmanship."*[2] Today God
still bestows these abilities and thousands of others, so
people can serve him.

All of our abilities come from God. Even abilities
used to sin are God-given; they are just being misused
or abused. The Bible says, *"God has given each of us the
ability to do certain things well."*[3] Since your natural
abilities are from God, they are just as important and as
"spiritual" as your spiritual gifts. The only difference is
that you were given them at birth.

One of the most common excuses people give for not
serving is "I just don't have any abilities to offer." This
is ludicrous. You have dozens, probably hundreds, of
untapped, unrecognized, and unused abilities that are
lying dormant inside you. Many studies have revealed
that the average person possesses from 500 to 700
different skills and abilities — far more than you realize.

For instance, your brain can store 100 trillion facts. Your mind can handle 15,000 decisions a second, as is the case when your digestive system is working. Your nose can smell up to 10,000 different odors. Your touch can detect an item 1/25,000th of an inch thick, and your tongue can taste one part of quinine in 2 million parts of water. You are a bundle of incredible abilities, an amazing creation of God. Part of the church's responsibility is to identify and release your abilities for serving God.

Every ability can be used for God's glory. Paul said, *"Whatever you do, do it all for the glory of God."*[4] The Bible is filled with examples of different abilities that God uses for his glory. Here are just a few of those mentioned in Scripture: artistic ability, architectural ability, administering, baking, boat making, candy making, debating, designing, embalming, embroidering, engraving, farming, fishing, gardening, leading, managing, masonry, making music, making weapons, needlework, painting, planting, philosophizing, machinability, inventing, carpentry, sailing, selling, being a soldier, tailoring, teaching, writing literature and poetry. The Bible says, *"There are different abilities to perform service, but the same God gives ability to all for their particular service."*[5] God has a place in his church where your specialties can shine and you can make a difference. It's up to you to find that place.

God gives some people the ability to make a lot of

money. Moses told the Israelites, *"Remember the Lord your God, for it is he who gives you the ability to produce wealth."*[6] People with this ability are good at building a business, making deals or sales, and reaping a profit. If you have this business ability, you should be using it for God's glory. How? First, realize your ability came from God and give him the credit. Second, use your business to serve a need of others and to share your faith with unbelievers. Third, return at least a tithe (10 percent) of the profit to God as an act of worship.[7] Finally, make your goal to be a *Kingdom Builder* rather than just a *Wealth Builder.* I will explain this in chapter 34.

What I'm *able* to do, God *wants* me to do. You are the only person on earth who can use your abilities. No one else can play your role, because they don't have the unique shape that God has given you. The Bible says that God equips you *"with all you need for doing his will."*[8] To discover God's will for your life, you should seriously examine what you are good at doing and what you're not good at.

If God hasn't given you the ability to carry a tune, he isn't going to expect you to be an opera singer. God will never ask you to dedicate your life to a task you have no talent for. On the other hand, the abilities you *do* have are a strong indication of what God wants you to do with your life. They are clues to knowing God's will for you. If you're good at designing or recruiting or drawing or organizing, it is a safe assumption that God's plan for your life includes that skill somehow. God doesn't waste abilities; he matches our calling and our capabilities.

Your abilities were not given just to make a living; God gave them to you for your ministry. Peter said, *"God has given each of you some special abilities; be sure to use them to help each other, passing on to others God's many kinds of blessings."*[9]

> *What I'm able to do, God wants me to do.*

At this writing, nearly 7,000 people are using their abilities in ministry at Saddleback Church, providing every kind of service you could imagine: repairing donated cars to be given to the needy; finding the best deal for church purchases; landscaping; organizing files; designing art, programs, and buildings; providing health care; preparing meals; composing songs; teaching music; writing grant proposals; coaching teams; doing research for sermons or translating them; and hundreds of other specialized tasks. New members are told, "Whatever you're good at, you should be doing for your church!"

SHAPE: Using Your *Personality*

We don't realize how truly unique each of us is. DNA molecules can unite in an infinite number of ways. The number is 10 to the 2,400,000,000th power. That number is the likelihood that you'd ever find somebody just like you. If you were to write out that number with each zero being one inch wide, you'd need a strip of paper 37,000 miles long!

To put this in perspective, some scientists have guessed that all the particles in the universe are probably less than 10 with 76 zeros behind it, far less than the possibilities of your DNA. Your uniqueness is a scientific fact of life. When God made you, he broke the mold. There never has been, and never will be, anybody exactly like you.

It is obvious that God loves variety — just look around! He created each of us with a unique combination of personality traits. God made *introverts* and *extroverts*. He made people who love *routine* and those who love *variety.* He made some people *"thinkers"* and others *"feelers."* Some people work best when given an individual assignment while others work better with a team. The Bible says, *"God works through different people in different ways, but it is the same God who achieves his purpose through them all."*[10]

> It feels good *to do what God made you to do.*

The Bible gives us plenty of proof that God uses all types of personalities. Peter was a *sanguine.* Paul was a *choleric.* Jeremiah was a *melancholy.* When you look at the personality differences in the twelve disciples, it's easy to see why they sometimes had interpersonal conflict.

There is no "right" or "wrong" temperament for ministry. We need all kinds of personalities to balance the church and give it flavor. The world would be a very boring place if we were all plain vanilla. Fortunately, people come in more than thirty-one flavors.

Your personality will affect *how* and *where* you use your spiritual gifts and abilities. For instance, two people may have the same gift of evangelism, but if one is introverted and the other is extroverted, that gift will be expressed in different ways.

Woodworkers know that it's easier to work with the grain rather than against it. In the same way, when you are forced to minister in a manner that is "out of character" for your temperament, it creates tension and discomfort, requires extra effort and energy, and produces less than the best results. This is why mimicking someone else's ministry never works. You don't have *their* personality. Besides, God made you to be you! You can *learn* from the examples of others, but you must filter what you learn through your own *shape.* Today there are many books and tools that can help you understand your personality so you can determine how to use it for God.

Like stained glass, our different personalities reflect God's light in many colors and patterns. This blesses the family of God with depth and variety. It also blesses us personally. It *feels good* to do what God made you to do. When you minister in a manner consistent with the personality God gave you, you experience fulfillment, satisfaction, and fruitfulness.

SHAPE: Employing Your *Experiences*

You have been shaped by your experiences in life, most of which were beyond your control. God allowed them for his purpose of molding you.[11] In determining your shape for serving God, you should examine at least six kinds of experiences from your past:

- *Family* experiences: What did you learn growing up in your family?
- *Educational* experiences: What were your favorite subjects in school?
- *Vocational* experiences: What jobs have you been most effective in and enjoyed most?
- *Spiritual* experiences: What have been your most meaningful times with God?
- *Ministry* experiences: How have you served God in the past?
- *Painful* experiences: What problems, hurts, thorns, and trials have you learned from?

It is this last category, *painful* experiences, that God uses the most to prepare you for ministry. *God never wastes a hurt!* In fact, your *greatest* ministry will most likely come out of your greatest hurt. Who could better minister to the parents of a Down syndrome child than another couple who have a child afflicted in the same way? Who could better help an alcoholic recover than someone who fought that demon and found freedom? Who could better comfort a wife whose husband has left her for an affair than a woman who went through that agony herself?

God intentionally allows you to go through painful experiences to equip you for ministry to others. The Bible says, *"He comforts us in all our troubles so that we can comfort others. When others are troubled, we will be able to give them the same comfort God has given us."*[12]

If you really desire to be used by God, you *must* understand a powerful truth: The very experiences that you have resented or regretted most in life — the ones you've wanted to hide and forget — are the experiences God wants to use to help others. They *are* your ministry!

For God to use your painful experiences, you must be willing to share them. You have to stop covering them up, and you must honestly admit your faults, failures, and fears. Doing this will probably be your most effective ministry. People are always more encouraged when we share how God's grace helped us in weakness than when we brag about our strengths.

> For God to use your painful experiences, you must be willing to share them.

Paul understood this truth, so he was honest about his bouts with depression. He admitted, *"I think you ought to know, dear brothers, about the hard time we went through in Asia. We were really crushed and overwhelmed, and*

*feared we would never live through it. We felt we were
doomed to die and saw how powerless we were to help
ourselves; but that was good, for then we put everything
into the hands of God, who alone could save us, for he can
even raise the dead. And he did help us and saved us from
a terrible death; yes, and we expect him to do it again and
again."*[13]

If Paul had kept his experience of doubt and
depression a secret, millions of people would never have
benefited from it. Only shared experiences can help
others. Novelist Aldous Huxley said, "Experience is not
what happens to you. It is what you do with what happens
to you." What will you do with what you've been through?
Don't waste your pain; use it to help others.

As we have looked at these five ways God has shaped
you for service, I hope you have a deeper appreciation
for God's sovereignty and a clearer idea of how he has
prepared you for the purpose of serving him. Using your
shape is the secret of both fruitfulness and fulfillment
in ministry.[14] You will be most effective when you use
your *spiritual gifts* and *abilities* in the area of your *heart's
desire,* and in a way that best expresses your *personality*
and *experiences.* The better the fit, the more successful
you will be.

DAY 31

Thinking about My Purpose

POINT TO PONDER: Nobody else can be me.

VERSE TO REMEMBER: *"God has given each of you some special abilities; be sure to use them to help each other, passing on to others God's many kinds of blessings."* 1 PETER 4:10 (LB)

QUESTION TO CONSIDER: What God-given ability or personal experience can I offer to my church?

MESSAGE TO HEAR: *www.purposedriven.com/day31*

DAY 32

Using What God Gave You

*Since we find ourselves fashioned into all
these excellently formed and marvelously
functioning parts in Christ's body, let's just
go ahead and be what we were made to be.*
ROMANS 12:5 (MSG)

purposedriven.com/
day32

*What you are is God's gift to you; what
you do with yourself is your gift to God.*
DANISH PROVERB

GOD DESERVES YOUR BEST.

He shaped you for a purpose, and he expects you to
make the most of what you have been given. He doesn't
want you to worry about or covet abilities you don't have.
Instead he wants you to focus on talents he has given you
to use.

When you attempt to serve God in ways you're not
shaped to serve, it feels like forcing a square peg into a
round hole. It's frustrating and produces limited results.
It also wastes your time, your talent, and your energy.
The best use of your life is to serve God out of your shape.

318

To do this you must discover your shape, learn to accept and enjoy it, and then develop it to its fullest potential.

Discover Your Shape

The Bible says, *"Don't act thoughtlessly, but try to find out and do whatever the Lord wants you to."*[1] Don't let another day go by. Start finding out and clarifying what God intends for you to be and do.

Begin by assessing your gifts and abilities. Take a long, honest look at what you are good at and what you're not good at. Paul advised, *"Try to have a sane estimate of your capabilities."*[2] Make a list. Ask other people for their candid opinion. Tell them you're searching for the truth, not fishing for a compliment. Spiritual gifts and natural abilities are always confirmed by others. If you think you are gifted to be a teacher or a singer and no one else agrees, guess what? If you want to know if you have the gift of leadership, just look over your shoulder! If no one is following you, you're not a leader.

Ask questions like these: Where have I seen fruit in my life *that other people confirmed?* Where have I already been successful?

Spiritual gift tests and ability inventories can have some value, but they are limited in their usefulness. In the first place, they are standardized, so they don't take into account your uniqueness. Second, there are no definitions of the spiritual gifts given in the Bible, so any definitions are arbitrary and usually represent a denominational bias. Another problem is that the more mature you become, the more likely you are to manifest the characteristics of a number of the gifts. You may be serving or teaching or giving generously out of maturity rather than because it is your spiritual gift.

The best way to discover your gifts and abilities is to *experiment* with different areas of service. I could have taken a hundred gift and ability tests as a young man and would have never discovered that I was gifted at teaching because I had never done it! It was only *after* I began accepting opportunities to speak that I saw the results, received confirmation from others, and realized, "God has gifted me to do this!"

Many books get the discovery process backwards. They say, "Discover your spiritual gift and then you will know what ministry you're supposed to have." It actually works the exact opposite way. Just start serving, experimenting with different ministries, and then you'll discover your gifts. Until you're actually involved in serving, you're not going to know what you're good at.

You will never know what you're good at until you try.

You have dozens of hidden abilities and gifts you don't know you've got because you have never tried them out. So I encourage you to try doing some things you have never done before. No matter how old you are, I urge you to never stop experimenting. I have met many people who discovered hidden talents in their seventies and eighties. I know a woman in her nineties who runs and wins 10K races and didn't discover that she enjoyed running until she was seventy-eight!

Don't try to figure out your gifts before volunteering to serve somewhere. Just start serving. You discover your gifts by getting involved in ministry. Try teaching or leading or organizing or playing an instrument or working with teenagers. You will never know what you're good at until you try. When it doesn't work out, call it an "experiment," not a failure. You will eventually learn what you're good at.

Consider your heart and your personality. Paul advised, *"Make a careful exploration of who you are and the work you have been given, and then sink yourself into that."*[3] Again, it helps to get feedback from those who know you best. Ask yourself questions: What do I really enjoy doing most? When do I feel the most fully alive? What am I doing when I lose track of time? Do I like routine or variety? Do I prefer serving with a team or by myself? Am I more introverted or extroverted? Am I more a thinker or a feeler? Which do I enjoy more — competing or cooperating?

Examine your experiences and extract the lessons you have learned. Review your life and think about how it has shaped you. Moses told the Israelites, *"Remember today what you have learned about the LORD through* *your experiences with him.*"[4] Forgotten experiences are worthless; that's a good reason to keep a spiritual journal. Paul worried that the believers in Galatia would waste the pain they had been through. He said, *"Were all your experiences wasted? I hope not!"*[5]

We rarely see God's good purpose in pain or failure or embarrassment while it is happening. When Jesus washed Peter's feet, he said, *"You do not realize now what I am doing, but later you will understand."*[6] Only in hindsight do we understand how God intended a problem for good.

Extracting the lessons from your experiences takes time. I recommend that you take an entire weekend for a *life review retreat,* where you pause to see how God has worked in the various defining moments of your life and consider how he wants to use those lessons to help others. There are resources that can help you do this.[7]

Accept and Enjoy Your Shape

Since God knows what's best for you, you should gratefully accept the way he has fashioned you. The Bible says, *"What right have you, a human being, to cross-examine God? The pot has no right to say to the potter: 'Why did you make me this shape?' Surely a potter can do what he likes with the clay!"*[8]

Your shape was sovereignly determined by God for *his* purpose, so you shouldn't resent it or reject it. Instead of trying to reshape yourself to be like someone else, you should celebrate the shape God has given only to you. *"Christ has given each of us special abilities — whatever he wants us to have out of his rich storehouse of gifts."*[9]

Part of accepting your shape is recognizing your limitations. Nobody is good at everything, and no one is called to be everything. We all have defined roles. Paul understood that his calling was not to accomplish everything or please everyone but to focus only on the particular ministry God had shaped him for.[10] He said, *"Our goal is to stay within the boundaries of God's plan for us."*[11]

> God wants you to enjoy using the shape he has given you.

The word *boundaries* refers to the fact that God assigns each of us a field or sphere of service. Your shape determines your specialty. When we try to overextend our ministry reach beyond what God shaped us for, we experience stress. Just as each runner in a race is given a different lane to run in, we must individually *"run with patience the particular race that God has set before us."*[12] Don't be envious of the runner in the lane next to you; just focus on finishing *your* race.

God wants you to enjoy using the shape he has given you. The Bible says, *"Be sure to do what you should, for then you will enjoy the personal satisfaction of having done your work well, and you won't need to compare yourself to anyone else."*[13] Satan will try to steal the joy of service from you in a couple of ways: by tempting you to *compare* your ministry with others, and by tempting you to *conform* your ministry to the expectations of others. Both are deadly traps that will distract you from serving in the ways God intended. Whenever you lose your joy in ministry, start by considering if either one of these temptations is the cause.

The Bible warns us never to compare ourselves with others: *"Do your own work well, and then you will have something to be proud of. But don't compare yourself with others."*[14] There are two reasons why you should never compare your shape, ministry, or the results of your ministry with anyone else. First, you will always be able to find someone who seems to be doing a better job than you and you will become discouraged. Or you will always be able to find someone who doesn't seem as effective as you and you will get full of pride. Either attitude will take you out of service and rob you of your joy.

DAY 32:
Using What God Gave You

Paul said it is foolish to compare ourselves with others. He said, *"We do not dare to classify or compare ourselves with some who commend themselves. When they measure themselves by themselves and compare themselves with themselves, they are not wise."*[15] The Message paraphrase says, *"In all this comparing and grading and competing, they quite miss the point."*[16]

You will find that people who do not understand your shape for ministry will criticize you and try to get you to conform to what *they* think you should be doing. Ignore them. Paul often had to deal with critics who misunderstood and maligned his service. His response was always the same: Avoid comparisons, resist exaggerations, and seek only God's commendation.[17]

One of the reasons Paul was used so greatly by God was that he refused to be distracted by criticism or by comparing his ministry with others or by being drawn into fruitless debates about his ministry. As John Bunyan said, "If my life is fruitless, it doesn't matter who praises me, and if my life is fruitful, it doesn't matter who criticizes me."

Keep Developing your Shape

Jesus' parable of the talents illustrates that God expects us to make the most of what he gives us. We are to cultivate our gifts and abilities, keep our hearts aflame, grow our character and personality, and broaden our experiences so we will be increasingly more effective in our service. Paul told the Philippians to *"keep on growing in your knowledge and understanding,"*[18] and he reminded Timothy, *"Kindle afresh the gift of God which is in you."*[19]

If you don't exercise your muscles, they weaken and atrophy. In the same way, if you don't utilize the abilities and skills God has given you, you will lose them. Jesus taught the parable of the talents to emphasize this truth. Referring to the servant who failed to use his one talent, the master said, *"Take the talent from him and give it to the one who has the ten talents.*"[20] Fail to use what you've been given and you'll lose it. Use the ability you've got and God will increase it. Paul told Timothy, *"Be sure to use the abilities God has given you.... Put these abilities to work."*[21]

Whatever gifts you have been given can be enlarged and developed through practice. For instance, no one gets the gift of teaching fully developed. But with study, feedback, and practice, a "good" teacher can become a *better* teacher, and with time, grow to be a *master* teacher. Don't settle for a half-developed gift. Stretch yourself and learn all you can. *"Concentrate on doing your best for God, work you won't be ashamed of."*[22] Take advantage of every training opportunity to develop your shape and sharpen your serving skills.

In heaven we are going to serve God forever. Right now, we can prepare for that eternal service by practicing on earth. Like athletes preparing for the Olympics, we keep training for that big day: *"They do it for a gold medal that tarnishes and fades. You're after one that's gold eternally."*[23]

We're getting ready for *eternal* responsibilities and rewards.

DAY 32

Thinking about My Purpose

POINT TO PONDER: God deserves my best.

VERSE TO REMEMBER: *"Do your best to present yourself to God as one approved, a workman who does not need to be ashamed and who correctly handles the word of truth."* 2 TIMOTHY 2:15 (NIV)

QUESTION TO CONSIDER: How can I make the best use of what God has given me?

MESSAGE TO HEAR: *www.purposedriven.com/day32*

DAY 33

How Real Servants Act

"Whoever wants to be great
must become a servant."

MARK 10:43 (MSG)

You can tell what they are
by what they do.

MATTHEW 7:16 (CEV)

purposedriven.com/
day33

WE SERVE GOD BY SERVING OTHERS.

The world defines greatness in terms of power, possessions, prestige, and position. If you can demand service from others, you have arrived. In our self-serving culture with its *me-first* mentality, acting like a servant is not a popular concept.

Jesus, however, measured greatness in terms of service, not status. God determines your greatness by how many people you serve, not how many people serve you. This is so contrary to the world's idea of greatness that we have a hard time understanding it, much less practicing it. The disciples argued about who deserved the most prominent position, and 2,000 years later, Christian leaders still jockey for position and prominence in churches, denominations, and parachurch ministries.

Thousands of books have been written on leadership, but few on servanthood. Everyone wants to lead; no one wants to be a servant. We would rather be generals than privates. Even Christians want to be *"servant-leaders,"* not just plain servants. But to be like Jesus is to be a servant. That's what he called himself.

While knowing your shape is important for serving God, having the heart of a servant is even more important. Remember, God shaped you for *service,* not for self-centeredness. Without a servant's heart, you will be tempted to misuse your shape for personal gain. You will also be tempted to use it as an excuse to exempt yourself from meeting some needs.

God often tests our hearts by asking us to serve in ways we're *not* shaped. If you see a man fall into a ditch, God expects you to help him out, not say, "I don't have the gift of mercy or service." While you may not be gifted for a particular task, you may be called to do it if no one gifted at it is around. Your *primary* ministry should be in the area of your shape, but your *secondary* service is wherever you're needed at the moment.

> *Your shape reveals your ministry, but your servant's heart will reveal your maturity.*

Your shape reveals your ministry, but your servant's heart will reveal your maturity. No special talent or gift is required to stay after a meeting to pick up trash or stack chairs. Anyone can be a servant. All it requires is character.

It is possible to serve in church for a lifetime without ever being a *servant.* You must have a servant's heart. How can you know if you have the heart of a servant? Jesus said, *"You can tell what they are by what they do."*[1]

Real servants make themselves available to serve. Servants don't fill up their time with other pursuits that could limit their availability. They want to be ready to jump into service when called on. Much like a soldier, a servant must always be standing by for duty: *"No soldier in active service entangles himself in the affairs of everyday life, so that he may please the one who enlisted him."*[2] If you only serve when it's convenient for you, you're not a real servant. Real servants do what's needed, even when it's inconvenient.

Are you available to God anytime? Can he mess up your plans without you becoming resentful? As a servant, you don't get to pick and choose when or where you will serve. Being a servant means giving up the right to control your schedule and allowing God to interrupt it whenever he needs to.

If you will remind yourself at the start of every day that you are God's servant, interruptions won't frustrate you as much, because your agenda will be whatever God wants to bring into your life. Servants see interruptions as divine appointments for ministry and are happy for the opportunity to practice serving.

Real servants pay attention to needs. Servants are always on the lookout for ways to help others. When they see a need, they seize the moment to meet it, just as the Bible commands us: *"Whenever we have the opportunity, we have to do what is good for everyone, especially for the family of believers."*[3] When God puts someone in need right in front of you, he is giving you the opportunity to grow in servanthood. Notice that God says the needs of your church family are to be given preference, not put at the bottom of your "things to do" list.

We miss many occasions for serving because we lack sensitivity and spontaneity. Great opportunities to serve never last long. They pass quickly, sometimes never to return again. You may only get one chance to serve that person, so take advantage of the moment. *"Never tell your neighbors to wait until tomorrow if you can help them now."*[4]

John Wesley was an incredible servant of God. His motto was "Do all the good you can, by all the means you can, in all the ways you can, in all the places you can, at all the times you can, to all the people you can, as long as you ever can." *That* is greatness. You can begin by looking for small tasks that no one else wants to do. Do these little things as if they were great things, because God is watching.

Real servants do their best with what they have.
Servants don't make excuses, procrastinate, or wait for
better circumstances. Servants never say, "One of these
days" or "When the time is right." They just do what
needs to be done. The Bible says, *"If you wait for perfect
conditions, you will never get anything done."*[5] God
expects you to do what you can, with what you have,
wherever you are. Less-than-perfect service is always
better than the best intention.

One reason many people never serve is that they fear
they are *not good enough* to serve. They have believed the
lie that serving God is only for superstars. Some churches
have fostered this myth by making "excellence" an idol,
which makes people of average talent hesitant to get
involved.

You may have heard it said, "If it can't be done with
excellence, don't do it." Well, Jesus never said that! The
truth is, almost everything we do is done poorly when we
first start doing it — that's how we learn. At Saddleback
Church, we practice *the "good enough" principle*: It doesn't
have to be perfect for God to use and bless it. We would
rather involve thousands of regular folks in ministry than
have a perfect church run by a few elites.

Real servants do every task with equal dedication.
Whatever they do, servants *"do it with all their heart."*[6]
The size of the task is irrelevant. The only issue is, does it
need to be done?

You will never arrive at the state in life where you're

too important to help with menial tasks. God will never exempt you from the mundane. It's a vital part of your character curriculum. The Bible says, *"If you think you are too important to help someone in need, you are only fooling yourself. You are really a nobody."*[7] It is in these small services that we grow like Christ.

Jesus specialized in menial tasks that everyone else tried to avoid: washing feet, helping children, fixing breakfast, and serving lepers. Nothing was *beneath* him, because he came to serve. It wasn't *in spite of* his greatness that he did these things, but *because of* it, and he expects us to follow his example.[8]

Small tasks often show a big heart. Your servant's heart is revealed in little acts that others don't think of doing, as when Paul gathered brushwood for a fire to warm everyone after a shipwreck.[9] He was just as exhausted as everyone else, but he did what everyone needed. No task is beneath you when you have a servant's heart.

> Great opportunities often disguise themselves in small tasks.

Great opportunities often disguise themselves in small tasks. The little things in life determine the big things. Don't look for great tasks to do for God. Just do the not-so-great stuff, and God will assign you whatever he wants you to do. But before attempting the extraordinary, try serving in ordinary ways.[10]

There will always be more people willing to do "great" things for God than there are people willing to do the little things. The race to be a leader is crowded, but the field is wide open for those willing to be servants. Sometimes you serve *upward* to those in authority, and sometimes you serve *downward* to those in need. Either way, you develop a servant's heart when you're willing to do anything needed.

Real servants are faithful to their ministry. Servants finish their tasks, fulfill their responsibilities, keep their promises, and complete their commitments. They don't leave a job half undone, and they don't quit when they get discouraged. They are trustworthy and dependable.

Faithfulness has always been a rare quality.[11] Most people don't know the meaning of commitment. They make commitments casually, then break them for the slightest reason without any hesitation, remorse, or regret. Every week, churches and other organizations must improvise because volunteers didn't prepare, didn't show up, or didn't even call to say they weren't coming.

Can you be counted on by others? Are there promises you need to keep, vows you need to fulfill, or commitments you need to honor? This is a test. God is testing your faithfulness. If you pass the test, you're in good company: Abraham, Moses, Samuel, David, Daniel, Timothy, and Paul were all called *faithful* servants of God. Even better, God has promised to reward your faithfulness in eternity. Imagine what it will feel like one day to have God say to you, *"Well done, my good and faithful servant. You have been faithful in handling this small amount, so now I will give you many more responsibilities. Let's celebrate together!"*[12]

By the way, faithful servants never retire. They serve faithfully as long as they're alive. You can retire from your career, but you will never retire from serving God.

Real servants maintain a low profile. Servants don't promote or call attention to themselves. Instead of acting to impress and dressing for success, they *"put on the apron of humility, to serve one another."*[13] If recognized for their service, they humbly accept it but don't allow notoriety to distract them from their work.

Paul exposed a kind of service that *appears* to be spiritual but is really just a put-on, a show, an act to get attention. He called it *"eyeservice"*[14] — serving in order to impress people with how spiritual we are. This was a sin of the Pharisees. They turned helping others, giving, and even prayer into a performance for others. Jesus hated this attitude and warned, *"When you do good deeds, don't try to show off. If you do, you won't get a reward from your Father in heaven."*[15]

Self-promotion and servanthood don't mix. Real servants don't serve for the approval or applause of others. They live for an audience of One. As Paul said, *"If I were still trying to please men, I would not be a servant of Christ."*[16]

You won't find many real servants in the limelight; in fact, they avoid it when possible. They are content with quietly serving in the shadows. Joseph is a great example. He didn't draw attention to himself, but quietly served Potiphar, then his jailer, then Pharaoh's baker and wine taster, and God blessed that attitude. When Pharaoh promoted him to prominence, Joseph still maintained a servant's heart, even with his brothers, who had betrayed him.

Unfortunately, many leaders today start off as servants but end up as celebrities. They become addicted to attention, unaware that always being in the spotlight blinds you.

DAY 33:

How Real Servants Act

You may be serving in obscurity in some small place, feeling unknown and unappreciated. Listen: God put you where you are for a purpose! He has every hair on your head numbered, and he knows your address. You had better stay put until he chooses to move you. He will let you know if he wants you somewhere else. Your ministry matters to the kingdom of God. *"When Christ ... shows up again on this earth, you'll show up, too — the real you, the glorious you. Meanwhile, be content with obscurity."*[17]

There are more than 750 "Halls of Fame" in America and more than 450 "Who's Who" publications, but you won't find many real servants in these places. Notoriety means nothing to real servants because they know the difference between prominence and significance. You have several prominent features on your body that you could live without. It is the hidden parts of your body that are indispensable. The same is true in the Body of Christ. The most significant service is often the service that is unseen.[18]

In heaven God is going to openly reward some of his most obscure and unknown servants — people we have never heard of on earth, who taught emotionally disturbed children, cleaned up after incontinent elderly, nursed AIDS patients, and served in thousands of other unnoticed ways.

Knowing this, don't be discouraged when your service is unnoticed or taken for granted. Keep on serving God! *"Throw yourselves into the work of the Master, confident that nothing you do for him is a waste of time or effort."*[19] Even the smallest service is noticed by God and will be rewarded. Remember the words of Jesus: *"If, as my representatives, you give even a cup of cold water to a little child, you will surely be rewarded."*[20]

DAY 33

Thinking about My Purpose

POINT TO PONDER: I serve God by serving others.

VERSE TO REMEMBER: *"If you give even a cup of cold water to one of the least of my followers, you will surely be rewarded."* MATTHEW 10:42 (NLT)

QUESTION TO CONSIDER: Which of the six characteristics of real servants offers the greatest challenge to me?

MESSAGE TO HEAR: *www.purposedriven.com/day33*

Thinking Like a Servant

My servant Caleb thinks differently
and follows me completely.

NUMBERS 14:24 (NCV)

Think of yourselves the way
Christ Jesus thought of himself.

PHILIPPIANS 2:5 (MSG)

purposedriven.com/
day34

SERVICE STARTS IN YOUR MIND.

To be a servant requires a mental shift, a change in your attitudes. God is always more interested in *why* we do something than in what we do. Attitudes count more than achievements. King Amaziah lost God's favor because *"he did what was right in the sight of the LORD, yet not with a true heart."*[1] Real servants serve God with a mind-set of five attitudes.

Servants think more about others than about themselves. Servants focus on others, not themselves. This is true humility: not thinking less of ourselves but thinking of ourselves *less.* They are self-forgetful. Paul said, *"Forget yourselves long enough to lend a helping hand."*[2] This is what it means to "lose your life" — forgetting yourself in service to others. When we stop focusing on our own needs, we become aware of the needs around us.

Jesus *"emptied himself by taking on the form of a servant."*[3] When was the last time you *emptied* yourself for someone else's benefit? You can't be a servant if you're full of yourself. It's only when we forget ourselves that we do the things that deserve to be remembered.

Unfortunately, a lot of our service is often self-serving. We serve to get others to like us, to be admired, or to achieve our own goals. That is manipulation, not ministry. The whole time we're really thinking about ourselves and how noble and wonderful we are. Some people try to use service as a bargaining tool with God: "I'll do this for you God, if you'll do something for me." Real servants don't try to use God for their purposes. They let God use them for *his* purposes.

The quality of self-forgetfulness, like faithfulness, is extremely rare. Out of all the people Paul knew, Timothy was the only example he could point to.[4] Thinking like a servant is difficult because it challenges the basic problem of my life: I am, by nature, selfish. I think most about me. That's why humility is a daily struggle, a lesson I must relearn over and over. The opportunity to be a servant confronts me dozens of times a day, in which I'm given the choice to decide between meeting my needs or the needs of others. Self-denial is the core of servanthood.

We can measure our servant's heart by how we respond when others treat us like servants. How do you react when you're taken for granted, bossed around, or treated as an inferior? The Bible says, *"If someone takes unfair advantage of you, use the occasion to practice the servant life."*[5]

Servants think like stewards, not owners. Servants remember that God owns it all. In the Bible, a steward was a servant entrusted to manage an estate. Joseph was this kind of servant as a prisoner in Egypt. Potiphar entrusted Joseph with his home. Then the jailer entrusted Joseph with his jail. Eventually Pharaoh entrusted the entire nation to him. Servanthood and stewardship go together,[6] since God expects us to be trustworthy in both. The Bible says, *"The one thing required of such servants is that they be faithful to their master."*[7] How are you handling the resources God has entrusted to you?

> *Real servants don't try to use God for their purposes. They let God use them for his purposes.*

To become a real servant you are going to have to settle the issue of money in your life. Jesus said, *"No servant can serve two masters.... You cannot serve both God and Money."*[8] He didn't say, "You *should not*," but "You *cannot*." It is impossible. Living for ministry and living for money are mutually exclusive goals. Which one will you choose? If you're a servant of God, you can't moonlight for yourself. *All* your time belongs to God. He insists on exclusive allegiance, not part-time faithfulness.

Money has the greatest potential to replace God in your life. More people are sidetracked from serving by materialism than by anything else. They say, "After I achieve my financial goals, I'm going to serve God." That is a foolish decision they will regret for eternity. When Jesus is your Master, money serves you, but if money is your master, you become its slave. Wealth is certainly not a sin, but failing to use it for God's glory is. Servants of God are always more concerned about ministry than money.

DAY 34:

Thinking Like a Servant

The Bible is very clear: God uses money to test your faithfulness as a servant. That is why Jesus talked more about money than he did about either heaven or hell. He said, *"If you have not been trustworthy in handling worldly wealth, who will trust you with true riches?"*[9] How you manage your money affects how much God can bless your life.

In chapter 31, I mentioned two kinds of people: Kingdom Builders and Wealth Builders. Both are gifted at making a business grow, making deals or sales, and making a profit. Wealth Builders continue to amass wealth for themselves no matter how much they make, but Kingdom Builders change the rules of the game. They still try to make as much money as they can, but they do it in order to give it away. They use the wealth to fund God's church and its mission in the world.

At Saddleback Church, we have a group of CEOs and business owners who are trying to make as much as they can so they can give as much as they can to further the kingdom of God. I encourage you to talk with your pastor and begin a Kingdom Builders' group in your church. For help see appendix 2.

Servants think about their work, not what others are doing. They don't compare, criticize, or compete with other servants or ministries. They're too busy doing the work God has given them.

Competition between God's servants is illogical for many reasons: We are all on the same team; our goal is to make God look good, not ourselves; we have been given different assignments; and we are all uniquely shaped. Paul said, *"We will not compare ourselves with each other as if one of us were better and another worse. We have far more interesting things to do with our lives. Each of us is an original."*[10]

There's no place for petty jealousy between servants. When you're busy serving, you don't have time to be critical. Any time spent criticizing others is time that could be spent ministering. When Martha complained to Jesus that Mary was not helping with the work, she lost her servant's heart. Real servants don't complain of unfairness, don't have pity-parties, and don't resent those not serving. They just trust God and keep serving.

It is not our job to evaluate the Master's other servants. The Bible says, *"Who are you to criticize someone else's servant? The Lord will determine whether his servant has been successful."*[11] It is also not our job to defend ourselves against criticism. Let your Master handle it. Follow the example of Moses, who showed true humility in the face of opposition, as did Nehemiah, whose response to critics was simply, *"My work is too important to stop now and ... visit with you."*[12]

If you serve like Jesus, you can expect to be criticized. The world, and even much of the church, does not understand what God values. One of the most beautiful acts of love shown to Jesus was criticized by the disciples. Mary took the most valuable thing she owned, expensive perfume, and poured it over Jesus. Her lavish service was called *"a waste"* by the disciples, but Jesus called it *"significant,"*[13] and that's all that mattered. Your service for Christ is never wasted regardless of what others say.

Servants base their identity in Christ. Because they remember they are loved and accepted by grace, servants don't have to prove their worth. They willingly accept jobs that insecure people would consider "beneath" them. One of the most profound examples of serving from a secure self-image is Jesus' washing the feet of his disciples. Washing feet was the equivalent of being a shoeshine boy, a job devoid of status. But Jesus knew who he was, so the task didn't threaten his self-image. The Bible says, *"Jesus knew that the Father had put all things under his power,* *and that he had come from God ... so he got up from the meal, took off his outer clothing, and wrapped a towel around his waist.*"[14]

If you're going to be a servant, you must settle your identity in Christ. Only secure people can serve. Insecure people are always worrying about how they appear to others. They fear exposure of their weaknesses and hide beneath layers of protective pride and pretensions. The more insecure you are, the more you will want people to serve you, and the more you will need their approval.

The closer you get to Jesus, the less you need to promote yourself.

Henri Nouwen said, "In order to be of service to others we have to die to them; that is, we have to give up measuring our meaning and value with the yardstick of others.... thus we become free to be compassionate." When you base your worth and identity on your relationship to Christ, you are freed from the expectations of others, and that allows you to really serve them best.

Servants don't need to cover their walls with plaques and awards to validate their work. They don't insist on being addressed by titles, and they don't wrap themselves in robes of superiority. Servants find status symbols unnecessary, and they don't measure their worth by their achievements. Paul said, *"You may brag about yourself, but the only approval that counts is the Lord's approval."*[15]

If anyone had the chance of a lifetime to flaunt his connections and "name-drop," it was James, the half-brother of Jesus. He had the credentials of growing up with Jesus as his brother. Yet, in introducing his letter, he simply referred to himself as *"a servant of God and of the Lord Jesus Christ."*[16] The closer you get to Jesus, the less you need to promote yourself.

Servants think of ministry as an opportunity, not an obligation. They enjoy helping people, meeting needs, and doing ministry. They *"serve the LORD with gladness."*[17] Why do they serve with gladness? Because they love the Lord, they're grateful for his grace, they know serving is the highest use of life, and they know God has promised a reward. Jesus promised, *"The Father will honor and reward anyone who serves me."*[18] Paul said, *"He will not forget how hard you have worked for him and how you have shown your love to him by caring for other Christians."*[19]

Imagine what could happen if just 10 percent of all Christians in the world got serious about their role as real servants. Imagine all the good that could be done. Are you willing to be one of those people? It doesn't matter what your age is, God will use you if you will begin to act and think like a servant. Albert Schweitzer said, "The only really happy people are those who have learned how to serve."

DAY 34

Thinking about My Purpose

POINT TO PONDER: To be a servant I must think like a servant.

VERSE TO REMEMBER: *"Your attitude should be the same as that of Christ Jesus."* PHILIPPIANS 2:5 (NIV)

QUESTION TO CONSIDER: Am I usually more concerned about *being* served or finding ways to serve others?

MESSAGE TO HEAR: *www.purposedriven.com/day34*

DAY 35

God's Power in Your Weakness

*We are weak ... yet by God's power
we will live with him to serve you.*

2 CORINTHIANS 13:4 (NIV)

purposedriven.com/
day35

*I am with you; that is all you need.
My power shows up best in weak people.*

2 CORINTHIANS 12:9A (LB)

GOD LOVES TO USE WEAK PEOPLE.

Everyone has weaknesses. In fact, you have a *bundle* of flaws and imperfections: physical, emotional, intellectual, and spiritual. You may also have uncontrollable circumstances that weaken you, such as financial or relational limitations. The more important issue is what you do with these. Usually we deny our weaknesses, defend them, excuse them, hide them, and resent them. This prevents God from using them the way he desires.

God has a different perspective on your weaknesses. He says, *"My thoughts and my ways are higher than yours,"*[1] so he often acts in ways that are the exact opposite of what we expect. We think that God only wants to use our strengths, but he also wants to use our weaknesses for his glory.

The Bible says, *"God purposely chose ... what the world considers weak in order to shame the powerful."*[2] Your weaknesses are not an accident. God deliberately allowed them in your life for the purpose of demonstrating his power through you.

God has never been impressed with strength or self-sufficiency. In fact, he is drawn to people who are weak and admit it. Jesus regarded this recognition of our need as being *"poor in spirit."* It's the number one attitude he blesses.[3]

The Bible is filled with examples of how God loves to use imperfect, ordinary people to do extraordinary things in spite of their weaknesses. If God only used perfect people, nothing would ever get done, because none of us is flawless. That God uses imperfect people is encouraging news for all of us.

A weakness, or *"thorn"* as Paul called it,[4] is not a sin or a vice or a character defect that you can change, such as overeating or impatience. A weakness is any limitation that you inherited or have no power to change. It may be a *physical* limitation, like a handicap, a chronic illness, naturally low energy, or a disability. It may be an *emotional* limitation, such as a trauma scar, a hurtful memory, a personality quirk, or a hereditary disposition.

Or it may be a *talent* or *intellectual* limitation. We're not all super bright or talented.

When you think of the limitation in your life, you may be tempted to conclude, "God could never use me." But God is never limited by our limitations. In fact, he enjoys putting his great power into ordinary containers. The Bible says, *"We are like clay jars in which this treasure is stored. The real power comes from God and not from us."*[5] Like common pottery, we are fragile and flawed and break easily. But God will use us if we allow him to work through our weaknesses. For that to happen, we must follow the model of Paul.

Admit your weaknesses. Own up to your imperfections. Stop pretending to have it all together, and be honest about yourself. Instead of living in denial or making excuses, take the time to identify your personal weaknesses. You might make a list of them.

Two great confessions in the New Testament illustrate what we need for healthy living. The first was Peter's, who said to Jesus, *"You are the Christ, the Son of the living God."*[6] The second confession was Paul's, who said to an idolizing crowd, *"We are only human beings like you."*[7] If you want God to use you, you must know who God is and know who you are. Many Christians, especially leaders, forget the second truth: We're only human! If it takes a crisis to get you to admit this, God won't hesitate to allow it, because he loves you.

Be content with your weaknesses. Paul said, *"I am*

glad to boast about my weaknesses, so that the power of Christ may work through me. Since I know it is all for Christ's good, I am quite content with my weaknesses."[8] At first this doesn't make sense. We want to be freed from our weaknesses, not be content with them! But contentment is an expression of faith in the goodness of God. It says, "God, I believe you love me and know what's best for me."

Paul gives us several reasons to be content with our inborn weaknesses.

> If God only used perfect people, nothing would ever get done.

First, they cause us to depend on God. Referring to his own weakness, which God refused to take away, Paul said, *"I am quite happy about 'the thorn,' ... for when I am weak, then I am strong—the less I have, the more I depend on him."*[9] Whenever you feel weak, God is reminding you to depend on him.

Our weaknesses also prevent arrogance. They keep us humble. Paul said, *"So I wouldn't get a big head, I was given the gift of a handicap to keep me in constant touch with my limitations."*[10] God often attaches a major weakness to a major strength to keep our egos in check. A limitation can act as a governor to keep us from going too fast and running ahead of God.

When Gideon recruited an army of 32,000 to fight the Midianites, God whittled it down to just 300, making the odds 450 to 1 as they went out to fight 135,000 enemy troops. It *appeared* to be a recipe for disaster, but God did it so Israel would know it was God's power, not their own strength, that saved them.

Our weaknesses also encourage fellowship between believers. While strength breeds an independent spirit ("I don't need anyone else"), our limitations show how much we need each other. When we weave the weak strands of our lives together, a rope of great strength is created. Evangelist Vance Havner quipped, "Christians, like snowflakes, are frail, but when they stick together they can stop traffic."

Most of all, our weaknesses increase our capacity for sympathy and ministry. We are far more likely to be compassionate and considerate of the weaknesses of others. God wants you to have a Christlike ministry on earth. That means other people are going to find healing in your wounds. Your greatest life messages and your most effective ministry will come out of your deepest hurts. The things you're most embarrassed about, most ashamed of, and most reluctant to share are the very tools God can use most powerfully to heal others.

Your most effective ministry will come out of your deepest hurts.

The great missionary Hudson Taylor said, "All God's giants were weak people." Moses' weakness was his temper. It caused him to murder an Egyptian, strike the rock he was supposed to speak to, and break the tablets of the Ten Commandments. Yet God transformed Moses into *"the humblest man on earth."*[11]

Gideon's weakness was low self-esteem and deep insecurities, but God transformed him into a *"mighty man of valor."*[12] Abraham's weakness was fear. Not once, but twice, he claimed his wife was his sister to protect himself. But God transformed Abraham into *"the father of those who have faith."*[13] Impulsive, weak-willed Peter became *"a rock,"*[14] the adulterer David became *"a man after my own heart,"*[15] and John, one of the arrogant "Sons of Thunder," became the "Apostle of Love."

The list could go on and on. *"It would take too long to recount the stories of the faith of ... Barak, Samson, Jephthah, David, Samuel, and all the prophets.... their weakness was turned to strength."*[16] God specializes in turning weaknesses into strengths. He wants to take your greatest weakness and transform it.

Honestly share your weaknesses. Ministry begins with vulnerability. The more you let down your guard, take off your mask, and share your struggles, the more God will be able to use you in serving others.

Paul modeled vulnerability in all his letters. He openly shared

- His failures: *"When I want to do good, I don't, and when I try not to do wrong, I do it anyway."*[17]
- His feelings: *"I have told you all my feelings."*[18]

- His frustrations: *"We were crushed and completely overwhelmed, and we thought we would never live through it."*[19]

- His fears: *"When I came to you, I was weak and fearful and trembling."*[20]

Of course, vulnerability is risky. It can be scary to lower your defenses and open up your life to others. When you reveal your failures, feelings, frustrations, and fears, you risk rejection. But the benefits are worth the risk. Vulnerability is emotionally liberating. Opening up relieves stress, defuses your fears, and is the first step to freedom.

We have already seen that God *"gives grace to the humble,"* but many misunderstand humility. Humility is not putting yourself down or denying your strengths; rather, it is being honest about your weaknesses. The more honest you are, the more of God's grace you get. You will also receive grace from others. Vulnerability is an endearing quality; we are naturally drawn to humble people. Pretentiousness repels but authenticity attracts, and vulnerability is the pathway to intimacy.

DAY 35:
God's Power in Your Weakness

This is why God wants to use your weaknesses, not just your strengths. If all people see are your strengths, they get discouraged and think, "Well, good for her, but I'll never be able to do that." But when they see God using you in spite of your weaknesses, it encourages them to think, "Maybe God can use me!" Our strengths create competition, but our weaknesses create community.

At some point in your life you must decide whether you want to *impress* people or *influence* people. You can impress people from a distance, but you must get close to influence them, and when you do that, they will be able to see your flaws. That's okay. The most essential quality for leadership is not perfection, but credibility. People must be able to trust you, or they won't follow you. How do you build credibility? Not by pretending to be perfect, but by being honest.

Glory in your weaknesses. Paul said, *"I am going to boast only about how weak I am and how great God is to use such weakness for his glory."*[21] Instead of posing as self-confident and invincible, see yourself as a trophy of grace. When Satan points out your weaknesses, agree with him and fill your heart with praise for Jesus, who *"understands every weakness of ours,"*[22] and for the Holy Spirit, who *"helps us in our weakness."*[23]

Sometimes, however, God turns a strength into a weakness in order to use us even more. Jacob was a manipulator who spent his life scheming and then running from the consequences. One night he wrestled with God and said, "I'm not letting go until you bless me." God said, "All right," but then he grabbed Jacob's thigh and dislocated his hip. What is the significance of that?

God touched Jacob's strength (the thigh muscle is

the strongest in the body) and turned it into a weakness. From that day forward, Jacob walked with a limp so he could never run away again. It forced him to lean on God whether he liked it or not. If you want God to bless you and use you greatly, you must be willing to walk with a limp the rest of your life, because God uses weak people.

DAY 35

Thinking about My Purpose

POINT TO PONDER: God works best when I admit my weakness.

VERSE TO REMEMBER: *"My grace is sufficient for you, my power is made perfect in weakness."* 2 CORINTHIANS 12:9A (NIV)

QUESTION TO CONSIDER: Am I limiting God's power in my life by trying to hide my weaknesses? What do I need to be honest about in order to help others?

MESSAGE TO HEAR: *www.purposedriven.com/day35*

YOU WERE
MADE
FOR A MISSION

The fruit of the righteous is a tree of life,
and he who wins souls is wise.

PROVERBS 11:30 (NIV)

Made for a Mission

*In the same way that you gave
me a mission in the world, I give
them a mission in the world.*

JOHN 17:18 (MSG)

*The most important thing is that
I complete my mission, the
work that the Lord Jesus gave me.*

ACTS 20:24 (NCV)

purposedriven.com/
day36

YOU WERE MADE FOR A MISSION.

God is at work in the world, and he wants you to join
him. This assignment is called your *mission.* God wants
you to have both a ministry in the Body of Christ and
a mission in the world. Your ministry is your service to
believers,[1] and your mission is your service to *unbelievers.*
Fulfilling your mission in the world is God's fifth purpose
for your life.

Your life mission is both *shared* and *specific.* One
part of it is a responsibility you share with every other
Christian, and the other part is an assignment that is

359

unique to you. We will look at both parts in the chapters ahead.

Our English word *mission* comes from the Latin word for "sending." Being a Christian includes being *sent* into the world as a representative of Jesus Christ. Jesus said, *"As the Father has sent me, I am sending you."*[2]

Jesus clearly understood his life mission on earth. At age twelve he said, *"I must be about my Father's business,"*[3] and twenty-one years later, dying on the cross, he said, *"It is finished."*[4] Like bookends, these two statements frame a well-lived, purpose-driven life. Jesus completed the mission the Father gave him.

> Jesus calls us not only to come *to him,* but to go for *him.*

The mission Jesus had while on earth is now *our* mission because we are the Body of Christ. What he did in his physical body we are to continue as his spiritual body, the church. What is that mission? Introducing people to God! The Bible says, *"Christ changed us from enemies into his friends and gave us the task of making others his friends also."*[5]

God wants to redeem human beings from Satan and reconcile them to himself so we can fulfill the five purposes he created us for: to love him, to be a part of his family, to become like him, to serve him, and to tell others about him. Once we are his, God uses us to reach others. He saves us and then sends us out. The Bible says, *"We have been sent to speak for Christ."*[6] We are the messengers of God's love and purposes to the world.

The Importance of Your Mission

Fulfilling your life mission on earth is an essential part of living for God's glory. The Bible gives several reasons why your mission is so important.

Your mission is a continuation of Jesus' mission on earth. As his followers, we are to continue what Jesus started. Jesus calls us not only to *come to* him, but to *go for* him. Your mission is so significant that Jesus repeated it five times, in five different ways, in five different books of the Bible.[7] It is as if he was saying, "I *really* want you to get this!" Study these five commissions of Jesus and you will learn the details of your mission on earth — the when, where, why, and how.

In the Great Commission Jesus said, *"Go to the people of all nations and make them my disciples. Baptize them in the name of the Father, the Son, and the Holy Spirit, and teach them to do everything I have told you."*[8] This commission was given to *every* follower of Jesus, not to pastors and missionaries alone. This is *your* commission from Jesus, and it is not optional. These words of Jesus are not the *Great Suggestion*. If you are a part of God's family, your mission is mandatory. To ignore it would be disobedience.

You may have been unaware that God holds you

responsible for the unbelievers who live around you. The Bible says, *"You must warn them so they may live. If you don't speak out to warn the wicked to stop their evil ways, they will die in their sin. But I will hold you responsible for their death."*[9] You are the only Christian some people will ever know, and your mission is to share Jesus with them.

Your mission is a wonderful privilege. Although it is a big responsibility, it is also an incredible honor to be used by God. Paul said, *"God has given us the privilege of urging everyone to come into his favor and be reconciled to him."*[10] Your mission involves two great privileges: working with God and representing him. We get to partner with God in the building of his kingdom. Paul calls us *"co-laborers"* and says, *"We are workers together with God."*[11]

Jesus has secured our salvation, put us in his family, given us his Spirit, and then made us his agents in the world. What a privilege! The Bible says, *"We're Christ's representatives. God uses us to persuade men and women to drop their differences and enter into God's work of making things right between them. We're speaking for Christ himself now: Become friends with God."*[12]

Telling others how they can have eternal life is the greatest thing you can do for them. If your neighbor had cancer or AIDS and you knew the cure, it would be criminal to withhold that lifesaving information. Even worse is to keep secret the way to forgiveness, purpose, peace, and eternal life. We have the greatest news in the world, and sharing it is the greatest kindness you can show to anyone.

One problem long-term Christians have is that they forget how hopeless it felt to be without Christ. We must remember that no matter how contented or successful people *appear* to be, without Christ they are hopelessly lost and headed for eternal separation from God. The Bible says, *"Jesus is the only One who can save people."*[13] Everybody needs Jesus.

Your mission has eternal significance. It will impact the eternal destiny of other people, so it's more important than any job, achievement, or goal you will reach during your life on earth. The consequences of your mission will last forever; the consequences of your job will not. Nothing else you do will ever matter as much as helping people establish an eternal relationship with God.

This is why we must be urgent about our mission. Jesus said, *"All of us must quickly carry out the tasks assigned us by the one who sent me, because there is little time left before the night falls and all work comes to an end."*[14] The clock is ticking down on your life mission, so don't delay another day. Get started on your mission of reaching out to others

The Great Commission was given to every follower of Jesus.

now! We will have all of eternity to celebrate with those we have brought to Jesus, but we only have our lifetime in which to reach them.

This does not mean you should quit your job to become a full-time evangelist. God wants you to share the Good News where you are. As a student, mother, preschool teacher, salesman, or manager or whatever you do, you should continually look for people God places in your path with whom you can share the gospel.

Your mission gives your life meaning. William James said, "The best use of life is to spend it for something that outlasts it." The truth is, only the kingdom of God is going to last. *Everything* else will eventually vanish. That is why we must live purpose-driven lives — lives committed to worship, fellowship, spiritual growth, ministry, and fulfilling our mission on earth. The results of these activities *will* last — forever!

If you fail to fulfill your God-given mission on earth, you will have wasted the life God gave you. Paul said, *"My life is worth nothing unless I use it for doing the work assigned me by the Lord Jesus — the work of telling others the Good News about God's wonderful kindness and love."*[15] There are people on this planet whom *only* you will be able to reach, because of where you live and what God has made you to be. If just one person will be in heaven because of you, your life will have made a difference for eternity. Start looking around at your personal mission field and pray, "God, who have you put in my life for me to tell about Jesus?"

God's timetable for history's conclusion is connected to the completion of our commission.

Today there's a growing interest in the second coming of Christ and the end of the world. When will it happen? Just before Jesus ascended to heaven the disciples asked him this same question, and his response was quite revealing. He said, *"It is not for you to know the times or dates the Father has set by his own authority. But you will receive power when the Holy Spirit comes on you; and you will be my witnesses in Jerusalem, and in all Judea and Samaria, and to the ends of the earth."*[16]

When the disciples wanted to talk about prophecy, Jesus quickly switched the conversation to evangelism. He wanted them to concentrate on their mission in the world. He said in essence, "The details of my return are none of your business. What *is* your business is the mission I've given you. Focus on that!"

It is easy to get distracted, because Satan would rather have you do anything besides sharing your faith.

Speculating on the exact timing of Christ's return is futile, because Jesus said, *"No one knows about that day or hour, not even the angels in heaven, nor the Son, but only the Father."*[17] Since Jesus said he didn't know the day or hour, why should you try to figure it out? What we *do* know for sure is this: Jesus will not return until everyone God wants to hear the Good News has heard it. Jesus said, *"The Good News about God's kingdom will be preached in all the world, to every nation. Then the end will come."*[18] If you want Jesus to come back sooner, focus on fulfilling your mission, not figuring out prophecy.

It is easy to get distracted and sidetracked from your mission because Satan would rather have you do anything besides sharing your faith. He will let you do all kinds of good things as long as you don't take anyone to heaven with you. But the moment you become serious about your mission, expect the Devil to throw all kinds of diversions at you. When that happens, remember the words of Jesus: *"Anyone who lets himself be distracted from the work I plan for him is not fit for the Kingdom of God."*[19]

What It Costs to Fulfill Your Mission

To fulfill your mission will require that you abandon your agenda and accept God's agenda for your life. You can't just "tack it on" to all the other things you'd like to do with your life. You must say, like Jesus, *"Father, ... I want your will, not mine."*[20] You yield your rights, expectations, dreams, plans, and ambitions to him. You stop praying selfish prayers like "God bless what I want to do." Instead you pray, "God help me to do what you're blessing!" You hand God a blank sheet with your name signed at the bottom and tell him to fill in the details. The Bible says, *"Give yourselves completely to God — every part of you ... to be tools in the hands of God, to be used for his good purposes."*[21]

If you will commit to fulfilling your mission in life no

matter what it costs, you will experience the blessing of God in ways that few people ever experience. There is almost nothing God won't do for the man or woman who is committed to serving the kingdom of God. Jesus has promised, *"[God] will give you all you need from day to day if you live for him and make the Kingdom of God your primary concern."*[22]

One More for Jesus

My father was a minister for over fifty years, serving mostly in small, rural churches. He was a simple preacher, but he was a man with a mission. His favorite activity was taking teams of volunteers overseas to build church buildings for small congregations. In his lifetime, Dad built over 150 churches around the world.

In 1999, my father died of cancer. In the final week of his life the disease kept him awake in a semi-conscious state nearly twenty-four hours a day. As he dreamed, he would talk out loud about what he was dreaming. Sitting by his bedside, I learned a lot about my dad by just listening to his dreams. He relived one church building project after another.

DAY 36: *Made For a Mission*

One night near the end, while my wife, my niece, and I were by his side, Dad suddenly became very active and tried to get out of bed. Of course, he was too weak, and my wife insisted he lay back down. But he persisted in trying to get out of bed, so my wife finally asked, "Jimmy, what are you trying to do?" He replied, "Got to save one more for Jesus! Got to save one more for Jesus! Got to save one more for Jesus!" He began to repeat that phrase over and over.

During the next hour, he said the phrase probably a hundred times. "Got to save one more for Jesus!" As I sat by his bed with tears flowing down my cheeks, I bowed my head to thank God for my dad's faith. At that moment Dad reached out and placed his frail hand on my head and said, as if commissioning me, "Save one more for Jesus! Save one more for Jesus!"

I intend for that to be the theme of the rest of my life. I invite you to consider it as a focus for your life, too, because *nothing* will make a greater difference for eternity. If you want to be used by God, you must care about what God cares about; what he cares about most is the redemption of the people he made. He wants his lost children found! Nothing matters more to God; the Cross proves that. I pray that you will always be on the lookout to reach "one more for Jesus" so that when you stand before God one day, you can say, "Mission accomplished!"

DAY 36

Thinking about My Purpose

POINT TO PONDER: I was made for a mission.

VERSE TO REMEMBER: *"Go and make disciples of all nations, baptizing them in the name of the Father and of the Son and of the Holy Spirit, and teaching them to obey everything I have commanded you. And surely I am with you always, to the very end of the age."* MATTHEW 28:19 — 20 (NIV)

QUESTION TO CONSIDER: What fears have kept me from fulfilling the mission God made me to accomplish? What keeps me from telling others the Good News?

MESSAGE TO HEAR: *www.purposedriven.com/day36*

DAY 37

Sharing Your Life Message

Those who believe in the Son of God have the testimony of God in them.

1 JOHN 5:10A (GWT)

purposedriven.com/
day37

Your lives are echoing the Master's Word.... The news of your faith in God is out. We don't even have to say anything anymore—you're the message!

1 THESSALONIANS 1:8 (MSG)

GOD HAS GIVEN YOU A LIFE MESSAGE TO SHARE.

When you became a believer, you also became God's messenger. God wants to speak to the world through you. Paul said, *"We speak the truth before God, as messengers of God."*[1]

You may feel you don't have anything to share, but that's the Devil trying to keep you silent. You have a storehouse of experiences that God wants to use to bring others into his family. The Bible says, *"Those who believe*

in the Son of God have the testimony of God in them."[2]
Your Life Message has four parts to it:

- Your *testimony:* the story of how you began a
  relationship with Jesus

- Your *life lessons:* the most important lessons God
  has taught you

- Your *godly passions:* the issues God shaped you
  to care about most

- The *Good News:* the message of salvation

Your Life Message includes your testimony.
Your testimony is the story of how Christ has made a
difference in your life. Peter tells us that we were chosen
by God *"to do his work and speak out for him, to tell
others of the night-and-day difference he made for you."*[3]
This is the essence of witnessing — simply sharing your
personal experiences regarding the Lord. In a courtroom,
a witness isn't expected to argue the case, prove the
truth, or press for a verdict; that is the job of attorneys.
Witnesses simply report what happened to them or what
they saw.

Jesus said, *"You will be my witnesses,"*[4] not "You will
be my attorney." He wants you to share your story with
others. Sharing your testimony is an essential part of
your mission on earth because it is unique. There is no
other story just like yours, so only you can share it. If
you don't share it, it will be lost forever. You may not

be a Bible scholar, but you *are* the authority on your life, and it's hard to argue with personal experience. Actually, your personal testimony is more effective than a sermon, because unbelievers see pastors as professional salesmen, but see you as a "satisfied customer," so they give you more credibility.

Shared stories build a relational bridge that Jesus can walk across from your heart to others.

Personal stories are also easier to relate to than principles, and people love to hear them. They capture our attention, and we remember them longer. Unbelievers would probably lose interest if you started quoting theologians, but they have a natural curiosity about experiences they've never had. Shared stories build a relational bridge that Jesus can walk across from your heart to theirs.

Another value of your testimony is that it bypasses intellectual defenses. Many people who won't accept the authority of the Bible will listen to a humble, personal story. That is why on six different occasions Paul used his testimony to share the gospel instead of quoting Scripture.[5]

The Bible says, *"Be ready at all times to answer anyone who asks you to explain the hope you have in you, but do it with gentleness and respect."*[6] The best way to "be ready" is to write out your testimony and then memorize the main points. Divide it into four parts:

1. What my life was like before I met Jesus

2. How I realized I needed Jesus

3. How I committed my life to Jesus

4. The difference Jesus has made in my life

Of course, you have many other testimonies besides your salvation story. You have a story for *every* experience in which God has helped you. You should make a list of all the problems, circumstances, and crises that God has brought you through. Then be sensitive and use the story that your unbelieving friend will relate to best. Different situations call for different testimonies.

Your Life Message includes your life lessons. The second part of your life message is the truths that God has taught you from experiences with him. These are lessons and insights you have learned about God, relationships, problems, temptations, and other aspects of life. David prayed, *"God, teach me lessons for living so I can stay the course."*[7] Sadly, we never learn from a lot that happens to us. Of the Israelites, the Bible says, *"Over and over God rescued them, but they never learned — until finally their sins destroyed them."*[8] You have probably met people like that.

While it is wise to learn from experience, it is *wiser* to learn from the experiences of others. There isn't enough time to learn everything in life by trial and error. We must learn from the life lessons of one another. The Bible says, *"A warning given by an experienced person to someone willing to listen is more valuable than ... jewelry made of the finest gold.*"[9]

Write down the major life lessons you have learned so you can share them with others. We should be grateful Solomon did this, because it gave us the books of Proverbs and Ecclesiastes, which are filled with practical lessons on living. Imagine how much needless frustration could be avoided if we learned from each other's life lessons.

> *While it is wise to learn from experience, it is wiser to learn from the experiences of others.*

Mature people develop the habit of extracting lessons from everyday experiences. I urge you to make a list of your life lessons. You haven't really thought about them unless you have written them down. Here are a few questions to jog your memory and get you started:[10]

- What has God taught me from failure?
- What has God taught me from a lack of money?
- What has God taught me from pain or sorrow or depression?
- What has God taught me through waiting?
- What has God taught me through illness?
- What has God taught me from disappointment?
- What have I learned from my family, my church, my relationships, my small group, and my critics?

Your Life Message includes sharing your godly passions. God is a passionate God. He passionately *loves* some things and passionately *hates* other things. As you grow closer to him, he will give you a passion for something he cares about deeply so you can be a spokesman for him in the world. It may be a passion about a problem, a purpose, a principle, or a group of people. Whatever it is, you will feel compelled to speak up about it and do what you can to make a difference.

You cannot keep yourself from talking about what you care about most. Jesus said, *"A man's heart determines his speech."*[11] Two examples are David, who said, *"My zeal for God and his work burns hot within me,"*[12] and Jeremiah, who said, *"Your message burns in my heart and bones, and I cannot keep silent."*[13]

God gives some people a godly passion to champion a cause. It's often a problem they personally experienced such as abuse, addiction, infertility, depression, a disease, or some other difficulty. Sometimes God gives people a passion to speak up for a group of others who can't speak for themselves: the unborn, the persecuted, the poor, the imprisoned, the mistreated, the disadvantaged, and those who are denied justice. The Bible is filled with commands to defend the defenseless.

God uses passionate people to further his kingdom. He may give you a godly passion for starting new churches, strengthening families, funding Bible translations, or training Christian leaders. You may be given a godly passion for reaching a particular group of people with the gospel: businessmen, teenagers, foreign exchange students, young mothers, or those with a particular hobby or sport. If you ask God, he will burden your heart for a specific country or ethnic group that desperately needs a strong Christian witness.

God gives us different passions so that everything he wants done in the world will get done. You should not expect everyone else to be passionate about your passion. Instead, we must listen to and value each other's life message because nobody can say it all. Never belittle someone else's godly passion. The Bible says, *"It is fine to be zealous, provided the purpose is good."*[14]

Your Life Message includes the Good News. What is the Good News? *"The Good News shows how God makes people right with himself—that it begins and ends with faith."*[15] *"For God was in Christ, reconciling the world to himself, no longer counting people's sins against them. This is the wonderful message he has given us to tell others."*[16] The Good News is that when we trust God's grace to save us through what Jesus did, our sins are forgiven, we get a purpose for living, and we are promised a future home in heaven.

There are hundreds of great books on how to share the Good News. I can provide a list of books that have been helpful to me (see appendix 2). But all the training in the world won't motivate you to witness for Christ until you internalize the eight convictions covered in the previous chapter. Most important, you must learn to love lost people the way God does.

God has never made a person he didn't love. Everybody matters to him. When Jesus stretched his arms out wide on the cross, he was saying, "I love you *this* much!" The Bible says, *"For Christ's love compels us, because we are convinced that one died for all."*[17] Whenever you feel apathetic about your mission in the world, spend some time thinking about what Jesus did for you on the cross.

> God gives us different passions so that everything he wants done in the world will get done.

We must care about unbelievers because God does. Love leaves no choice. The Bible says, *"There is no fear in love; perfect love drives out all fear."*[18] A parent will run into a burning building to save a child because their love for that child is greater than their fear. If you've been afraid to share the Good News with those around you, ask God to fill your heart with his love for them.

The Bible says, *"[God] does not want anyone to be lost, but he wants all people to change their hearts and lives."*[19] As long as you know one person who doesn't know Christ, you *must* keep praying for them, serving them in love, and sharing the Good News. And as long as there is one person in your community who isn't in the family of God, your church *must* keep reaching out. The church that doesn't want to grow is saying to the world, "You can go to hell."

What are *you* willing to do so that the people you know will go to heaven? Invite them to church? Share your story? Give them this book? Take them a meal? Pray for them every day until they are saved? Your mission field is all around you. Don't miss the opportunities God is giving you. The Bible says, *"Make the most of your chances to tell others the Good News. Be wise in all your contacts with them."*[20]

Is anyone going to be in heaven because of you? Will anyone in heaven be able to say to you, "I want to thank you. I'm here because you cared enough to share the Good News with me"? Imagine the joy of greeting people in heaven whom you helped get there. The eternal salvation of a single soul is more important than anything else you will ever achieve in life. Only people are going to last forever.

DAY 37:
Sharing Your Life Message

In this book you have learned God's five purposes for your life on earth: He made you to be a *member* of his family, a *model* of his character, a *magnifier* of his glory, a *minister* of his grace, and a *messenger* of his Good News to others. Of these five purposes, the fifth can *only* be done on earth. The other four you will keep doing in eternity in some way. That's why spreading the Good News is so important; you only have a short time to share your life message and fulfill your mission.

DAY 37

Thinking about My Purpose

POINT TO PONDER: God wants to say something to the world through me.

VERSE TO REMEMBER: *"Be ready at all times to answer anyone who asks you to explain the hope you have in you, but do it with gentleness and respect."* 1 PETER 3:15B — 16 (TEV)

QUESTION TO CONSIDER: As I reflect on my personal story, who does God want me to share it with?

MESSAGE TO HEAR: *www.purposedriven.com/day37*

Becoming a World-Class Christian

Jesus said to his followers,
"Go everywhere in the world,
and tell the Good News to everyone."

MARK 16:15 (NCV)

purposedriven.com/
day38

Send us around the world with
the news of your saving power and
your eternal plan for all mankind.

PSALM 67:2 (LB)

THE GREAT COMMISSION IS YOUR COMMISSION.

You have a choice to make. You will be either a *world-class* Christian or a *worldly* Christian.[1]

Worldly Christians look to God primarily for personal fulfillment. They are saved, but self-centered. They love to attend concerts and enrichment seminars, but you would never find them at a missions conference because they aren't interested. Their prayers focus on their own needs, blessings, and happiness. It's a "me-first" faith: How can God make *my* life more comfortable? They want to use God for their purposes instead of *being* used for *his* purposes.

In contrast, world-class Christians know they were saved to serve and made for a mission. They are eager to receive a personal assignment and excited about the privilege of being used by God. World-class Christians are the only *fully alive* people on the planet. Their joy, confidence, and enthusiasm are contagious because they know they're making a difference. They wake up each morning expecting God to work through them in fresh ways. Which type of Christian do you want to be?

God invites you to participate in the greatest, largest, most diverse, and most significant cause in history — his kingdom. History is *his story*. He's building his family for eternity. Nothing matters more, and nothing will last as long. From the book of Revelation we know that God's global mission *will* be accomplished. Someday the Great Commission will be the Great Completion. In heaven an enormous crowd of people from *"every race, tribe, nation, and language"*[2] will one day stand before Jesus Christ to worship him. Getting involved as a world-class Christian will allow you to experience a little of what heaven will be like *in advance.*

When Jesus told his followers to *"go everywhere in the world, and tell the Good News to everyone,"* that small band of poor, Middle Eastern disciples were overwhelmed. Were they supposed to walk or ride slow animals? That's all they had for transportation, and there were no ocean-crossing ships, so there were real physical barriers to going to the whole world.

Today we have airplanes, ships, trains, buses, and automobiles. It's a small world after all, and it's shrinking daily. You can fly across the ocean in a matter of *hours* and be home the next day if you need to be. The opportunities for normal, everyday Christians to become involved in short-term international missions are now literally limitless. Every corner of the world is available to you — just ask the travel industry. We have no excuse not to spread the Good News.

Now, with the Internet, the world has gotten even smaller. In addition to phones and faxes, any believer with Internet access can personally communicate with people in virtually every country on earth. The whole world is at your fingertips!

> *It has never been easier in history to fulfill your commission to go to the whole world.*

Even many remote villages get email, so you can now carry on *"e-vangelistic"* conversations with people on the other side of the world, without even leaving your home! It has never been easier in history to fulfill your commission to go to the whole world. The great barriers are no longer distance, cost, or transportation. The only barrier is the way we *think.* To be a world-class Christian you must make some mental shifts. Your perspective and attitudes must change.

How to Think Like a World-Class Christian

Shift from self-centered thinking to other-centered thinking. The Bible says, *"My friends, stop thinking like children. Think like mature people."*[3] This is the first step to becoming a world-class Christian. Children only think of themselves; grown-ups think of others. God commands, *"Don't think only about your own affairs, but be interested in others, too."*[4]

Of course, this is a difficult mental shift because we're naturally self-absorbed and almost all advertising encourages us to think of ourselves. The only way we can make this paradigm switch is by a moment-by-moment dependence on God. Fortunately he doesn't leave us to struggle on our own. *"God has given us his Spirit. That's why we don't think the same way that the people of this world think."*[5]

Begin asking the Holy Spirit to help you to think of the spiritual need of unbelievers whenever you talk to them. With practice you can develop the habit of praying silent "breath prayers" for those you encounter. Say, "Father, help me to understand what is keeping this person from knowing you."

Your goal is to figure out where others are in their spiritual journey and then do whatever will bring them a step closer to knowing Christ. You can learn how to do this by adopting the mind-set of Paul, who said, *"I don't think about what would be good for me but about what would be good for many people so that they might be saved."*[6]

Shift from local thinking to global thinking. God is a global God. He has always cared about the entire world. *"God so loved the world...."*[7] From the beginning he has wanted family members from every nation he created. The Bible says, *"From one person God made all nations who live on earth, and he decided when and where every nation would be. God has done all this, so that we will look for him and reach out and find him."*[8]

Much of the world already thinks globally. The largest media and business conglomerates are all multinational. Our lives are increasingly intertwined with those in other nations as we share fashions, entertainment, music, sports, and even fast food. Probably most of the clothes you are wearing and much of what you ate today were produced in another country. We are more connected than we realize.

These are exciting days to be alive. There are more Christians on earth right now than ever before. Paul was right: *"This same Good News that came to you is going out all over the world. It is changing lives everywhere, just as it changed yours."*[9]

The first way to start thinking globally is to begin praying for specific countries. World-class Christians pray for the world. Get a globe or map and pray for nations by name. The Bible says, *"If you ask me, I will give you the nations; all the people on earth will be yours."*[10]

Prayer is the most important tool for your mission in the world. People may refuse our love or reject our message, but they are defenseless against our prayers. Like an intercontinental missile, you can aim a prayer at a person's heart whether you are ten feet or 10,000 miles away.

> *People may refuse our love or reject our message, but they are defenseless against our prayers.*

What should you pray for? The Bible tells us to pray for opportunities to witness,[11] for courage to speak up,[12] for those who will believe,[13] for the rapid spread of the message,[14] and for more workers.[15] Prayer makes you a partner with others around the world.

You should also pray for missionaries and everyone else involved in the global harvest. Paul told his prayer partners, *"You are also joining to help us when you pray for us."*[16] If you would like suggestions for praying intelligently for the world and Christian workers, see appendix 2.

Another way to develop global thinking is to read and watch the news with *"Great Commission eyes."* Wherever there is change or conflict, you can be sure that God will use it to bring people to him. People are most receptive to God when they are under tension or in transition.

Because the rate of change is increasing in our world, more people are open to hearing the Good News now than ever before.

The best way to switch to global thinking is to just get up and go on a short-term mission project to another country! There's simply no substitute for hands-on, real life experience in another culture. Quit studying and discussing your mission and just do it! I dare you to dive into the deep end. In Acts 1:8 Jesus gave us a pattern for involvement: *"You will tell everyone about me in Jerusalem, in all Judea, in Samaria, and everywhere in the world."*[17] His followers were to reach out to their community (Jerusalem), to their country (Judea), to other cultures (Samaria), and to other nations (everywhere in the world). Note that our commission is simultaneous, not sequential. While not everyone has the missionary gift, *every* Christian is called to be on a mission to all four groups in some way. Are you an Acts 1:8 Christian?

Set a goal to participate in a mission project to each of these four targets. I urge you to save and do whatever it takes to participate in a short-term mission trip overseas *as soon as possible.* Nearly every mission agency can help you do this. It will enlarge your heart, expand your vision, stretch your faith, deepen your compassion, and fill you with a kind of joy you have never experienced. It could be the turning point in your life.

Shift from "here and now" thinking to eternal thinking. To make the most of your time on earth, you must maintain an eternal perspective. This will keep you from majoring on minor issues and help you distinguish between what's urgent and what's ultimate. Paul said, *"We fix our eyes not on what is seen, but on what is unseen. For what is seen is temporary, but what is unseen is eternal."*[18]

So much of what we waste our energy on will not matter even a year from now, much less for eternity. Don't trade your life for temporary things. Jesus said, *"Anyone who lets himself be distracted from the work I plan for him is not fit for the Kingdom of God."*[19] Paul warned, *"Deal as sparingly as possible with the things the world thrusts on you. This world as you see it is on its way out."*[20]

What are you allowing to stand in the way of your mission? What's keeping you from being a world-class Christian? Whatever it is, let it go. *"Let us strip off anything that slows us down or holds us back."*[21]

Jesus told us to *"store up your treasures in heaven."*[22]

> *"You can't take it with you"* — but the Bible says you can send it on ahead by investing in people who are going there!

How can we do this? In one of his most misunderstood statements Jesus said, *"I tell you, use worldly wealth to gain friends for yourselves, so that when it is gone, you will be welcomed into eternal dwellings."*[23] Jesus did not mean for you to "buy" friends with money. What he meant was that you should use the money God gives you to bring people to Christ. They will then be friends for eternity who will welcome you when you get to heaven! It's the best financial investment you'll ever make.

You have probably heard the expression "You can't take it with you" — but the Bible says you *can* send it on ahead by investing in people who are going there! The Bible says, *"By doing this they will be storing up real treasure for themselves in heaven — it is the only safe investment for eternity! And they will be living a fruitful Christian life down here as well."*[24]

Shift from thinking of excuses to thinking of creative ways to fulfill your commission. If you are willing, there is always a way to do it, and there are agencies that will help you. Here are some common excuses:

- *"I only speak English."* This is actually an advantage in many countries where millions of people want to learn English and are eager to practice it.

- *"I don't have anything to offer."* Yes, you do. Every ability and experience in your shape can be used somewhere.

- *"I'm too old (or too young)."* Most mission agencies have age-appropriate short-term projects.

Whether it was Sarah claiming she was too old to be used by God or Jeremiah claiming he was too young, God rejected their excuses. *"'Don't say that,' the LORD replied, 'for you must go wherever I send you and say whatever I tell you. And don't be afraid of the people, for I will be with you and take care of you.'"*[25]

Maybe you have believed that you needed a special "call" from God, and you have been waiting for some supernatural feeling or experience. But God has already stated his call repeatedly. We are *all* called to fulfill God's five purposes for our lives: to worship, to fellowship, to grow like Christ, to serve, and to be on mission with God in the world. God doesn't want to use just *some* of his people; he wants to use *all* of his people. We are all called to be *on-mission* for God. He wants his whole church to take the whole gospel to the whole world.[26]

Many Christians have missed God's plan for their lives because they have never even *asked God* if he wanted them to serve as a missionary somewhere. Whether out of fear or ignorance, they have automatically closed their minds to the possibility of serving as a resident missionary in a cross-cultural location. If you are tempted to say no, you ought to check out all the different ways and possibilities that are now available (this will surprise you), and you ought to seriously pray and ask God what he wants from you in the years ahead. Untold thousands of resident missionaries are desperately needed at this critical point in history, when so many doors are opening wide like never before.

DAY 38:

Becoming a

World-Class

Christian

If you want to be like Jesus, you must have a heart

for the whole world. You can't be satisfied with just your family and friends coming to Christ. There are over 6 billion people on earth, and Jesus wants *all* his lost children found. Jesus said, *"Only those who throw away their lives for my sake and for the sake of the Good News will ever know what it means to really live!"*[27] The Great Commission is *your* commission, and doing your part is the secret to living a life of significance.

DAY 38

Thinking about My Purpose

POINT TO PONDER: The Great Commission is *my* commission.

VERSE TO REMEMBER: *"Send us around the world with the news of your saving power and your eternal plan for all mankind."* PSALM 67:2 (LB)

QUESTION TO CONSIDER: What steps can I take to prepare to go on a short-term missions experience in the next year?

MESSAGE TO HEAR: *www.purposedriven.com/day38*

Balancing Your Life

Live life with a due sense of responsibility,
not as those who do not know the meaning
of life but as those who do.

EPHESIANS 5:15 (PH)

Don't let the errors of evil people
lead you down the wrong path
and make you lose your balance.

2 PETER 3:17 (CEV)

purposedriven.com/
day39

BLESSED ARE THE BALANCED; THEY SHALL OUTLAST
everyone.

One of the events in the summer Olympics is the
pentathlon. It is composed of five events: pistol shooting,
fencing, horseback riding, running, and swimming. The
pentathlete's goal is to succeed in all five areas, not just
one or two.

Your life is a pentathlon of five purposes, which you
must keep in balance. These purposes were practiced
by the first Christians in Acts 2, explained by Paul in
Ephesians 4, and modeled by Jesus in John 17, but they

391

are summarized in the Great Commandment and the Great Commission of Jesus. These two statements sum up what this book is all about — God's five purposes for your life:

1. **"Love God with all your heart"**: You were planned for God's pleasure, so your purpose is to love God through *worship*.

2. **"Love your neighbor as yourself"**: You were shaped for serving, so your purpose is to show love for others through *ministry*.

3. **"Go and make disciples"**: You were made for a mission, so your purpose is to share God's message through *evangelism*.

4. **"baptize them into ..."**: You were formed for God's family, so your purpose is to identify with his church through *fellowship*.

5. **"teach them to do all things ..."**: You were created to become like Christ, so your purpose is to grow to maturity through *discipleship*.

A great commitment to the Great Commandment and the Great Commission will make you a great Christian.

Keeping these five purposes in balance is not easy. We all tend to overemphasize the purposes we feel most passionate about and neglect the others. Churches do the same thing. But you can keep your life balanced and on track by joining a small group for accountability, by regularly evaluating your spiritual health, by recording your progress in a personal journal, and by passing on what you learn to others. These are four important activities for purpose-driven living. If you are serious about staying on track, you will need to develop these habits.

Talk it through with a spiritual partner or small group. The best way to *internalize* the principles in this book is to discuss them with others in a small-group setting. The Bible says, *"As iron sharpens iron, so people can improve each other."*[1] We learn best in community. Our minds are sharpened and our convictions are deepened through conversation.

I *strongly* urge you to gather a small group of friends and form a Purpose Driven Life Reading Group to review these chapters on a weekly basis. Discuss the implications and the applications of each chapter. Ask "So what?" and

> A great commitment to the Great Commandment and the Great Commission will make you a great Christian.

"What now?" What does this mean for me, my family, and our church? What am I going to do about it? Paul said, *"Put into practice what you learned."*[2] In appendix 1, I have prepared a list of discussion questions for your small group or Sunday school class to use.

A small reading group provides many benefits that a book by itself cannot. You can give and receive feedback about what you're learning. You can discuss real-life examples. You can pray for, encourage, and support each other as you begin to live out these purposes. Remember, we are meant to grow together, not separately. The Bible says, *"Encourage each other and give each other strength."*[3] After you have gone through this book together as a group, you might consider studying other purpose-driven life studies that are available for classes and groups (see appendix 2).

I also encourage you to do personal Bible study. I have footnoted over a thousand Scriptures used in this book for you to study in their context. Please read appendix 3, which explains why this book uses so many different translations and paraphrases. To keep these chapters to a size for daily reading, I was unable to explain the fascinating context of most of the verses used. But the Bible is intended to be studied by paragraphs, chapters, and even entire books. My book *Personal Bible Study Methods* can show you how to do inductive studies.

Give yourself a regular spiritual checkup. The best way to *balance* the five purposes in your life is to evaluate yourself periodically. God places a high value on the habit of self-evaluation. At least five times in Scripture we are told to test and examine our own spiritual health.[4] The Bible says, *"Test yourselves to make sure you are solid in the faith. Don't drift along taking everything for granted. Give yourselves regular checkups.... Test it out. If you fail the test, do something about it."*[5]

To maintain your physical health, you need regular checkups with a doctor who can assess your vital signs —blood pressure, temperature, weight, and so on. For your spiritual health you need to regularly check the five vital signs of worship, fellowship, growth in character, ministry, and mission. Jeremiah advised, *"Let's take a good look at the way we're living and reorder our lives under God."*[6]

At Saddleback Church we have developed a simple personal evaluation tool that has helped thousands of people stay on-purpose for God. If you would like a copy of this purpose-driven life spiritual health assessment, you can email me (see appendix 2). You will be amazed at how much this little tool will help you balance your life for health and growth. Paul urged, *"Let your enthusiastic idea at the start be equaled by your realistic action now."*[7]

Write down your progress in a journal. The best way to *reinforce* your progress in fulfilling God's purposes for your life is to keep a spiritual journal. This is not a diary of events, but a record of the life lessons you don't want to forget. The Bible says, *"It's crucial that we keep a firm grip on what we've heard so that we don't drift off."*[8] We remember what we record.

Writing helps clarify what God is doing in your life. Dawson Trotman used to say, "Thoughts disentangle themselves when they pass through your fingertips." The Bible has several examples of God telling people to keep a spiritual journal. It says, *"At the LORD's direction, Moses kept a written record of their progress."*[9] Aren't you glad Moses obeyed God's command to record Israel's spiritual journey? If he had been lazy, we would be robbed of the powerful life lessons of the Exodus.

While it's unlikely that your spiritual journal will be as widely read as Moses' was, yours is still important. The New International Version says, *"Moses recorded the stages in their journey."* Your life is a journey, and a journey deserves a journal. I hope you will write about the stages of your spiritual journey in living a purpose-driven life.

Don't just write down the pleasant things. As David did, record your doubts, fears, and struggles with God. Our greatest lessons come out of pain, and the Bible says God keeps a record of our tears.[10] Whenever problems occur, remember that God uses them to fulfill *all five* purposes in your life: Problems force you to focus on God, draw you closer to others in fellowship, build Christlike character, provide you with a ministry, and give you a testimony. Every problem is purpose-driven.

You owe it to future generations to preserve the testimony of how God helped you fulfill his purposes on earth.

In the middle of a painful experience, the psalmist wrote, *"Write down for the coming generation what the LORD has done, so that people not yet born will praise him."*[11] You owe it to future generations to preserve the testimony of how God helped you fulfill his purposes on earth. It is a witness that will continue to speak long after you're in heaven.

Pass on what you know to others. If you want to keep growing, the best way to learn more is to pass on what you have already learned. Proverbs tells us, *"The one who blesses others is abundantly blessed; those who help others are helped."*[12] Those who pass along insights get more from God.

Now that you understand the purpose of life, it is your responsibility to carry the message to others. God is calling you to be his messenger. Paul said, *"Now I want you to tell these same things to followers who can be trusted to tell others."*[13] In this book I have passed on to you what others taught me about the purpose of life; now it's your duty to pass that on to others.

You probably know hundreds of people who do not know the purpose of life. Share these truths with your children, your friends, your neighbors, and those you work with. If you give this book to a friend, add your personal note on the dedication page.

The more you know, the more God expects you to use that knowledge to help others. James said, *"Anyone who knows the right thing to do, but does not do it, is sinning."*[14] Knowledge increases responsibility. But passing along the purpose of life is more than an obligation; it's one of life's greatest privileges. Imagine how different the world would be if everyone knew their purpose. Paul said, *"If you teach these things to other followers, you will be a good servant of Christ Jesus."*[15]

It's All for God's Glory

The reason we pass on what we learn is for the glory of God and the growth of his kingdom. The night before he was crucified, Jesus reported to his Father, *"I have brought you glory on earth by completing the work you gave me to do."*[16] When Jesus prayed these words, he had not yet died for our sins, so what "work" had he completed? In this instance he was referring to something other than the atonement. The answer lies in what he said in the next twenty verses of his prayer.[17]

Jesus told his Father what he had been doing for the last three years: preparing his disciples to live for God's purposes. He helped them to know and love God (worship), taught them to love each other (fellowship), gave them the Word so they could grow to maturity (discipleship), showed them how to serve (ministry), and sent them out to tell others (mission). Jesus modeled a purpose-driven life, and he taught others how to live it, too. That was the "work" that brought glory to God.

Today God calls each of us to the same work. Not only does he want us to live out his purposes, he also wants us to help others do the same. God wants us to introduce people to Christ, bring them into his fellowship, help them grow to maturity and discover their place of service, and then send them out to reach others, too.

This is what purpose-driven living is all about. Regardless of your age, the rest of your life can be the best of your life, and you can start living on purpose today.

DAY 39

Thinking about My Purpose

POINT TO PONDER: Blessed are the balanced.

VERSE TO REMEMBER: *"Live life with a due sense of responsibility, not as those who do not know the meaning of life but as those who do."*
EPHESIANS 5:15 (PH)

QUESTION TO CONSIDER: Which of the four activities will I begin in order to stay on track and balance God's five purposes for my life?

MESSAGE TO HEAR: *www.purposedriven.com/day39*

Living with Purpose

Many are the plans in a man's heart,
but it is the Lord's purpose that prevails.
PROVERBS 19:21 (NIV)

For David ... served the purpose
of God in his own generation.
ACTS 13:36 (NASB)

purposedriven.com/
day40

LIVING ON PURPOSE IS THE ONLY WAY TO *REALLY* LIVE.
Everything else is just existing.

Most people struggle with three basic issues in
life. The first is *identity:* "Who am I?" The second is
importance: "Do I matter?" The third is *impact:* "What is
my place in life?" The answers to all three questions are
found in God's five purposes for you.

In the Upper Room, as Jesus was concluding his last
day of ministry with his disciples, he washed their feet
as an example and said, *"Now that you know these things,*
you will be blessed if you do them."[1] Once you know what

God wants you to do, the blessing comes in actually doing it. As we come to the end of our forty-day journey together, now that you know God's purposes for your life, you will be blessed if you *do* them!

This probably means you will have to stop doing some other things. There are many "good" things you can do with your life, but God's purposes are the five essentials you *must* do. Unfortunately, it's easy to get distracted and forget what is most important. It's easy to drift away from what matters most and slowly get off course. To prevent this, you should develop a purpose statement for your life and then review it regularly.

What Is a Life Purpose Statement?

It's a statement that summarizes God's purposes for your life. In your own words you affirm your commitment to God's five purposes for your life. A purpose statement is *not* a list of goals. Goals are temporary; purposes are eternal. The Bible says, *"His plans endure forever; his purposes last eternally."*[2]

It's a statement that points the direction of your life. Writing down your purposes on paper will force you to think specifically about the path of your life. The Bible says, *"Know where you are headed, and you will stay on solid ground."*[3] A life purpose statement not only spells out what you intend to do with your time, life, and money, but also implies what you *aren't* going to do. Proverbs says, *"An intelligent person aims at wise action, but a fool starts off in many directions."*[4]

It's a statement that defines "success" for you. It states what you believe is important, not what the world says is important. It clarifies your values. Paul said, *"I want you to understand what really matters."*[5]

It's a statement that clarifies your roles. You will have different roles at different stages in life, but your purposes will never change. They are greater than any role you will have.

It's a statement that expresses your shape. It reflects the unique ways God made you to serve him.

Take your time writing out your life purpose statement. Don't try to complete it in a single sitting, and don't aim for perfection in your first draft; just write down your thoughts as fast as they come to you. It is always easier to edit than to create. Here are five questions you should consider as you prepare your statement:

Life's Five Greatest Questions

What will be the *center* of my life? This is the question of *worship.* Who are you going to live for? What are you going to build your life around? You can center your life around your career, your family, a sport or hobby, money, having fun, or many other activities. These are all good things, but they don't belong at the center of your life.

None is strong enough to hold you together when life starts breaking apart. You need an unshakable center.

King Asa told the people of Judah to *"center their lives in God."*[6] Actually, whatever is at the center of your life is your god. When you committed your life to Christ, he moved into the center, but you must keep him there through worship. Paul says, *"I pray that Christ will be more and more at home in your hearts."*[7]

> When God is at the center of your life, you worship. When he's not, you worry.

How do you know when God is at the center of your life? When God is at the center, you worship. When he's not, you worry. Worry is the warning light that God has been shoved to the sideline. The moment you put him back at the center, you will have peace again. The Bible says, *"A sense of God's wholeness ... will come and settle you down. It's wonderful what happens when Christ displaces worry at the center of your life."*[8]

What will be the *character* of my life? This is the question of *discipleship.* What kind of person will you be? God is far more interested in what you *are* than what you *do.* Remember, you will take your character into eternity, but not your career. Make a list of the character qualities you want to work on and develop in your life. You might begin with the fruit of the Spirit[9] or the Beatitudes.[10]

Peter said, *"Don't lose a minute in building on what you've been given, complementing your basic faith with good character, spiritual understanding, alert discipline, passionate patience, reverent wonder, warm friendliness, and generous love."*[11] Don't get discouraged and give up when you stumble. It takes a lifetime to build Christlike character. Paul told Timothy, *"Keep a firm grasp on both your character and your teaching. Don't be diverted. Just keep at it."*[12]

What will be the *contribution* of my life? This is the question of *service.* What will be your ministry in the Body of Christ? Knowing your combination of spiritual gifts, heart, abilities, personality, and experiences (SHAPE), what would be your best role in the family of God? How can you make a difference? Is there a specific group in the Body that I am shaped to serve? Paul pointed out two wonderful benefits when you fulfill your ministry: *"This service you perform not only meets the needs of God's people, but also produces an outpouring of gratitude to God."*[13]

While you are shaped to serve others, even Jesus didn't meet the needs of *everyone* while on earth. You have to choose whom you can best help, based on your shape. You need to ask, "Who do I have a desire to help most?" Jesus said, *"I commissioned you to go out and to bear fruit, fruit that will last."*[14] Each of us bears different fruit.

What will be the *communication* of my life? This is the question of your *mission* to unbelievers. Your *mission statement* is a part of your life purpose statement. It should include your commitment to share your testimony and the Good News with others. You should also list the life lessons and godly passions you feel God has given you to share with the world. As you grow in Christ, God may give you a special target group of people to focus on reaching. Be sure to add this to your statement.

If you are a parent, part of your mission is to raise your children to know Christ, to help them understand his purposes for their lives, and to send them out on their mission in the world. You might include Joshua's statement in yours: *"As for me and my family, we will serve the LORD."*[15]

Of course, our lives must support and validate the message we communicate. Before most unbelievers accept the Bible as credible they want to know that *we* are credible. That is why the Bible says, *"Be sure that you live in a way that brings honor to the Good News of Christ."*[16]

> *Before most unbelievers accept the Bible as credible they want to know that we are credible.*

What will be the *community* of my life? This is the question of *fellowship.* How will you demonstrate your commitment to other believers and connection to the family of God? Where will you practice the "one another" commands with other Christians? To which church family will you be joined as a functioning member? The more you mature, the more you will love the Body of Christ and want to sacrifice for it. The Bible says, *"Christ loved the church and gave his life for it."*[17] You should include an expression of your love for God's church in your statement.

As you consider your answers to these questions, include any Scriptures that speak to you about each of these purposes. There are many in this book. It may take you weeks or months to craft your life purpose statement just the way you want it. Pray, think about it, talk with close friends, and reflect on Scripture. You may go through several rewrites before you get to your final form. Even then, you will probably make minor changes as time goes by and God gives you more insight into your own shape. If you would like to see some examples from other people, just email me (see appendix 2).

In addition to writing a detailed life purpose statement, it is also helpful to have a shorter statement or slogan that summarizes the five purposes for your life in a way that's *memorable* and *inspires* you. Then you can remind yourself daily. Solomon advised, *"It will be good to keep these things in mind so that you are ready to repeat them."*[18] Here are a few examples:

- "My life purpose is to worship Christ with my heart, serve him with my shape, fellowship with his family, grow like him in character, and fulfill his mission in the world so he receives glory."

- "My life purpose is to be a member of Christ's family, a model of his character, a minister of his grace, a messenger of his word, and a magnifier of his glory."

- "My life purpose is to love Christ, grow in Christ, share Christ, and serve Christ through his church, and to lead my family and others to do the same."

- "My life purpose is to make a great commitment to the Great Commandment and the Great Commission."

- "My goal is Christlikeness; my family is the church; my ministry is _____; my mission is _____; my motive is the glory of God."

You may wonder, "What about God's will for my job or marriage or where I'm supposed to live or go to school?" Honestly, these are secondary issues in your life, and there may be multiple possibilities that would *all* be in God's will for you. What matters most is that you fulfill God's eternal purposes regardless of where you live or work or whom you marry. Those decisions should support your purposes. The Bible says, *"Many are the plans in a man's heart, but it is the LORD's purpose that prevails."*[19] Focus on God's purposes for your life, not your plans, since that's what will last forever.

DAY 40: *Living with Purpose*

I once heard the suggestion that you develop your life purpose statement based on what you would like other people to say about you at your funeral. Imagine your perfect eulogy, then build your statement on that. Frankly, that's a bad plan. At the end of your life it isn't going to matter at all what other people say about you. The only thing that will matter is *what God says* about you. The Bible says, *"Our purpose is to please God, not people."*[20]

One day God will review your answers to these life questions. Did you put Jesus at the center of your life? Did you develop his character? Did you devote your life to serving others? Did you communicate his message and fulfill his mission? Did you love and participate in his family? These are the only issues that will count. As Paul said, *"Our goal is to measure up to God's plan for us."*[21]

God Wants to Use You

About thirty years ago, I noticed a little phrase in Acts 13:36 that forever altered the direction of my life. It was only seven words but, like the stamp of a searing hot branding iron, my life was permanently marked by these words: *"David served God's purpose in his generation."*[22] Now I understood why God called David *"a man after my own heart."*[23] David dedicated his life to fulfilling God's purposes on earth.

There is no greater epitaph than that statement! Imagine it chiseled on *your* tombstone: That *you* served God's purpose in your generation. My prayer is that people will be able to say that about me when I die. It is also my prayer that people will say it about you, too. That is why I wrote this book for you.

This phrase is the ultimate definition of a life well lived. You do the eternal and timeless (God's purpose) in a contemporary and timely way (in your generation). That is what the *purpose-driven life* is all about. Neither past nor future generations can serve God's purpose in this generation. Only we can. Like Esther, God created you *"for such a time as this."*[24]

God is still looking for people to use. The Bible says, *"The eyes of the LORD search the whole earth in order to strengthen those whose hearts are fully committed to him."*[25] Will you be a person God can use for his purposes? Will you serve God's purpose in *your* generation?

> You can start living on purpose today.

Paul lived a purpose-driven life. He said, *"I run straight to the goal with purpose in every step."*[26] His only reason for living was to fulfill the purposes God had for him. He said, *"For to me, to live is Christ and to die is gain."*[27] Paul was not afraid of either living or dying. Either way, he would fulfill God's purposes. He couldn't lose!

One day history will come to a close, but eternity will go on forever. William Carey said, "The future is as bright as the promises of God." When fulfilling your purposes seems tough, don't give in to discouragement. Remember your reward, which will last forever. The Bible says, *"For our light and momentary troubles are achieving for us an eternal glory that far outweighs them all."*[28]

Imagine what it is going to be like one day, with all of us standing before the throne of God presenting our lives in deep gratitude and praise to Christ. Together we will say, *"Worthy, Oh Master! Yes, our God! Take the glory! the honor! the power! You created it all; It was created because you wanted it!"*[29] We will praise him for his plan and live for his purposes forever!

DAY 40

Thinking about My Purpose

POINT TO PONDER: Living with purpose is the only way to *really* live.

VERSE TO REMEMBER: *"For David ... served the purpose of God in his own generation."* ACTS 13:36 (NASB)

QUESTION TO CONSIDER: When will I take the time to write down my answers to life's five great questions? When will I put my purpose on paper?

MESSAGE TO HEAR: *www.purposedriven.com/day40*

The Envy Trap

A heart at peace gives life to the body,
but envy rots the bones.

PROVERBS 14:30 (NIV)

"I observed all the work and
ambition motivated by envy.
What a waste!"

ECCLESIASTES 4:4 (MSG)

purposedriven.com/
day41

YOU CANNOT FULFILL GOD'S PURPOSE FOR YOUR LIFE IF you envy the lives of others.

While God created each of us for the same five eternal purposes, *the way you fulfill those purposes* — the time, place, plan, and style — *is absolutely unique.* God never creates clones, never copies what he's already made, and never duplicates a life plan. God only creates original masterpieces. As we discussed in Day 30 and 31, God distinctively *shaped* you for a life unlike any other. Only you can be you. Only you can live the life God designed you to live. But it's also true that you cannot live a life that God designed for someone else. To attempt to be what you weren't created to be always leads to frustration, fatigue, and failure.

As humans, we are naturally interested in the lives of others. It's part of our wiring. We are fascinated with how others look, act, talk, and live. We notice what they wear, what they do, and what they have. There is nothing wrong with this, especially if you can appreciate the limitless variety of people God chose to create instead of making all exactly alike. It only becomes a problem when we resent how God made others, reject how he made us, and start envying what they have. Envy is a trap. In today's world, where technology allows us to see how everyone else is living, envy may be the most common reason people miss God's unique plan for their lives. Envy is a global sin. I have witnessed it among every age group, economic group, and ethnic group and every place I have traveled to around the world.

"Why does *she* get to live in *that* house?" "Why did *he* get that job?" "Why can't I be *that* attractive, that rich, that smart, that famous?" Envy distracts your focus away from what God wants to do in your life and refocuses it on all that you don't have. Every time you envy, you take your eyes off what God created you to do. You get side-tracked from God's custom-made plan for you. Envy detours your life, and it always leads to a dead-end. Envy exacts a huge emotional cost without a payoff. You miss your purpose and lose your joy at the same time.

The worst part of envy is that it's an insult to God! Every time you wish you were someone else, have what they have, or do what they do, you are saying, "God, you made a huge mistake with me! You could have done better. You could have made me like *that* person, but you didn't!

"Why did you mess up with me? If I were God, I would have made me more like that person!"

Envy is actually a form of spiritual rebellion based on ignorance and arrogance. It assumes that I have a better plan for my life than my Creator does! Really? The Bible reminds us how presumptuous this is: *"Who are you, a mere human being, to argue with God? Should the thing that was created say to the one who created it, 'Why have you made me like this?'"*[1]

Envy is such a destructive attitude that God outlawed it in the Ten Commandments. The last commandment says, *"You shall not covet!"*[2] Coveting is another word for envy. God absolutely prohibits us from envying what others have, how they look, what they accomplish, and who they are because he knows the damage envy does.

Four Harmful Effects of Envy

Envy denies your uniqueness. Just as no two snowflakes are alike, no two human beings are alike. Even identical twins aren't completely identical! As I mentioned earlier in this book, you have a unique thumbprint, eye print, voiceprint, foot print, and heartbeat. No one has ever been, or ever will be, like you. The Bible says *"We are God's masterpiece."*[3] But when you envy others, you can't see the amazing value of your own unique shape. Envy blinds you to yourself.

When you stand before God someday, he's not going to say, "Why weren't you more like your parents or neighbor or some celebrity?" It is more likely that God will say, "Why weren't you more of what I intended *you* to be?"

Envy divides your attention. You can't give your full concentration to becoming what God wants you to be and envy others at the same time. Jesus said, *"Anyone who lets himself be distracted from the work I plan for him is not fit for the Kingdom of God."*[4] If you are always preoccupied watching what others do, or wishing you had what they have, you will miss seeing what God is doing in you.

Envy misuses your time and energy. Solomon noted that envy is the reason why most people overwork! *"I have also learned why people work so hard to succeed: it is because they envy the things their neighbors have. But it is useless. It is like chasing the wind."*[5] The result is, *"... he is always working, never satisfied with the wealth he has. For whom is he working so hard and denying himself any pleasure? This is useless, too—and a miserable way to live."*[6]

Envy is the enemy of contentment. Envy says, "I've

always got to have *more*: more money, more possessions, more power, more prestige, pleasure, and popularity." Many people work themselves to death trying to match or surpass those they envy. The Bible says that is foolish: *"Don't wear yourself out trying to get rich; be wise enough to control yourself."*[7]

Envy leads you to other sins. Envy is one of the so-called "Seven Deadly Sins." These are root sins that many other sins grow out of. The Bible says, *"Where you have envy and selfish ambition, there you find disorder and every evil practice."*[8] Note that envy causes "disorder." Whenever envy raises its head, it creates disharmony, competition, conflict, and confusion. Anytime a relationship seems "out of order," you should check for either envy or selfish ambition as a possible cause.

James 3:16 also says that envy is a source of "every evil practice." Can envy cause a person to lie? Yes. Cause a person to steal? Yes. Murder? Of course. Murders motivated by envy make the daily news, and the Bible is filled with examples of envy-based crimes: Cain killed his brother Abel out of envy. Joseph's brothers sold him into slavery out of envy. Saul tried to kill David several times out of envying his popularity. The Bible clearly states that the religious leaders had Jesus put to death because they deeply envied him![9]

> *Envy* infects *everything* inside *you and* affects *everything* around *you.*

Envy *infects* everything *inside* you and *affects* everything *around* you. So how do you eradicate envy from your life? The Bible gives us a pathway.

Steps to Eradicating Envy

Stop comparing yourself to others! This is the starting point. Comparing is the root of all envy. Unfortunately, from about the time we each began to walk, we also began to compare. Can you remember all those times you complained that your brother or sister got more ice cream than you? We grow up comparing everything: appearance, grades in school, athletic ability, and other talents. As adults we compare clothes, cars (or the lack of one), homes, how much we earn, and a thousand other things. But God says such comparisons are foolish. The Bible says, *"When they measure themselves by themselves and compare themselves to themselves, they show how foolish they are."*[10]

DAY 41:

The Envy Trap

Why is it foolish to compare yourself with others? Because you are *incomparable!* So is everyone else. God made each of us "one of a kind." Besides, comparing leads to one of two negative reactions: pride or envy. You can always find someone you think you're better than, and you will be prideful. On the other hand, you will always find people that you think are doing better than you, and you will become envious and discouraged. What matters is not who's better off, but are you doing what God created you to do? Are you making the most of what you've been given?

God doesn't judge you for talents you don't have or for opportunities you didn't get. He evaluates your faithfulness by how you lived and what you did with what you were given.

Remember this: God has not called you to be the best *in the world* at anything! He has called you to be *the best you can be,* given your background, experiences, opportunities, and abilities. So ... decide right now that you are going to break the habit of comparing yourself to others. It will take some time, but you can train yourself to refocus on something else whenever you are tempted to compare. Just tell yourself, "I'm not going to go down that path," and start thinking of something else.

Celebrate God's goodness to others. Instead of resenting others, rejoice with them! The Bible tells us to be happy when God blesses those around us. *"Rejoice with those who rejoice, and weep with those who weep."*[11] Now, the second part of that verse is easy to obey. It's not hard to offer comfort when people hurt or experience loss, even if they are a rival. It's much harder to celebrate others' success, especially if you aren't succeeding in that area.

How do you handle the promotions of coworkers? If you're single, how do you handle the weddings and baby showers of friends? What's your first gut reaction to news that someone you know has experienced a windfall of good fortune? When was the last time you thanked God for what he did for *somebody else?*

One reason we sometimes find it hard to "rejoice with those who rejoice" is because we fear that there is only a limited supply of God's goodness and grace, so if others get a bigger slice of cake, then I may not get as much. But God's grace is boundless. There is plenty to give to everyone and still have an infinite amount left over! Ephesians 3:8 speaks of *"the unending, boundless, fathomless, incalculable, and exhaustless riches of Christ."*[12]

The embarrassing truth about envy is that the people we envy most are usually those who are closest to us: Family members envy each other. Neighbors envy neighbors. Teammates envy teammates. Musicians envy musicians. Farmers envy other farmers, and preachers envy other preachers.

If you would like to increase the amount of happiness you experience in life, here is one of the secrets: learn to enjoy the successes and joys of others. If you are only happy when good things happen to you, then you will be unhappy for much of your life, since no one experiences only good things. But if you learn to enjoy other people's victories too, you will always have something to be happy about.

Be grateful for who you are and whatever you have. Everything you have is a gift from God. The Bible says, *"Isn't everything you have and everything you are sheer* *gifts from God? So what's the point of all this comparing and competing? You already have all you need.*"[13] When you find yourself beginning to envy someone else, instead of wishing you had their job or talent or boyfriend or children or whatever, remind yourself that "God has given me some unique gifts they don't have, and besides that, I don't know the downside of being them."

Envy is based on the popular myth that having more will make me more happy. But both the Bible and the testimony of millions show that is not true. Solomon, the wealthiest man who ever lived, had this to say about the desire to acquire more: "*Those who love money will never have enough. How meaningless to think that wealth brings true happiness! The more you have, the more people come to help you spend it. So what good is wealth — except perhaps to watch it slip through your fingers!*"[14]

> If you don't know how to be happy with what you have, you will never be happy with more.

Happiness is a choice. You are as happy as you choose to be. If you don't know how to be happy with what you have, you will never be happy with more.

Envy asks, "Why them? Why do they get what I don't have?" Gratitude asks, "Why me? Why do I get all that I have?" David modeled this kind of gratitude when he prayed, *"Who am I, O Sovereign LORD, and what is my family, that you have brought me this far?"*[15] Years later, his son would write, *"It is better to be satisfied with what you have than to be always wanting something else."*[16]

Let me be clear: Having ambitious dreams, a desire to be better, and faith goals are all good things, *if* they come from God, benefit others, and are pursued in faith for his glory. You should want to make the most of your life, create beauty, and help others. But envy poisons everything it touches and prevents God's blessing on your efforts. *Why* you do what you do matters the most to God.

Trust God when life seems unfair. One of the signs that envy has entered my heart is when I start feeling, "It's not fair! It's not fair that I don't have what they have!" Anytime we accuse God of unfairness, we are actually doubting his goodness. Envy is the fever, the symptom, but doubting God is the disease.

Anytime you envy others, you are doubting that God knows what's best for you. You question his love, his justice, and even his wisdom. Anytime I accuse God of being unfair, I am foolishly implying, "God, I'd make a better god than you, because if I was God, I'd be more fair than you are."

The next time you start to rant about God's unfairness to you, remind yourself of these facts:

1. Everything I have is an undeserved gift from God.
   I wouldn't even exist if it weren't for God's grace.
   The next breath of air I take is a gift of God.

2. I don't know what God knows and I can't see what God sees, so I should trust him.

3. Life on earth *is* unfair because of sin, not because of God. Our rebellion against God has broken everything on the planet. This isn't heaven, where everything works perfectly. Nothing works perfectly here.

4. God sent Jesus to save us from the judgment day when he will balance the books, right all wrongs, and administer justice.

5. It was not fair for Jesus to die in my place for my sins. But he did.

In Matthew 20, Jesus told the story of a landowner who hired several men at different times of the day to work in his field. At the end of the day, the landowner unexpectedly paid all of them the same amount for their work. Obviously this didn't bother the last-minute hires, but the men who had worked all day complained loudly that the landowner was being unfair. They said, *"These last workers put in only one easy hour, and you just made them equal to us, who slaved all day under a scorching sun!"*[17]

I love the landowner's reply: *"Friend, I didn't cheat you. I paid you exactly what we agreed on. Take your money now and go! What business is it of yours if I want to pay them the same that I paid you? Don't I have the right to do what I want with my own money? Why should you be jealous, if I want to be generous?"*[18] I love the landowner's frankness: *"Take what is yours and go your way!"*[19] In other words, "Stop resenting my grace to others, be grateful for what you've got, and move on with your life now!" That advice will keep you from getting caught in the envy trap and being detoured from the path God has laid out for you.

DAY 41

The Envy Trap

POINT TO PONDER: I cannot fulfill God's purpose for me if I am envying others.

VERSE TO REMEMBER: *"A heart at peace gives life to the body, but envy rots the bones."* PROVERBS 14:30 (NIV)

QUESTION TO CONSIDER: In what areas of my life do I most often compare myself with and envy others?

MESSAGE TO HEAR: *www.purposedriven.com/day41*

The People-Pleaser Trap

*"It is dangerous to be concerned
with what others think of you,
but if you trust the Lord, you are safe."*

PROVERBS 29:25 (TEV)

*"I'm not trying to be a people pleaser!
No, I am trying to please God.
If I were still trying to please people,
I would not be Christ's servant."*

GALATIANS 1:10 (NLT)

purposedriven.com/
day42

WHOSE APPROVAL ARE YOU LIVING FOR?

Because God wired us for relationships, each of us carries a desire to be loved, to be valued, and to be appreciated. We long to feel accepted and approved by others. This *longing for belonging*, the desire to "fit in" and feel connected to others, is the driving force behind many of the choices we make. In both small choices, like the clothes we wear or the style of our hair, and in major decisions such as where we live and work, what other people think has a greater influence on us than we are aware of.

There is nothing wrong with our desire to be accepted, appreciated, and approved by other people. In fact, without the affirmation of others we never fully blossom into our full potential. Our growth is stunted. We can only become what God created us to be *with the help of others.*

As I explained in earlier chapters, God shaped us to need each other. We all need someone to believe in us, to cheer us on, and to affirm our value and progress. If you are not in a small group and church family that do that, you need to find one that does. Encouragement is absolutely essential to your spiritual health and development.

But as with all of the healthy and good desires God puts in our hearts, the desire for approval can be misused, abused, and confused. It can become an obsession that dominates our life and a fear that destroys our soul. Like a flesh-eating bacteria, *the disease to please* can consume all our time, energy, and happiness. The American actor Bill Cosby once said, "I do not know the key to success, but I do know that the way to fail is to try to please everyone."

People-pleasing is the flip side of envy. Envy says, "I must be *like you* to be happy!" People-pleasing says, "I must be *liked BY you* to be happy." Both traps will prevent us from living a purpose driven life for God's glory.

The dark side of the desire for approval is the fear of disapproval. After talking with people living in over a hundred different countries, I have come to believe that fear of being criticized or rejected by others is the most common reason people get detoured from the path God planned for them. I believe it is Satan's favorite tool to distract you. Once you know what you were created to do, he whispers, "But what will other people think?" What if they dislike the changes you make? What if they criticize what you say or do? What if they make fun of what you believe?

This fear of rejection is often such an overwhelming force that we back away from what we know is the right thing to do. It is why peer-pressure is so effective in controlling what we do and say. Peer pressures — whether at school, at work, in our neighborhood — is rooted in the fear of disapproval or rejection. When schools or businesses or governments use "political correctness" to stifle our God-given freedom to speak and live our conscience, they prey on this fear.

> *The Bible warns us not to let the fear of disapproval keep us from doing what we know God wants us to do.*

Of course, the Bible repeatedly commands us to be considerate of other's feelings. In matters of behavior where God allows great freedom, "*We may know that these things make no difference, but we cannot just go ahead and do them to please ourselves. We must be considerate of the doubts and fears of those who think these things are wrong.*"[1] It is unloving to ignore how our choices affect others. Paul reminds us, *"For none of us lives to himself alone and none of us dies to himself alone."*[2]

But the Bible also warns us not to let the fear of disapproval keep us from doing what we know God wants us to do. Proverbs 29:25 says, *"It is dangerous to be concerned with what others think of you."*[3] Another translation of this verse says, *"Fearing people is a dangerous trap."*[4]

The people-pleaser trap is baited with a lie. The lie is this: "If I can just get everyone to like me, then I'll be happy!" But that lie will only make us miserable. We cannot live under the constant stress of worrying about what others think of us. The Bible says, *"Too much honey is bad for you, and so is trying to win too much praise."*[5]

The Dangers of People-Pleasing

Let me share five harmful effects of letting other people's approval or disapproval determine what you do with your life.

People-pleasing will cause me to miss God's will for my life. Remember, God didn't create you to fulfill the expectations of others! You were planned for *God's* pleasure. God loves watching you be you. God's Word is unmistakably clear: *"Our purpose is to please God, not people. He alone examines the motives of our hearts."*[6] Note that God inspects and tests "the motives of our hearts." God is always more interested in *why* you do what you do rather than where or how you do it. You can do all kinds of good work, but if your motive is just to impress others, gain recognition, or avoid their disapproval, you miss the point of doing good. Paul said, *"You may brag about yourself, but the only approval that counts is the Lord's approval."*[7] Besides, if you're always focused on what other people want you to be, you can't become who God wants you to be. The expectations of others will box you in, limit your potential, and keep you from fulfilling the dream God placed in your heart to fulfill.

People-pleasing prevents my faith from growing. The fear of disapproval keeps me from taking risks in faith. Without risk-taking, my faith cannot be stretched and developed. Many people never even take the first step to faith in Christ because they fear their friends or family will disapprove or look down on them. That is a fatal mistake. The Bible says, *"You try to get praise from each other, but you do not try to get the praise that comes from the only God. So how can you believe?"*[8] Never allow anyone else to stand in the way of your relationship to Christ.

People-pleasing is an emotional handicap. It immobilizes your potential. The Message paraphrase of Proverbs 29:25 says, *"The fear of human opinion disables."*[9] Of course, *any* fear will hinder your spiritual growth, but worrying about what others think is especially disabling. When the opinions of others loom large in your life, God's role in your life is reduced. But when God's approval matters most to you, the views of others lose their grip on your life.

DAY 42:

The People-Pleasing Trap

Whose opinion matters *most* to you? Whoever that person is, is your god. When you value anyone's opinions more than God's, you give that person power and authority that belongs only to God. That creates all kinds of insecurity within you. On the other hand, when God's approval matters the most to you, it sets you free from insecurity, because he will never reject you.

People-pleasing leads me to other sins. Scripture is filled with examples of people who did wrong because they gave in to peer pressure: Reuben agreed to sell Joseph, his younger brother, into slavery because the other brothers pressured him. Aaron built a golden idol to worship when the people pressured him. Samson broke his vow to God when his girlfriend pressured him. Peter denied knowing Jesus when he feared what others might say. And Pilate, even though he knew Jesus had done nothing worthy of punishment, allowed Jesus to be crucified because he feared the disapproval of the crowd.

If you're honest, you can recall times when you have caved in to peer pressure the way these people did. Right now would be a great time to pause and confess your cowardice to God. Pray the words of King Saul, who said, *"I've sinned! I've trampled roughshod over God's Word and your instructions. I cared more about pleasing the people. I let them tell me what to do.*"[10]

Let me be frank: If your friends are causing you to downplay your commitment to Jesus, deny your beliefs, compromise your values, or give up on the dream God gave you, you need to find new friends! The Bible warns, *"Do not follow the crowd in doing wrong."*[11] It also says, *"If bad companions tempt you, don't go along with them."*[12] Friends who discourage your walk with God are not true friends. *"Do not be misled: 'Bad company corrupts good character.' Come back to your senses as you ought, and stop sinning."*[13]

People-pleasing causes hypocrisy. The English word *hypocrite* comes from an ancient Greek word used to describe stage actors who played multiple roles in the same play by wearing different masks for different scenes. People-pleasers wear masks, and they switch roles, depending on the audience. They wear one mask at home, another mask at church, and an entirely different mask at work. They are hypocrites.

If you fall into the trap of people-pleasing, you hide your true self, afraid that you will be rejected. You will compromise your convictions in order to be socially acceptable and politically correct. Jesus was referring to this kind of hypocrisy when he told the Pharisees, *"You are always making yourselves look good, but God sees what is in your heart. The things that most people think are important are worthless as far as God is concerned."*[14]

People-pleasing silences my life-message. Until you break free from the fear of disapproval, God can't use you the way he wants to. You will be reluctant the share the powerful message God wants to communicate through you. Your testimony will be stifled, and you will miss out on life's greatest privilege: being used by God to change the eternal destiny of another human being.

For centuries Satan has used the fear of rejection to silence believers. Even during Jesus' ministry on earth, in the face of one miracle after another, John the disciple tells us, *"No one had the courage to speak favorably about him [Jesus] in public, for they were afraid of getting in trouble with the Jewish leaders."*[15] Later John wrote, *"Nevertheless, many even of the authorities did believe in him. But they would not admit it for fear of the Pharisees, in case they should be excommunicated. They were more concerned to have the approval of men than to have the approval of God."*[16] If you are always reluctant to share your faith with others, you have a problem with people-pleasing. For the sake of others and their eternal destinies, you need to ask God to help you break free from the trap.

How to Break Free from the People-Pleaser Trap

What is the cure for approval addiction? How do we break out of the people-pleaser prison? Well, since this prison is mental, not physical, the solution is to change the way we think. The Bible word for this mental shift is *repentance*. We break free from the pressure to conform by having our thoughts transformed by God: *"Do not conform any longer to the pattern of this world, but be transformed by the renewing of your mind."*[17] So what does God use to transform our minds? The answer is *truth!* Cultural lies conform us, but eternal truths transform us.

> What does God use to transform our minds? The answer *is* truth!

Jesus famously said, *"The truth will set you free."*[18] Here are six truths to remember the next time you are tempted to give in to peer pressure.

Remember that even God can't please everyone! At every sporting event, fans on each side pray for their team to win. In every election, voters in each party pray that their candidates will win. Someone is always disappointed! Some days farmers are praying for rain while children are praying for sunshine. Other days, some people pray for snow while others pray for no snow. The list could go on and on. Even God can't please everybody. Only a fool would try to do what even God can't do. It is impossible to make everyone happy at the same time.

Even if you could make everyone like you, it wouldn't be a good idea. It would only mean that you have no convictions you deeply believe in and no principles you are willing to stand for.

Jesus said, *"Woe to you when all men speak well of you!"*[19]

Remember that I don't need anyone's approval to be happy. Happiness is a choice. You are as happy as you choose to be. What other people think of you cannot rob your happiness unless you allow them to rob it.

It is a fact of life that on our broken planet filled with broken people, there will always be those who will demean how you look, dislike what you do, disapprove of what you believe, dispute what you say, and disrespect who you are. But they cannot control your emotions unless you let them. Disapproval doesn't have to devastate you.

As a pastor, I have talked to thousands of people who have invested much of their time and energy in trying to please an unappeasable person, most often a parent or other family member. When I ask if all their effort has paid off, the answer is always "no." I then share the truth that is tough to take at first but is ultimately liberating: "If you haven't gotten their approval by now, you're not going to get it. The problem isn't you. They are the problem. They are unappeasable."

But here is the good news, the truth that will set you free: You don't need their approval to be happy! So let it go! Stop wasting emotional energy on something that is never going to happen and something that isn't necessary for you to be happy. They are miserable, but you don't have to be. There is no sane reason for both of you to be miserable!

Instead of focusing on that unappeasable person, refocus on Jesus, who accepts you unconditionally. The more important Jesus becomes to you, the more free you will be from the disapproval of others. Jesus promised it. He said, *"If the Son sets you free, you will be free indeed."*[20]

Getting to know Jesus personally and intimately can free you from many things: the burden of guilt, the poison of resentment, the stress of overwork, the pressure of materialism, the habits of addiction, and the fear of death. But one of the greatest freedoms Jesus offers is being liberated from the fear of disapproval. That is a key to peace of mind.

If you are looking to *any* human being to either make you happy or keep you happy, you are going to be disappointed eventually. No human being has the capacity to meet all your needs and keep you constantly happy. Only God can meet all your needs. No person has the ability to give you *all* the security, approval, acceptance, and love you need, regardless of what they may promise you. If you expect them to meet needs that only God can meet, you are being unfair to them, you are setting them up for failure, and you are setting yourself up to become bitter.

On the other hand, God has repeatedly promised to never forsake you, never abandon you, and never reject you. The Bible says, *"Even if my father and mother abandon me, the Lord will hold me close."*[21] This is a truth you can count on, a solid rock on which you can build your identity, your security, and your happiness.

Remember that what seems so important now

is only temporary. In the light of eternity, what other people think of you right now isn't going to matter at all. In fact, it probably won't even matter in just a few years. Can you remember the people whose opinions mattered the most to you in high school? How important are those people's opinions of you today? It's probable that they don't matter at all today. What seemed *so* important then is now irrelevant. People-pleasing is always a short-term thinking activity. The benefits never last.

Everything around us today tells us that wealth, success, and fame will earn us the approval of others, but the truth is, none of these values will last. They are all temporary. God says, *"The world and everything in it that people desire is passing away; but those who do the will of God live forever."*[22]

Remember that I only have to please one person! If what I do pleases God, it is always the right thing to do, and I can stop worrying about everyone else's reactions. This dramatically simplifies life. It also keeps me from the sin of idolatry.

The first two of the Ten Commandments are (1) "You must not have any other god but me," and (2) "You shall not make for yourself an idol of any kind."[23] An idol is anything I put first in my life before God. If someone's approval matters more to me than God's, then that person has become an idol in my life. Jesus pointed out that it is impossible to have two gods in your life: *"No one can serve two masters."*[24] You have to decide. As Paul said,

"I'm not trying to win the approval of people but of God. If pleasing people were my goal, I would not be Christ's servant."[25]

This truth, that I have to please only God, is an important key to becoming resistant to being manipulated by disapproval from others. The reason Jesus was not swayed by criticism or the fear of rejection is that he lived for an audience of One. He said, *"I don't try to please myself, but I try to please the One who sent me."*[26] To be like him, we must do the same.

Remember that one day I will give an account of my life to God. There will be a day of reckoning. The Bible says, *"Yes, each of us will give a personal account to God."*[27] You're going to be asked for an explanation of everything you have said and everything you have done. That is a sobering thought! If you keep this fact in mind, it will change how you live each day and who you live it for. It will strengthen your courage to say no to things that you would rather not have to explain to God someday.

> *If what I do pleases God, I can stop worrying about everyone else's reactions.*

In those moments when you are tempted to water down the truth, compromise your beliefs, or deny your faith, remember that Jesus didn't deny you. He died publicly on the cross for you. *"So now Jesus and the ones he makes holy have the same Father. That is why Jesus is not ashamed to call them his brothers and sisters."*[28] Jesus is not ashamed of you. He claims you as part of his family if you have repented of your sins and trusted him for salvation.

But here's a question: Because of your fear of disapproval, have you been ashamed of Jesus? Remember, one day you will give an account to him, and Jesus has said, *"If anyone is ashamed of me and my words, the Son of Man will be ashamed of him when he comes in his glory."*[29] Will Jesus be ashamed of you one day because you were ashamed of him?

Remember that God shaped me to be me, not somebody else. This is the final truth to hold on to. Earlier in this book I mentioned that when you get to heaven, God isn't going to say, "Why weren't you more like your brother or your mother or father?" God isn't going to ask, "Were you popular? Did everyone like you, and did you fulfill all their expectations?" No. God is going to say, "Did you fulfill the purpose I created you for?"

In these last two chapters I have explained the two biggest hindrances to living the life God designed you to live: Wanting to be like others (envy), and wanting to be liked by others (people-pleasing.) These traps are subtle, but they distract and detour millions of people from the purposes they were created to fulfill. Having talked with thousands of people, I know that we all need continued support. That's why I have committed the rest of my life to help you on your journey. Please let me know when you have finished this book, and I will help you with your next steps. Email me at *Rick@purposedriven.com* or sign in at my personal website, *www.PastorRick.com*. I will pray for you, and I will send you additional free teaching materials on what to do next. My sincere prayer is that you will begin to experience all that God has in store for you. *"No mere man has ever seen, heard, or even imagined what wonderful things God has ready for those who love the Lord!"*[30]

DAY 42

Thinking about My Purpose

POINT TO PONDER: Happiness is my choice. I don't need anyone's approval to be happy.

VERSE TO REMEMBER: *"Even if my father and mother abandon me, the Lord will hold me close."*
PSALM 27:10 (NLT)

QUESTION TO CONSIDER: Whose opinion matters most to me? Whose approval am I living for?

MESSAGE TO HEAR: *www.purposedriven.com/day42*

Discussion Questions

In addition to the questions at the end of each chapter, you can use these discussion questions in your small group or Sunday school class setting.

What on Earth Am I Here For?

- What do you think are implications of the first sentence of this book, "It's not about you"?

- What do you feel most people's lives are driven by? What has been the driving force in your life?

- Up to this point, what image or metaphor has best described your life? A race, a circus, something else?

- If everyone understood that life on earth is really *preparation for eternity,* how would we act differently?

- What do people get attached to on earth that keeps them from living for God's purposes?

• What have you been attached to that could keep you from living for God's purposes?

You Were Planned for God's Pleasure

• How is *"living your whole life for God's pleasure"* different from the way most people understand "worship"?

• How is a friendship with God similar to any other friendship, and how is it different?

• Share something you learned from a time when God seemed distant.

• Which is easier for you — public or private worship? In which do you usually feel closer to God?

• When is it appropriate to express anger to God?

• What fears surface when you think of surrendering your complete life to Christ?

You Were Formed for God's Family

- How is *"being as committed to each other as we are to Jesus Christ"* different from the way most people understand "fellowship"?

- What are the barriers that keep us from loving and caring for other believers?

- What would make it easier for you to be able to share your needs, hurts, fears, and hopes with others?

- What are the most common excuses people give for not joining a church, and how would you answer them?

- What could our group do to protect and promote the unity in our church?

- Is there someone you need to restore a relationship with that we could pray for you about?

You Were Created to Become Like Christ

- How is *"becoming like Jesus Christ"* different from the way most people understand "discipleship"?

- What are some of the changes you have seen in your life since you became a believer? What have others noticed?

- A year from now, how would you like to be more Christlike? What can you do today to move toward that goal?

- Where in your spiritual growth are you having to be patient because there seems to be little progress?

- How has God used pain or trouble to help you grow?

- When are you most vulnerable to temptation? Which of the steps to defeating temptation could help you most?

You Were Shaped for Serving God: Ministry

- How is *"using your shape to serve others"* different from the way most people understand "ministry"?

- What do you *love* to do that you could use to serve others in the family of God?

- Think of a painful experience you have gone through that God could use to help others who are going through the same kind of situation.

- How does comparing ourselves with others keep us from fully developing our unique shape?

- How have you seen God's power demonstrated through you when you felt weak?

- How can we help every member of our small group or class find a place of ministry? What can our group do to serve our church family?

You Were Made for a Mission: Evangelism

- What are some typical fears and stereotypes that people have when they hear the word "evangelism"? What keeps *you* from sharing the Good News with others?

- What do you feel might be a part of the Life Message that God has given you to share with the world?

- Share the name of an unbelieving friend that everyone in your group can begin praying for.

- What can our group do together to help fulfill the Great Commission?

- How has reading through this book together refocused or redirected your life purpose? What have been some of the most helpful insights to you?

- Who does God bring to mind that you could share the life-changing message of this book with?

- What are we going to study next? (See appendix 2 for suggestions.)

Please email me your group's story. I'd like to continue to help you!

Rick@purposedriven.com

Resources

Resources for the Purpose Driven Life

At *www.saddlebackresources.com* or your local bookstore.

1. ***The Purpose Driven Life Journal.*** The companion to this book. (Zondervan)

2. ***The Purpose Driven Life Video Series.*** Six sessions taught by Rick Warren and used by churches and groups during *"What on Earth Am I Here For?"*—a 40-day spiritual growth emphasis. Study guides available.

3. ***What on Earth Am I Here For?*** The first seven chapters of *The Purpose Driven Life* in a pocket booklet format for you to share with friends as a testimony.

4. ***The Purpose Driven Church.*** The classic, groundbreaking book that has sold more than a million copies in 17 languages. This book explains

how your church can organize to help people live out God's five purposes. Available in book and DVD in 20 languages. Millions of people have studied this in churches and groups. (Zondervan and Purpose Driven Ministries)

5. ***40 Days in the Word.*** A six-week course based on the book *Rick Warren's Bible Study Methods.* This will teach you how to feed yourself from God's Word.

6. ***Foundations: 11 Core Truths to Build Your Life on.*** A popular Saddleback Church curriculum on the biblical foundation of purpose-driven living. This 24-week study for small groups or adult classes includes extensive teachings notes, teacher's guide, learner's guide, small-group discussion questions, and PowerPoint slides. (Zondervan)

7. ***Doing Life Together.*** A 30-week small group curriculum that focuses on applying God's purposes to your life. (Zondervan)

8. ***Planned for God's Pleasure.*** This beautiful book and inspirational music CD take the groundbreaking message of *The Purpose Driven Life* and apply it in a way that encourages everyone to find meaning and significance through reflection on God's purposes for one's life. (Zondervan)

Free Subscriptions

For a free subscription, email *Rick@purposedriven.com* or sign up at *www.purposedriven.com*

Daily Hope, my daily inspirational devotional for you.

Pastor Toolbox, a weekly email newsletter for all church leaders and those in ministry.

Why Use So Many Translations?

This book contains nearly a thousand quotations from Scripture. I have intentionally varied the Bible translations used for two important reasons. First, no matter how wonderful a translation is, it has limitations. The Bible was originally written using 11,280 Hebrew, Aramaic, and Greek words, but the typical English translation uses only around 6,000 words. Obviously, nuances and shades of meaning can be missed, so it is always helpful to compare translations.

Second, and even more important, is the fact that we often miss the full impact of familiar Bible verses, *not* because of poor translating, but simply because they have become so familiar! We *think* we know what a verse says because we have read it or heard it so many times. Then when we find it quoted in a book, we skim over it and miss the full meaning. Therefore I have deliberately used paraphrases in order to help you see God's truth in new, *fresh* ways. English-speaking people should thank God that we have so many different versions to use for devotional reading.

Also, since the verse divisions and number were not included in the Bible until 1560 A.D., I haven't always quoted the *entire* verse, but rather focused on the phrase that was appropriate. My model for this is Jesus and how he and the apostles quoted the Old Testament. They often just quoted a phrase to make a point.

AMP   *The Amplified Bible*
Grand Rapids: Zondervan (1965)

CEV   *Contemporary English Version*
New York: American Bible Society (1995)

GWT   *God's Word Translation*
Grand Rapids: World Publishing, Inc. (1995)

KJV   *King James Version*

LB   *Living Bible*
Wheaton, IL: Tyndale House Publishers (1979)

MSG   *The Message*
Colorado Springs: Navpress (1993)

NAB   *New American Bible*
Chicago: Catholic Press (1970)

NASB   *New American Standard Bible*
Anaheim, CA: Foundation Press (1973)

NCV   *New Century Version*
Dallas: Word Bibles (1991)

NIV   *New International Version*
Colorado Springs: Biblica, Inc. (1978, 1984)

NJB   *New Jerusalem Bible*
Garden City, NY: Doubleday (1985)

NLT   *New Living Translation*
Wheaton, IL: Tyndale House Publishers (1996)

NRSV   *New Revised Standard Version*
Grand Rapids: Zondervan (1990)

PH   *New Testament in Modern English* by J. B. Phillips
New York: Macmillan (1958)

TEV   *Today's English Version*
New York: American Bible Society (1992)
(Also called *Good News Translation*)

Notes

A Journey with Purpose

1. Romans 12:2 (NLT).
2. 2 Timothy 2:7 (NIV).

DAY 1: It All Starts with God

1. Job 12:10 (TEV).
2. Romans 8:6 (MSG).
3. Matthew 16:25 (MSG).
4. Hugh S. Moorhead, comp., *The Meaning of Life According to Our Century's Greatest Writers and Thinkers* (Chicago: Chicago Review Press, 1988).
5. 1 Corinthians 2:7 (MSG).
6. Ephesians 1:11 (MSG).
7. David Friend, ed., *The Meaning of Life* (Boston: Little, Brown, 1991), 194.

DAY 2: You Are Not an Accident

1. Psalm 138:8a (NIV).
2. Psalm 139:15 (MSG).
3. Psalm 139:16 (LB).

4. Acts 17:26 (NIV).
5. Ephesians 1:4a (MSG).
6. James 1:18 (NCV).
7. Michael Denton, *Nature's Destiny: How the Laws of Biology Reveal Purpose in the Universe* (New York: Free Press, 1998), 389.
8. Isaiah 45:18 (GWT).
9. 1 John 4:8.
10. Isaiah 46:3 – 4 (NCV).
11. Russell Kelfer. Used by permission.

DAY 3: What Drives Your Life?

1. Genesis 4:12 (NIV).
2. Psalm 32:1 (LB).
3. Job 5:2 (TEV).
4. 1 John 4:18 (MSG).
5. Matthew 6:24 (NLT).
6. Isaiah 49:4 (NIV).
7. Job 7:6 (LB).

8. Job 7:16 (TEV).

9. Jeremiah 29:11 (NCV).

10. Ephesians 3:20 (LB).

11. Proverbs 13:7 (MSG).

12. Isaiah 26:3 (TEV).

13. Ephesians 5:17 (MSG).

14. Philippians 3:13 (NLT).

15. Philippians 3:15 (MSG).

16. Romans 14:10b, 12 (NLT).

17. John 14:6 (NIV).

DAY 4: Made to Last Forever

1. Ecclesiastes 3:11 (NLT).

2. 2 Corinthians 5:1 (TEV).

3. Philippians 3:7 (NLT).

4. 1 Corinthians 2:9 (LB).

5. Matthew 25:34 (NIV).

6. C. S. Lewis, *The Last Battle* (New York: Collier Books, 1970), 184.

7. Psalm 33:11 (TEV).

8. Ecclesiastes 7:2 (CEV).

9. Hebrews 13:14 (LB).

10. 2 Corinthians 5:6 (LB).

DAY 5: Seeing Life from God's View

1. Romans 12:2 (TEV).

2. 2 Chronicles 32:31 (NLT).

3. 1 Corinthians 10:13 (TEV).

4. James 1:12 (GWT).

5. Psalm 24:1 (TEV).

6. Genesis 1:28 (TEV).

7. 1 Corinthians 4:7b (NLT).

8. 1 Corinthians 4:2 (NCV).

9. Matthew 25:14 – 29.

10. Matthew 25:21 (NIV).

11. Luke 16:11 (NLT).

12. Luke 12:48b (NIV).

DAY 6: Life Is a Temporary Assignment

1. Job 8:9 (NLT).

2. Psalm 39:4 (LB).

3. Psalm 119:19 (NLT).

4. 1 Peter 1:17 (GWT).

5. Philippians 3:19 – 20 (NLT).

6. James 4:4 (MSG).

7. 2 Corinthians 5:20 (NLT).

8. 1 Peter 2:11 (MSG).

9. 1 Corinthians 7:31 (NLT).

10. 2 Corinthians 4:18b (MSG).

11. John 16:33; 16:20; 15:18 – 19.

12. 2 Corinthians 4:18 (NIV).

13. 1 Peter 2:11 (GWT).

14. Hebrews 11:13, 16 (NCV).

DAY 7: The Reason for Everything

1. Psalm 19:1 (NIV).

2. Genesis 3:8; Exodus 33:18 – 23; 40:33 – 38; 1 Kings 7:51; 8:10 – 13; John 1:14; Ephesians 2:21 – 22; 2 Corinthians 4:6 – 7.

3. Exodus 24:17; 40:34; Psalm 29:3; Isaiah 6:3 – 4; 60:1; Luke 2:9.

4. Revelation 21:23 (NIV).

5. Hebrews 1:3 (NIV); also 2 Corinthians 4:6b (LB).

6. John 1:14 (GWT).

7. 1 Chronicles 16:24; Psalm 29:1; 66:2; 96:7; 2 Corinthians 3:18.

8. Revelation 4:11a (NLT).

9. Romans 3:23 (NIV).

10. Isaiah 43:7 (TEV).

11. John 17:4 (NLT).

12. Romans 6:13b (NLT).

13. 1 John 3:14 (CEV).

14. Romans 15:7 (NLT).

15. John 13:34 – 35 (NIV).

16. 2 Corinthians 3:18 (NLT).

17. Philippians 1:11 (NLT); see also John 15:8 (GWT).

18. 1 Peter 4:10 – 11 (NLT); see also 2 Corinthians 8:19b (NCV).

19. 2 Corinthians 4:15 (NLT).

20. John 12:27 – 28 (NASB).

21. John 12:25 (MSG).

22. 2 Peter 1:3 (MSG).

23. John 1:12 (NIV).

24. John 3:36a (MSG).

DAY 8: Planned for God's Pleasure

1. Ephesians 1:5 (TEV).

2. Genesis 6:6; Exodus 20:5; Deuteronomy 32:36; Judges 2:20; 1 Kings 10:9; 1 Chronicles 16:27; Psalms 2:4; 5:5; 18:19; 35:27; 37:23; 103:13; 104:31; Ezekiel 5:13; 1 John 4:16.

3. Psalm 147:11 (CEV).

4. John 4:23.

5. Isaiah 29:13 (NIV).

6. Psalm 105:4 (TEV).

7. Psalm 113:3 (LB).

8. Psalms 119:147; 5:3; 63:6; 119:62.

9. Psalm 34:1 (GWT).

10. 1 Corinthians 10:31 (NIV).

11. Colossians 3:23 (NIV).

12. Romans 12:1 (MSG).

DAY 9: What Makes God Smile?

1. Ephesians 5:10 (MSG).

2. Genesis 6:8 (LB).

3. Genesis 6:9b (NLT).

4. Hosea 6:6 (LB).

5. Matthew 22:37 – 38 (NIV).

6. Hebrews 11:7 (MSG).

7. Genesis 2:5 – 6.

8. Psalm 147:11 (TEV).

9. Hebrews 11:6 (NIV).

10. Genesis 6:22 (NLT); see also Hebrews 11:7b (NCV).

11. Psalm 100:2 (LB).

12. Psalm 119:33 (LB).

13. James 2:24 (CEV).

14. John 14:15 (TEV).

15. Genesis 8:20 (NIV).

16. Hebrews 13:15 (KJV).

17. Psalm 116:17 (KJV).

18. Psalm 69:30 – 31 (NIV).

19. Psalm 68:3 (TEV).

20. Genesis 9:1, 3 (NIV).

21. Psalm 37:23 (NLT).

22. Psalm 33:15 (MSG).

23. Isaiah 45:9 (CEV).

24. 1 Timothy 6:17 (TEV).

25. Psalm 103:14 (GWT).

26. 2 Corinthians 5:9 (TEV).

27. Psalm 14:2 (LB).

DAY 10: The Heart of Worship

1. 1 John 4:9 – 10, 19.

2. Romans 12:1 (TEV).

3. Psalm 145:9.

4. Psalm 139:3.

5. Matthew 10:30.

6. 1 Timothy 6:17b.

7. Jeremiah 29:11.

8. Psalm 86:5.

9. Psalm 145:8.

10. Romans 5:8 (NRSV).

11. Genesis 3:5.

12. Luke 5:5 (NIV).

13. Psalm 37:7a (GWT).

14. Matthew 6:24.

15. Matthew 6:21.

16. Mark 14:36 (NLT).

17. Job 22:21 (NLT).

18. Romans 6:17 (MSG).

19. Joshua 5:13 – 15.

20. Luke 1:38 (NLT).

21. James 4:7a (NCV).

22. Romans 12:1 (KJV).

23. Romans 12:1 (CEV).

24. 2 Corinthians 5:9 (NIV).

25. Philippians 4:13 (AMP).

26. 1 Corinthians 15:31.

27. Luke 9:23 (NCV).

DAY 11: Becoming Best Friends with God

1. Psalms 95:6; 136:3; John 13:13; Jude 1:4; 1 John 3:1; Isaiah 33:22; 47:4; Psalm 89:26.

2. Exodus 33:11, 17; 2 Chronicles 20:7; Isaiah 41:8; James 2:23; Acts 13:22; Genesis 6:8; 5:22 (nlt); Job 29:4.

3. Romans 5:11 (NLT).

4. 2 Corinthians 5:18a (TEV).

5. 1 John 1:3.

6. 1 Corinthians 1:9.

7. 2 Corinthians 13:14.

8. John 15:15 (NIV).

9. John 3:29.

10. Exodus 34:14 (NLT).

11. Acts 17:26 – 27 (MSG).

12. Jeremiah 9:24 (TEV).

13. See "How to Have a Meaningful Quiet Time" in *Personal Bible Study Methods*, Rick Warren, 1981. Available from *www. pastors.com*.

14. 1 Thessalonians 5:17.

15. Ephesians 4:6b (NCV).

16. Brother Lawrence, *The Practice of the Presence of God* (Grand Rapids: Revell/Spire Books, 1967), Eighth Letter.

17. 1 Thessalonians 5:17 (MSG).

18. Psalms 23:4; 143:5; 145:5; Joshua 1:8; Psalm 1:2.

19. 1 Samuel 3:21.

20. Job 23:12 (NIV).

21. Psalm 119:97 (NIV).

22. Psalm 77:12 (NLT).

23. Genesis 18:17; Daniel 2:19; 1 Corinthians 2:7 – 10.

24. Psalm 25:14 (LB).

DAY 12: Developing Your Friendship with God

1. Matthew 11:19.

2. Job 42:7 – 8 (MSG).

3. Exodus 33:1 – 17.

4. Exodus 33:12 – 17 (MSG).

5. Consider Job (Job 7:17 – 21), Asaph (Psalm 83:13 – 18), Jeremiah (Jeremiah 20:7), Naomi (Ruth 1:20).

6. Psalm 142:2 – 3a (NLT).

7. John 15:14 (NIV).

8. John 15:9 – 11 (NLT).

9. 1 Samuel 15:22 (NCV).

10. Matthew 3:17 (NLT).

11. 2 Corinthians 11:2 (MSG).

12. Psalm 69:9 (NLT).

13. Psalm 27:4 (LB).

14. Psalm 63:3 (CEV).

15. Genesis 32:26 (NIV).

16. Philippians 3:10 (AMP).

17. Jeremiah 29:13 (MSG).

18. 1 Timothy 6:21a (LB).

DAY 13: Worship That Pleases God

1. Hebrews 12:28 (TEV).

2. John 4:23 (NIV).

3. 1 Samuel 16:7b (NIV).

4. Hebrews 13:15; Psalm 7:17;

Ezra 3:11; Psalms 149:3; 150:3; Nehemiah 8:6.

5. Gary Thomas, *Sacred Pathways* (Grand Rapids: Zondervan, 2000).

6. John 4:23 (MSG).

7. Matthew 6:7 (KJV).

8. See 11-week tape series on the names of God, *"How God Meets Your Deepest Needs,"* by Saddleback Pastors (1999), *www.pastors.com*.

9. 1 Corinthians 14:40 (NIV).

10. 1 Corinthians 14:16 – 17 (CEV).

11. Romans 12:1 (NIV).

12. Psalm 50:14 (TEV); Hebrews 13:15 (CEV); Psalms 51:17; 54:6 (NIV); Philippians 4:18 (NIV); Psalm 141:2 (GWT); Hebrews 13:16; Mark 12:33 (MSG); Romans 12:1 (NIV).

13. 2 Samuel 24:24 (TEV).

14. Matt Redman, "Heart of Worship" (Kingsway's Thankyou Music, 1997).

DAY 14: When God Seems Distant

1. Philip Yancey, *Reaching for the Invisible God* (Grand Rapids: Zondervan, 2000), 242.

2. 1 Samuel 13:14; Acts 13:22.

3. Psalm 10:1 (LB).

4. Psalm 22:1 (NLT).

5. Psalm 43:2 (TEV); see also Psalms 44:23 (TEV); 74:11 (TEV); 88:14 (MSG); 89:49 (LB).

6. Deuteronomy 31:8; Psalm 37:28; John 14:16 – 18; Hebrews 13:5.

7. Isaiah 45:15.

8. Floyd McClung, *Finding Friendship with God* (Ann Arbor, MI: Vine Books, 1992), 186.

9. Job 23:8 – 10 (NLT).

10. Psalm 51; Ephesians 4:29 – 30; 1 Thessalonians 5:19; Jeremiah 2:32; 1 Corinthians 8:12; James 4:4 (NLT).

11. Job 1:20 – 21 (NIV).

12. Job 7:11 (TEV).

13. Job 29:4 (NIV).

14. Psalm 116:10 (NCV).

15. Job 10:12.

16. Job 42:2; 37:5, 23.

17. Job 23:10; 31:4.

18. Job 34:13.

19. Job 23:14.

20. Job 19:25.

21. Job 23:12 (NIV).

22. Job 13:15 (CEV).

23. 2 Corinthians 5:21 (TEV).

DAY 15: Formed for God's Family

1. Ephesians 1:5 (NLT).
2. James 1:18 (LB).
3. 1 Peter 1:3b (LB); see also Romans 8:15 – 16 (TEV).
4. Mark 8:34; Acts 2:21; Romans 10:13; 2 Peter 3:9.
5. Galatians 3:26 (NLT).
6. Ephesians 3:14 – 15 (LB).
7. 1 John 3:1; Romans 8:29; Galatians 4:6 – 7; Romans 5:2; 1 Corinthians 3:23; Ephesians 3:12; 1 Peter 1:3 – 5; Romans 8:17.
8. Galatians 4:7b (NLT).
9. Philippians 4:19 (NIV).
10. Ephesians 1:7; Romans 2:4; 9:23; 11:33; Ephesians 3:16; 2:4.
11. Ephesians 1:18b (NLT).
12. 1 Thessalonians 5:10; 4:17.
13. 1 John 3:2; 2 Corinthians 3:18.
14. Revelation 21:4.
15. Mark 9:41; 10:30; 1 Corinthians 3:8; Hebrews 10:35; Matthew 25:21, 23.
16. Romans 8:17; Colossians 3:4; 2 Thessalonians 2:14; 2 Timothy 2:12; 1 Peter 5:1.
17. 1 Peter 1:4 (NLT).
18. Colossians 3:23 – 24a (NIV).
19. Matthew 28:19 (NLT).
20. 1 Corinthians 12:13 (NLT).
21. Acts 2:41; 8:12 – 13, 35 – 38.
22. Hebrews 2:11 (CEV).
23. Matthew 12:49 – 50 (NLT).

DAY 16: What Matters Most

1. Galatians 5:14 (LB).
2. 1 Peter 2:17b (CEV).
3. Galatians 6:10 (NCV).
4. John 13:35 (LB).
5. 1 Corinthians 14:1a (LB).
6. 1 Corinthians 13:3 (MSG).
7. Matthew 22:37 – 40 (NLT).
8. 1 Corinthians 13:13 (NCV).
9. Matthew 25:34 – 46.
10. Matthew 25:40 (NRSV).
11. Galatians 5:6 (NIV).
12. 1 John 3:18 (TEV).
13. Ephesians 5:2 (LB).
14. John 3:16a.
15. Galatians 6:10 (NLT).
16. Ephesians 5:16 (NCV).
17. Proverbs 3:27 (TEV).

DAY 17: A Place to Belong

1. Genesis 2:18.
2. 1 Corinthians 12:12; Ephesians 2:21, 22; 3:6; 4:16; Colossians 2:19; 1 Thessalonians 4:17.

3. Romans 12:5 (NIV).

4. Romans 12:4 – 5;
1 Corinthians 6:15; 12:12 – 27.

5. Romans 12:4 – 5 (MSG).

6. Ephesians 4:16.

7. Matthew 16:18 (NLT).

8. Ephesians 5:25 (GWT).

9. 2 Corinthians 11:2;
Ephesians 5:27;
Revelation 19:7.

10. 1 Peter 2:17b (MSG).

11. 1 Corinthians 5:1 – 13;
Galatians 6:1 – 5.

12. Ephesians 2:19b (LB).

13. John 13:35 (NLT).

14. Galatians 3:28 (MSG);
see also John 17:21.

15. 1 Corinthians 12:27 (NCV).

16. 1 Corinthians 12:26 (NCV).

17. Ephesians 4:16; Romans
12:4 – 5; Colossians 2:19,
1 Corinthians 12:25.

18. 1 John 3:16 (NIV).

19. Ephesians 4:16b (NLT).

20. 1 Corinthians 12:7 (NLT).

21. Ephesians 2:10 (MSG).

22. 1 Corinthians 10:12;
Jeremiah 17:9;
1 Timothy 1:19.

23. Hebrews 3:13 (NIV).

24. James 5:19 (MSG).

25. Acts 20:28 – 29; 1 Peter 5:1 – 4;
Hebrews 13:7, 17.

26. Hebrews 13:17 (NLT).

27. Acts 2:42 (MSG).

28. 2 Corinthians 8:5 (TEV).

DAY 18: Experiencing Life Together

1. Matthew 18:20 (NASB).

2. 1 John 1:7 – 8 (NCV).

3. James 5:16a (MSG).

4. 1 Corinthians 12:25 (MSG).

5. Romans 1:12 (NCV).

6. Romans 12:10 (NRSV).

7. Romans 14:19 (NIV).

8. Colossians 3:12 (GWT).

9. Philippians 3:10;
Hebrews 10:33 – 34.

10. Galatians 6:2 (NLT).

11. Job 6:14 (NIV).

12. 2 Corinthians 2:7 (CEV).

13. Colossians 3:13 (LB).

14. Colossians 3:13 (NLT).

DAY 19: Cultivating Community

1. Ephesians 4:3 (NCV).

2. 1 Timothy 3:14 – 15 (NCV).

3. Ephesians 4:15.

4. Proverbs 24:26 (TEV).

5. Galatians 6:1 – 2 (NCV).

6. Ephesians 4:25 (MSG).

7. Proverbs 28:23 (NLT).

8. Ecclesiastes 8:6 (TEV).

9. 1 Timothy 5:1–2 (GWT).

10. 1 Corinthians 5:3–12 (MSG).

11. 1 Peter 5:5b (NIV).

12. 1 Peter 5:5c (NIV).

13. Romans 12:16 (NLT).

14. Philippians 2:3–4 (NCV).

15. Romans 15:1–2 (LB).

16. Titus 3:2 (MSG).

17. Romans 12:10 (GWT).

18. Proverbs 16:28 (TEV).

19. Titus 3:10 (NIV).

20. Hebrews 10:25 (TEV).

21. Acts 2:46 (LB).

DAY 20: Restoring Broken Fellowship

1. 2 Corinthians 5:18 (GWT).

2. Philippians 2:1–2 (MSG).

3. Romans 15:5 (MSG).

4. John 13:35.

5. 1 Corinthians 6:5 (TEV).

6. 1 Corinthians 1:10 (MSG).

7. Matthew 5:9 (NLT).

8. 2 Corinthians 5:18 (MSG).

9. James 4:1–2 (NIV).

10. Matthew 5:23–24 (MSG).

11. 1 Peter 3:7; Proverbs 28:9.

12. Job 5:2 (TEV); 18:4 (TEV).

13. Philippians 2:4 (TEV).

14. Psalm 73:21–22 (TEV).

15. Proverbs 19:11 (NIV).

16. Romans 15:2 (LB).

17. Romans 15:3 (NJB).

18. Matthew 7:5 (NLT).

19. 1 John 1:8 (MSG).

20. Proverbs 15:1 (MSG).

21. Proverbs 16:21 (TEV).

22. Ephesians 4:29 (TEV).

23. Romans 12:18 (TEV).

24. Romans 12:10; Philippians 2:3.

25. Matthew 5:9 (MSG).

26. 1 Peter 3:11 (NLT).

27. Matthew 5:9.

DAY 21: Protecting Your Church

1. John 17:20–23.

2. Ephesians 4:3 (NIV).

3. Romans 14:19 (PH).

4. Romans 10:12; 12:4–5; 1 Corinthians 1:10; 8:6; 12:13; Ephesians 4:4–5; 5:5; Philippians 2:2.

5. Romans 14:1; 2 Timothy 2:23.

6. 1 Corinthians 1:10 (NLT).

7. Ephesians 4:2 (NLT).

8. Dietrich Bonhoffer, *Life Together* (New York: HarperCollins, 1954).

9. Romans 14:13; James 4:11; Ephesians 4:29; Matthew 5:9; James 5:9.

10. Romans 14:4 (CEV).

11. Romans 14:10 (PH).

12. Revelation 12:10.

13. Romans 14:19 (MSG).

14. Proverbs. 17:4; 16:28; 26:20; 25:9; 20:19.

15. Proverbs 17:4 (CEV).

16. Jude 1:19 (MSG).

17. Galatians 5:15 (AMP).

18. Proverbs 20:19 (NRSV).

19. Proverbs 26:20 (LB).

20. Matthew 18:15 – 17a (MSG).

21. Matthew 18:17; 1 Corinthians 5:5.

22. Hebrews 13:17 (MSG).

23. Hebrews 13:17 (NIV).

24. 2 Timothy 2:14, 23 – 26; Philippians 4:2; Titus 2:15 – 3:2, 10 – 11.

25. 1 Thessalonians 5:12 – 13a (MSG).

26. 1 Corinthians 10:24 (NLT).

DAY 22: Created to Become Like Christ

1. Genesis 1:26 (NCV).

2. Genesis 9:6; Psalm 139:13 – 16; James 3:9.

3. 2 Corinthians 4:4 (NLT); Colossians 1:15 (NLT); Hebrews 1:3 (NIV).

4. Ephesians 4:24 (GWT).

5. Genesis 3:5 (KJV).

6. Ephesians 4:22 – 24 (MSG).

7. Matthew 5:1 – 12.

8. Galatians 5:22 – 23.

9. 1 Corinthians 13.

10. 2 Peter 1:5 – 8.

11. John 10:10.

12. 2 Corinthians 3:18b (NLT).

13. Philippians 2:13 (NLT).

14. 1 Kings 19:12 (NIV).

15. Colossians 1:27 (NLT).

16. Joshua 3:13 – 17.

17. Luke 13:24; Romans 14:19; Ephesians 4:3 (all NIV); 2 Timothy 2:15 (NCV); Hebrews 4:11; 12:14; 2 Peter 1:5; 2 Peter 3:14 (all NIV).

18. Ephesians 4:22 (MSG).

19. Ephesians 4:23 (CEV).

20. Romans 12:2.

21. Ephesians 4:24 (NIV).

22. Ephesians 4:13 (CEV).

23. 1 John 3:2 (NLT).

24. 1 Corinthians 10:31; 16:14; Colossians 3:17, 23.

25. Romans 12:2 (MSG).

DAY 23: How We Grow

1. Matthew 9:9 (NLT).

2. 2 Peter 3:11 (NLT).

3. Philippians 2:12 – 13 (NIV).

4. Proverbs 4:23 (TEV).

5. Romans 12:2b (NLT).

6. Ephesians 4:23 (NLT).

7. Philippians 2:5 (CEV).

8. 1 Corinthians 14:20 (NIV).

9. Romans 8:5 (NCV).

10. 1 Corinthians 13:11 (NIV).

11. Romans 15:2 – 3a (CEV).

12. 1 Corinthians 2:12a (CEV).

DAY 24: Transformed by Truth

1. John 17:17 (NIV).

2. 2 Timothy 3:17 (MSG).

3. Hebrew 4:12; Acts 7:38; 1 Peter 1:23.

4. John 6:63 (NASB).

5. James 1:18 (NCV).

6. Job 23:12 (NIV).

7. 1 Peter 2:2; Matthew 4:4, 1 Corinthians 3:2; Psalm 119:103.

8. 1 Peter 2:2 (NIV).

9. John 8:31 (NASB, 1978 edition).

10. Proverbs 30:5 (NIV).

11. 2 Timothy 3:16 (CEV).

12. Acts 24:14 (NIV).

13. Luke 8:18 (NIV).

14. James 1:21b (AMP).

15. Deuteronomy 17:19a (NCV).

16. Rick Warren, *Twelve Personal Bible Study Methods.* This book has been translated into six languages. Available from *www .pastors.com.*

17. James 1:25 (NCV).

18. Psalms 119:11; 119:105; 119:49 – 50; Jeremiah 15:16; Proverbs 22:18; 1 Peter 3:15.

19. Colossians 3:16a (LB).

20. 2 Corinthians 3:18 (NIV).

21. Acts 13:22 (NIV).

22. Psalm 119:97 (NCV).

23. John 15:7; Joshua 1:8; Psalm 1:2 – 3.

24. James 1:22 (KJV).

25. Matthew 7:24 (NIV).

26. John 13:17 (NIV).

DAY 25: Transformed by Trouble

1. John 16:33.
2. 1 Peter 4:12 (LB).
3. Psalm 34:18 (NLT).
4. Joni Eareckson Tada, *31 Days Toward Intimacy with God* (Portland, OR: Multnomah Books, 2005.
5. Genesis 39:20 – 22.
6. Daniel 6:16 – 23.
7. Jeremiah 38:6.
8. 2 Corinthians 11:25.
9. Daniel 3:1 – 26.
10. 2 Corinthians 1:9 (LB).
11. Psalm 139:16.
12. Romans 8:28 – 29 (NLT).
13. Matthew 6:10 (KJV).
14. Matthew 1:1 – 16.
15. Romans 5:3 – 4 (NCV).
16. 1 Peter 1:7a (NCV).
17. James 1:3 (MSG).
18. Hebrews 5:8 – 9.
19. Romans 8:17 (MSG).
20. Jeremiah 29:11 (NIV).
21. Genesis 50:20 (NIV).
22. Isaiah 38:17 (CEV).
23. Hebrews 12:10b (MSG).
24. Hebrews 12:2a (LB).
25. Corrie ten Boom, *The Hiding Place* (Grand Rapids: Chosen Books, 1971).
26. Hebrews 11:26 (NIV).
27. 2 Corinthians 4:17 (NLT).
28. Romans 8:17 – 18 (NLT).
29. 1 Thessalonians 5:18 (NIV).
30. Philippians 4:4 (NIV).
31. Luke 6:23 (NCV).
32. James 1:3 – 4 (PH).
33. Hebrews 10:36 (MSG).

DAY 26: Growing through Temptation

1. Galatians 5:22 – 23 (NLT).
2. 2 Corinthians 2:11 (NLT).
3. Mark 7:21 – 23 (NLT).
4. James 4:1 (LB).
5. Hebrews 3:12 (CEV).
6. John 8:44.
7. James 1:14 – 16 (TEV).
8. 1 Corinthians 10:13 (NLT).
9. Hebrews 4:15.
10. 1 Peter 5:8 (MSG).
11. Matthew 26:41; Ephesians 6:10 – 18; 1 Thessalonians 5:6, 8; 1 Peter 1:13; 4:7; 5:8.
12. Ephesians 4:27 (TEV).
13. Proverbs 4:26 – 27 (TEV).
14. Proverbs 16:17 (CEV).
15. Psalm 50:15 (GWT).

16. Hebrews 4:15 (NLT).

17. Hebrews 4:16 (TEV).

18. James 1:12 (NCV).

DAY 27: **Defeating Temptation**

1. James 4:7.

2. Job 31:1 (NLT).

3. Psalm 119:37a (TEV).

4. Romans 12:21.

5. Hebrews 3:1 (NIV).

6. 2 Timothy 2:8 (GWT).

7. Philippians 4:8 (TEV).

8. Proverbs 4:23 (TEV).

9. 2 Corinthians 10:5 (NCV).

10. Ecclesiastes 4:9 – 10 (CEV).

11. James 5:16 (NIV).

12. 1 Corinthians 10:13.

13. Romans 3:23.

14. James 4:6 – 7a (NLT).

15. Ephesians 6:17 (NLT).

16. Jeremiah 17:9 (NIV).

17. Proverbs 14:16 (TEV).

18. 1 Corinthians 10:12 (MSG).

DAY 28: **It Takes Time**

1. Philippians 1:6 (NIV).

2. Ephesians 4:13 (PH).

3. Colossians 3:10a (NCV).

4. 2 Corinthians 3:18b (MSG).

5. Deuteronomy 7:22.

6. Romans 13:12; Ephesians 4:22 – 25; Colossians 3:7 – 10, 14.

7. 1 Timothy 4:15 (GWT).

8. Ecclesiastes 3:1 (CEV).

9. Psalm 102:18; 2 Timothy 3:14.

10. Hebrews 2:1 (MSG).

11. James 1:4 (MSG).

12. Habakkuk 2:3 (LB).

DAY 29: **Accepting Your Assignment**

1. Ephesians 2:10b (TEV).

2. Colossians 3:23 – 24; Matthew 25:34 – 45; Ephesians 6:7.

3. Jeremiah 1:5 (NCV).

4. 2 Timothy 1:9 (LB).

5. 1 Corinthians 6:20 (CEV).

6. Romans 12:1 (TEV).

7. 1 John 3:14 (CEV).

8. Matthew 8:15 (NCV).

9. Ephesians 4:4 – 14; see also Romans 1:6 – 7; 8:28 – 30; 1 Corinthians 1:2, 9, 26; 7:17; Philippians 3:14; 1 Peter 2:9; 2 Peter 1:3.

10. 2 Timothy 1:9 (TEV).

11. 1 Peter 2:9 (GWT).

12. Romans 7:4 (TEV).

13. 1 Corinthians 12:27 (NLT).

14. Matthew 20:28 (LB).

15. Romans 14:12 (NLT).

16. Romans 2:8 (NLT).

17. Mark 8:35 (LB); see also Matthew 10:39; 16:25; Luke 9:24; 17:33.

18. Romans 12:5 (MSG).

19. 1 Corinthians 12:14a, 19 (MSG).

DAY 30: Shaped for Serving God

1. Ephesians 2:10 (NIV).

2. Psalm 139:13 – 14 (NLT).

3. Psalm 139:16 (NLT).

4. Romans 12:4 – 8; 1 Corinthians 12; Ephesians 4:8 – 15; 1 Corinthians 7:7.

5. 1 Corinthians 2:14 (TEV).

6. Ephesians 4:7 (CEV).

7. 1 Corinthians 12:11 (NLT).

8. 1 Corinthians 12:29 – 30.

9. 1 Corinthians 12:7 (NLT).

10. 1 Corinthians 12:5 (NLT).

11. Proverbs 27:19 (NLT).

12. Matthew 12:34; Proverbs 4:23.

13. Deuteronomy 11:13; 1 Samuel 12:20; Romans 1:9; Ephesians 6:6.

14. Proverbs 15:16 (MSG).

DAY 31: Understanding Your Shape

1. 1 Corinthians 12:4 – 6 (TEV).

2. Exodus 31:3 – 5 (NIV).

3. Romans 12:6a (NLT).

4. 1 Corinthians 10:31 (NIV).

5. 1 Corinthians 12:6 (TEV).

6. Deuteronomy 8:18 (NIV).

7. Deuteronomy 14:23 (LB); Malachi 3:8 – 11.

8. Hebrews 13:21 (LB).

9. 1 Peter 4:10 (LB).

10. 1 Corinthians 12:6 (PH).

11. Romans 8:28 – 29.

12. 2 Corinthians 1:4 (NLT).

13. 2 Corinthians 1:8 – 10 (LB).

14. For more help you can order the tapes of Class 301, *Discovering Your Shape for Ministry,* which includes a Shape identification tool.

DAY 32: Using What God Gave You

1. Ephesians 5:17 (LB).

2. Romans 12:3b (PH).

3. Galatians 6:4b (MSG).

4. Deuteronomy 11:2 (TEV).

5. Galatians 3:4 (NCV).

6. John 13:7 (NIV).

7. Contact *www. purposedrivenlife .com.*

8. Romans 9:20 – 21 (JB).

9. Ephesians 4:7 (LB).

10. Galatians 2:7 – 8.

11. 2 Corinthians 10:13 (NLT).

12. Hebrews 12:1 (LB).

13. Galatians 6:4 (NLT).

14. Galatians 6:4 (CEV).

15. 2 Corinthians 10:12 (NIV).

16. 2 Corinthians 10:12b (MSG).

17. 1 Corinthians 10:12 – 18.

18. Philippians 1:9 (NLT).

19. 2 Timothy 1:6 (NASB).

20. Matthew 25:28 (NIV).

21. 1 Timothy 4:14 – 15 (LB).

22. 2 Timothy 2:15 (MSG).

23. 1 Corinthians 9:25 (MSG).

DAY 33: How Real Servants Act

1. Matthew 7:16 (CEV).

2. 2 Timothy 2:4 (NASB).

3. Galatians 6:10 (GWT).

4. Proverbs 3:28 (TEV).

5. Ecclesiastes 11:4 (NLT).

6. Colossians 3:23.

7. Galatians 6:3 (NLT).

8. John 13:15.

9. Acts 28:3.

10. Luke 16:10 – 12.

11. Psalm 12:1; Proverbs 20:6; Philippians 2:19 – 22.

12. Matthew 25:23 (NLT).

13. 1 Peter 5:5 (TEV).

14. Ephesians 6:6 (KJV); Colossians 3:22 (KJV).

15. Matthew 6:1 (CEV).

16. Galatians 1:10 (NIV).

17. Colossians 3:4 (MSG).

18. 1 Corinthians 12:22 – 24.

19. 1 Corinthians 15:58 (MSG).

20. Matthew 10:42 (LB).

DAY 34: Thinking Like a Servant

1. 2 Chronicles 25:2 (NRSV).

2. Philippians 2:4 (MSG).

3. Philippians 2:7 (GWT).

4. Philippians 2:20 – 21.

5. Matthew 5:41 (MSG).

6. 1 Corinthians 4:1 (NJB).

7. 1 Corinthians 4:2 (TEV).

8. Luke 16:13 (NIV).

9. Luke 16:11 (NIV).

10. Galatians 5:26 (MSG).

11. Romans 14:4 (GWT).

12. Nehemiah 6:3 (CEV).

13. Matthew 26:10 (MSG).

14. John 13:3 – 4 (NIV).

15. 2 Corinthians 10:18 (CEV).

16. James 1:1.

17. Psalm 100:2 (KJV).

18. John 12:26 (MSG).

19. Hebrews 6:10 (NLT).

DAY 35: God's Power in Your Weakness

1. Isaiah 55:9 (CEV).

2. 1 Corinthians 1:27 (TEV).

3. Matthew 5:3.

4. 2 Corinthians 12:7.

5. 2 Corinthians 4:7 (CEV).

6. Matthew 16:16 (NIV).

7. Acts 14:15 (NCV).

8. 2 Corinthians 12:9 – 10a (NLT).

9. 2 Corinthians 12:10 (LB).

10. 2 Corinthians 12:7 (MSG).

11. Numbers 12:3.

12. Judges 6:12 (KJV).

13. Romans 4:11 (NLT).

14. Matthew 16:18 (TEV).

15. Acts 13:22 (NLT).

16. Hebrews 11:32 – 34 (NLT).

17. Romans 7:19 (NLT).

18. 2 Corinthians 6:11 (LB).

19. 2 Corinthians 1:8 (NLT).

20. 1 Corinthians 2:3 (NCV).

21. 2 Corinthians 12:5b (LB).

22. Hebrews 4:15 (CEV).

23. Romans 8:26a (NIV).

DAY 36: Made for a Mission

1. Colossians 1:25 (NCV); 1 Corinthians 12:5.

2. John 20:21 (NIV).

3. Luke 2:49 (KJV).

4. John 19:30.

5. 2 Corinthians 5:18 (TEV).

6. 2 Corinthians 5:20 (NCV).

7. Matthew 28:19 – 20; Mark 16:15; Luke 24:47; John 20:21; Acts 1:8.

8. Matthew 28:19 – 20 (CEV).

9. Ezekiel 3:18 (NCV).

10. 2 Corinthians 5:18 (LB).

11. 2 Corinthians 6:1 (NCV).

12. 2 Corinthians 5:20 (MSG).

13. Acts 4:12 (NCV).

14. John 9:4 (NLT).

15. Acts 20:24 (NLT).

16. Acts 1:7 – 8 (NIV).

17. Matthew 24:36 (NIV).

18. Matthew 24:14 (NCV).

19. Luke 9:62 (LB).

20. Luke 22:42 (NLT).

21. Romans 6:13b (LB).

22. Matthew 6:33 (NLT).

DAY 37: Sharing Your Life Message

1. 2 Corinthians 2:17b (NCV).
2. 1 John 5:10a (GWT).
3. 1 Peter 2:9 (MSG).
4. Acts 1:8 (NIV).
5. Acts 22 to 26.
6. 1 Peter 3:15 – 16 (TEV).
7. Psalm 119:33 (MSG).
8. Psalm 106:43 (MSG).
9. Proverbs 25:12 (TEV).
10. For some biblical examples of each of these, see Psalm 51; Philippians 4:11 – 13; 2 Corinthians 1:4 – 10; Psalm 40; Psalm 119:71; Genesis 50:20.
11. Matthew 12:34 (LB).
12. Psalm 69:9 (LB).
13. Jeremiah 20:9 (CEV).
14. Galatians 4:18 (NIV).
15. Romans 1:17 (NCV).
16. 2 Corinthians 5:19 (NLT).
17. 2 Corinthians 5:14 (NIV).
18. 1 John 4:18 (TEV).
19. 2 Peter 3:9 (NCV).
20. Colossians 4:5 (LB).

DAY 38: Becoming a World-Class Christian

1. Paul Borthwick's books *A Mind for Missions* (Colorado Springs: NavPress, 1987) and *How to Be a World-Class Christian* (Waynesboro, GA: Authentic Media, 1999), should be read by every Christian.
2. Revelation 7:9 (CEV).
3. 1 Corinthians 14:20 (CEV).
4. Philippians 2:4 (NLT).
5. 1 Corinthians 2:12 (CEV).
6. 1 Corinthians 10:33 (GWT).
7. John 3:16 (KJV).
8. Acts 17:26 – 27 (CEV).
9. Colossians 1:6 (NLT).
10. Psalm 2:8 (NCV).
11. Colossians 4:3 (NIV); Romans 1:10 (NLT).
12. Ephesians 6:19 (MSG).
13. John 17:20 (NIV).
14. 2 Thessalonians 3:1.
15. Matthew 9:38.
16. 2 Corinthians 1:11 (GWT).
17. Acts 1:8 (CEV).
18. 2 Corinthians 4:18 (NIV).
19. Luke 9:62 (LB).
20. 1 Corinthians 7:31 (MSG).
21. Hebrews 12:1 (LB).
22. Matthew 6:20 – 21 (CEV).
23. Luke 16:9 (NIV).
24. 1 Timothy 6:19 (LB).
25. Jeremiah 1:7 – 8 (NLT).

26. From the Lausanne Covenant (1974).

27. Mark 8:35 (LB).

DAY 39: Balancing Your Life

1. Proverbs 27:17 (NCV).

2. Philippians 4:9 (TEV).

3. 1 Thessalonians 5:11 (NCV).

4. Lamentations 3:40 (NLT); 1 Corinthians 11:28 (NLT), 11:31 (TEV); 2 Corinthians 13:5 (MSG); Galatians 6:4 (NIV).

5. 2 Corinthians 13:5 (MSG).

6. Lamentations 3:40 (MSG).

7. 2 Corinthians 8:11 (LB).

8. Hebrews 2:1 (MSG).

9. Numbers 33:2 (NLT).

10. Psalm 56:8 (TEV).

11. Psalm 102:18 (TEV).

12. Proverbs 11:25 (MSG).

13. 2 Timothy 2:2b (CEV).

14. James 4:17 (NCV).

15. 1 Timothy 4:6 (CEV).

16. John 17:4 (NIV).

17. John 17:6 – 26.

DAY 40: Living with Purpose

1. John 13:17 (NIV).

2. Psalm 33:11 (TEV).

3. Proverbs 4:26 (CEV).

4. Proverbs 17:24 (TEV).

5. Philippians 1:10 (NLT).

6. 2 Chronicles 14:4 (MSG).

7. Ephesians 3:17 (NLT).

8. Philippians 4:7 (MSG).

9. Galatians 5:22 – 23.

10. Matthew 5:3 – 12.

11. 2 Peter 1:5 – 7 (MSG).

12. 1 Timothy 4:16 (MSG).

13. 2 Corinthians 9:12 (TEV).

14. John 15:16a (NJB).

15. Joshua 24:15 (NLT).

16. Philippians 1:27 (NCV).

17. Ephesians 5:25 (TEV).

18. Proverbs 22:18 (NCV).

19. Proverbs 19:21 (NIV).

20. 1 Thessalonians 2:4b (NLT).

21. 2 Corinthians 10:13 (LB).

22. Acts 13:36a.

23. Acts 13:22.

24. Esther 4:14.

25. 2 Chronicles 16:9 (NLT).

26. 1 Corinthians 9:26 (NLT).

27. Philippians 1:21 (NIV).

28. 2 Corinthians 4:17 (NIV).

29. Revelation 4:11 (MSG).

DAY 41: The Envy Trap

1. Romans 9:20 (NLT).

2. Exodus 20:17 (NIV).

3. Ephesians 2:10 (NLT).

4. Luke 9:62 (LB).

5. Ecclesiastes 4:4 (TEV).

6. Ecclesiastes 4:8 (TEV).

7. Proverbs 23:4 (NCV).

8. James 3:16 (NIV).

9. Matthew 27:18; Mark 15:10. See LB.

10. 2 Corinthians 10:12 (GWT).

11. Romans 12:15 (NKJV).

12. Ephesians 3:8 (AMP).

13. 1 Corinthians 4:7b – 8a (MSG).

14. Ecclesiastes 5:10 – 11 (NLT).

15. 2 Samuel 7:18 (NLT).

16. Ecclesiastes 6:9 (TEV).

17. Matthew 20:12 (MSG).

18. Matthew 20:13 – 15 (CEV).

19. Matthew 20:14 (NKJV).

DAY 42: The People-Pleaser Trap

1. Romans 15:1 (NLT).

2. Romans 14:7 (NIV).

3. Proverbs 29:25 (TEV).

4. Proverbs 29:25 (NLT).

5. Proverbs 25:27 (TEV).

6. 1 Thessalonians 2:4 (NLT).

7. 2 Corinthians 10:18 (CEV).

8. John 5:44 (NCV).

9. Proverbs 29:25 (MSG).

10. 1 Samuel 15:24 (MSG).

11. Exodus 23:2 (NIV).

12. Proverbs 1:10 (MSG).

13. 1 Corinthians 15:33 – 34 (NIV).

14. Luke 16:15 (CEV).

15. John 7:13 (NLT).

16. John 12:42 – 43 (PH).

17. Romans 12:2 (NIV).

18. John 8:32 (NIV).

19. Luke 6:26 (NIV).

20. John 8:36 (NIV).

21. Psalm 27:10 (NLT).

22. 1 John 2:17 (TEV).

23. Exodus 20:3, 4 (NLT).

24. Matthew 6:24 (NIV).

25. Galatians 1:10 (NLT).

26. John 5:30 (NCV).

27. Romans 14:12 (NLT).

28. Hebrews 2:11 (NLT).

29. Luke 9:26 (NIV).

30. 1 Cor. 2:9 (LB).

The Purpose Driven® Church

Growth Without Compromising Your Message and Mission

Rick Warren

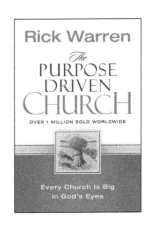

Every church is driven by something. Tradition, finances, programs, even buildings can be the controlling force in a church. But in order for a church to be healthy, it must become purpose-driven by Jesus.

Rick Warren, the founding pastor of Saddleback Church, shares a proven five-part strategy that will enable your church to grow …

- Warmer through fellowship
- Deeper through discipleship
- Stronger through worship
- Broader through ministry
- Larger through evangelism

Discover the same practical insights and principles for growing a healthy church that Rick has taught to over 100,000 pastors and church leaders from over 100 countries. *The Purpose Driven Church* shifts the focus away from church-building programs to emphasizing a people-building process. Warren says, "If you will concentrate on building people, God will build the church."

Available in stores and online!

God's Answers to Life's Difficult Questions

Rick Warren

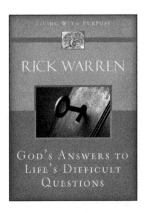

Life's difficult questions have answers.

Answers from the Bible that can change your outlook — and your life.

Rick Warren writes, "In each of these studies, you will discover simple ways to apply God's truth to your personal life, your family, and your job. The way to get the most out of this book is to act on it."

Rick Warren takes you inside the Scriptures to see what they reveal about twelve of the most pressing questions people ask. They are questions you yourself either have asked or most likely will ask. This book provides simple, straightforward answers you can begin to apply right away to move past your worst sticking points and enjoy a life of purpose, peace, and significance.

Available in stores and online!

ZONDERVAN®
.com

God's Power to Change Your Life

Rick Warren

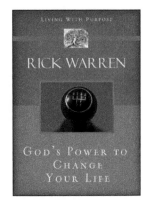

"In the years I have been a pastor," writes Rick Warren, "the number-one question I'm asked is, 'Rick, why can't I change?'" People want to change — but they're stuck.

Do you want to get unstuck? Here's how.

Drawing simple but powerful truths from the Bible, this book gives you practical guidance for specific types of change, and it links you up with the power to actually make the changes you long to make.

As you apply the truth of God's Word by the power of his Spirit, your life will change. You'll move out of your rut — and get on track with God's wonderful purposes for your life.

Available in stores and online!

Share Your Thoughts

With the Author: Your comments will be forwarded to the author when you send them to *zauthor@zondervan.com*.

With Zondervan: Submit your review of this book by writing to *zreview@zondervan.com*.

Free Online Resources at
www.zondervan.com

Zondervan AuthorTracker: Be notified whenever your favorite authors publish new books, go on tour, or post an update about what's happening in their lives at www.zondervan.com/ authortracker.

Daily Bible Verses and Devotions: Enrich your life with daily Bible verses or devotions that help you start every morning focused on God. Visit www.zondervan.com/newsletters.

Free Email Publications: Sign up for newsletters on Christian living, academic resources, church ministry, fiction, children's resources, and more. Visit www.zondervan.com/newsletters.

Zondervan Bible Search: Find and compare Bible passages in a variety of translations at www.zondervanbiblesearch.com.

Other Benefits: Register to receive online benefits like coupons and special offers, or to participate in research.

ZONDERVAN®

ZONDERVAN.com/
AUTHORTRACKER
follow your favorite authors

CPSIA information can be obtained
at www.ICGtesting.com
Printed in the USA
BVHW050225010323
659351BV00006B/26